THE MAGIC MIRROR

SUNY Series in the Philosophy of the Social Sciences
Lenore Langsdorf, editor

THE MAGIC MIRROR

Myth's Abiding Power

Elizabeth M. Baeten

STATE UNIVERSITY OF NEW YORK PRESS

Published by
State University of New York Press, Albany

For information, address State University of New York Press,
State University Plaza, Albany, N.Y., 12246

Production by Marilyn P. Semerad
Marketing by Nancy Farrell

Library of Congress Cataloging-in-Publication Data

Baeten, Elizabeth M., 1954-
   The magic mirror : myth's abiding power / Elizabeth M. Baeten.
      p.   cm. — (SUNY series in the philosophy of the social sciences)
   Includes bibliographical references and index.
   ISBN 0-7914-3091-X (alk. paper). — ISBN 0-7914-3092-8 (pbk. : alk. paper)
   1. Cassirer, Ernst, 1874-1945—Contributions in concept of myth. 2. Barthes, Roland—Contributions in concept of myth. 3. Eliade, Mircea, 1907-   —Contributions in concept of myth. 4. Hillman, James—Contributions in concept of myth. 5. Myth—History—20th century. I. Title. II. Series.
BL304.B25 1996
291.1'3'0904—dc20   96-27863
                                                        CIP

10 9 8 7 6 5 4 3 2 1

For Larry and Harry

Contents

Acknowledgments

Writing a book is a matter of many and varied conversations: with friends, colleagues, mentors, imaginary others, students, thinkers long gone, family, oneself. I'd like to thank a few of those who have given freely time, concern, sympathy, and appraisal along the way.

Robert Cummings Neville has seen this work through its many stages, from beginning to end, and his deft intellectual touch has been much appreciated. Bob has the unusual skill of encouraging without undue praise and criticizing without undue alarm.

Sidney Gelber, Peter Manchester, and Edward Casey read early versions of this work, and their careful reading and commentary was invaluable. Lenore Langsdorf, as editor of this series, carved a niche for my work as I was about to despair of it ever finding its place; I'd also like to thank her for her critical reading of chapter 6.

I owe a deep and abiding debt to the late Justus Buchler. He has provided me with a model of utmost respect for query and for those engaged in query. I hope someday to fulfill the promise he saw in me.

A book can grow only in the soil of a life. My life, and my work, have been made immensely richer by the fellows to whom this book is dedicated. My husband, Lawrence Cahoone, has been with me since before the beginning of this, offering his help with the project and offering wonderful respite from it. My son, Harrison Baeten Cahoone, appeared only near the finish of the work, though he lay dreaming in me long before. Thanks, guys.

Introduction

We start with three stories. First:

> In the beginning, Eurynome, the Goddess of All Things, rose naked from Chaos, but found nothing substantial for her feet to rest upon, and therefore divided the sea from the sky, dancing lonely upon its waves. She danced towards the south, and the wind set in motion behind her seemed something new and apart with which to begin a work of creation. Wheeling about, she caught hold of this north wind, rubbed it between her hands, and behold! the great serpent Ophion. Eurynome danced to warm herself, wildly and more wildly, until Ophion, grown lustful, coiled about those divine limbs and was moved to couple with her. . . .
>
> Next, [Eurynome] assumed the form of a dove, brooding on the waves and, in due process of time, laid the Universal Egg. At her bidding, Ophion coiled seven times about this egg, until it hatched and split in two. Out tumbled all things that exist, her children: sun, moon, planets, stars, the earth with its mountains and rivers, its trees, herbs and living creatures. . . .
>
> Next, the goddess created the seven planetary powers, setting a Titaness and Titan over each. . . . But the first man was Pelagus, ancestor of the Pelasgians; he sprang from the soil of Arcadia, followed by certain others, whom he taught to make huts and feed upon acorns, and sew pig-skin tunics.[1]

Perhaps all but the ancient Pelasgians would agree that this is a myth. For them, we can guess, this was an accurate account of the origin of the world and of all that inhabits the world, not a myth.

☙❦❧

A man speaks:

> Well, I will tell you a tale; not one of the tales which Odysseus tells of the hero Alcinous, yet this too is a tale of a hero, Er the son of Armenius, a Pamphylian by birth. He was slain in battle, and ten days afterwards, when the bodies of the dead were taken up already in a state of corruption, his body was found unaffected by decay, and carried away home to be buried. And on the twelfth day, as he was lying upon the funeral pile, he returned to life and told them what he had seen in the other world. He said that when his soul had left the body he went on a journey with a great company, and that they came to a mysterious place at which there were two openings in the earth; they were near together, and over against them were two other openings in the heaven above. In the intermediate space there were judges seated, who commanded the just, after they had given judgment on them and had bound their sentences in front of them, to ascend by the heavenly way on the right hand; and in like manner the unjust were bidden by them to descend by the lower way on the left hand; these also bore the symbols of their deeds, but fastened on their backs. He drew near, and they told him that he was to be the messenger who would carry the report of the other world to men, and they bade him hear and see all that was to be heard and seen in that place.

The speaker continues telling the tale of Er and of life after earthly death. Er discovers that our souls will return to embodied existence, and that we will be able to choose our soul's next abode. But the choice is difficult. Life before death ought to be spent in seeking truth, virtue, and justice, for only then will we be fit for making our choice. The tale ends with words of advice:

> And thus, Glaucon, the tale has been saved and has not perished, and will save us if we are obedient to the word spoken; and we shall pass safely over the river of Forgetfulness and our soul will not be defiled. Wherefore my counsel is that we hold fast ever to the heavenly way and follow after justice and virtue always, considering that the soul is immortal and able to endure every sort of good and every sort of evil.[2]

We are less likely in this case, the last sections of book X of Plato's *Republic*, to find consensus on its status as myth. Does it belong in the same category as the Pelasgian creation story? The story of Er is a story about the afterlife, stocked with gods and goddesses and heroes and impossible deeds. But Socrates must tell the story self-consciously, mustn't he? In Plato's great discussion of the possibilities inherent in human community, Socrates clearly shows antipathy to the revered tales and myths of his time. The community (and the soul) desiring truth, goodness, and justice will banish most poetry, will outlaw the telling of tales that are not true, that can never be the basis for real knowledge because they are but opinions and reflections of reflections. The story of Er is recounted as a nonphilosophical response to questions that properly belong to the domain of philosophy, or the pursuit of the wisdom. Socrates suggests, through his telling of the tale after making quite clear that telling tales cannot bring us to the truth, that rational discourse may not be able to disclose the truth about what follows embodied life nor about what one's life ought to be to prepare for death. Lacking knowledge, we should choose stories that are edifying, stories that will provide motivation for continued rational discourse in the face of the unknown and unknowable. Does the story of Er retain its character as myth when it is used in this way? Does a myth lose its mythical power when it is domesticated and used for reason's own ends?

☙❦❧

It is late at night. The speaker sits in robes before a blazing fire. He speaks from a dream within a dream:

> I dread waking from this sleep. If roused from my slumber I face demons and difficulties and puzzles so much exceeding those of my dreams. Just as a dreaming prisoner enjoys the sweetest liberty and fears to awaken, so I fear to awaken. But from what do I fear to wake? It is my life that is a dream. I find that I have been deceived about the simplest things. What I was told as a child were lies. I cannot trust my senses. I have no more reason to think myself a flesh and blood man than to think that I am made of glass. Am I insane? I can no longer tell if I am awake or asleep and dreaming. I cannot know if this hand in front of me exists or if I have merely imagined it and forgotten the imagining. I cannot rest in the most obvious truths. 2 + 2 = 4? There can be no assurance. Perhaps I am in another's dream. Perhaps some powerful being has created me

as his jester, laughing at my stupidity and blindness. I am held prisoner in my doubts, and dream the dream of the freedom of knowing.

All is Chaos. But I must not awaken from this dream within a dream. For if I do, I will believe to be true what I know in my dream I cannot know to be true. I will ride the waves of Chaos. Though my world has turned inside out, I will refuse a resting place. I remain obstinate in this refusal.

The speaker falls insensible. He sleeps. When he wakes, he repeats the incantation: I will doubt; I will doubt; I will doubt. Then he continues his tale:

One cannot chart Chaos. There are neither footholds nor toeholds in this vortex. There is nothing upon which to stand. I must remember my dream within a dream. I must remember that there is no center of the world. If there is to be a center, then it is my task to create it. I shut my eyes to Chaos, close my ears to the whirlwind, step back from space, from time, from body, from soul, all now fractured into kaleidoscopic unknowns. And what is there, in the stillness at the center of the whirlwind? I find He-Who-Does-Not-Know, I find myself. By doubting all, I find the doubter and know this *must* be so. Out of Chaos, I create a moment of truth—uncertainty reflecting itself. Out of Chaos come I, now double, I see I. I shun mother and father and give birth to myself, pure and unsullied. And out of this flows all else, the existence of God, the true and the false, all material things, and the bodies and souls of men.

Is this a myth? Of course my wild paraphrase of a work some consider to be the progenitor of the modern philosophic era may seem to do injustice to the serious nature of Descartes' *Meditations*. But Descartes himself gives us fuel for considering at least meditations I and II a mythical story. It has many of the right ingredients. It begins with a tenor of "Once upon a time . . .". It is a tale of a heroic task: there was a man who wanted to rebuild the world from the ground up. Descartes dons his robes and sits before a fire and speaks of demons and sirens and gods and nightmares and a world in which whatever seems most true is most false. Descartes himself is the hero of the tale; it is he who follows Ariadne's thread and finds his way to the very center of the world of intelligibility. And of course, every student of philosophy is initiated in the ritual performance. To find the still center, the origin of truth, we must each perform the dance of doubt.

Why is the Pelasgian creation story so obviously a myth? What makes the story of Er *not quite* mythical? What makes Descartes' *Meditations* philosophical rather than mythical? Perhaps none of these are myths. Perhaps all are myths.

What exactly *is* a myth?

☙

Casual references to myth and the mythical abound in public life. These terms are scattered throughout what we read and hear, from the most erudite philosophical treatises to the most inane television programs. But the concept of myth and the process of myth-making have gotten short shrift as a serious matter of investigation in twentieth-century philosophy. While we have borrowed heavily from history, philology, sociology, mathematics, psychology, linguistics, and physics, philosophers have brought little interest in myth into our work. Of course, there are important exceptions to this, and we will examine notable twentieth-century philosophical theories about myth. But, in general, when myth enters the philosophic conversation, it does so in some fairly predictable ways, ways not much different from the most casual of nonphilosophical uses. The sentiment expressed by W. V. O. Quine in contending that "[u]ncritical semantics is the myth of a museum in which the exhibits are meanings and the words are labels,"[3] is quite similar to the sentiment expressed in the newspaper headline, "More Myths about Seatbelts." Each locution uses the term "myth" as a near synonym for "mistaken belief," or perhaps, "widely or deeply held beliefs with no solid foundation in the facts of the matter."

In philosophical work, myth is rarely addressed as a legitimate subject of inquiry, but is employed as a means of curt dismissal of some foolishness or utilized as a foil for another concept or phenomenon. This derogates what is deemed mythical and offers a (sometimes) covert honorific sense to whatever is understood as opposed to myth. Thus we have the "capitalist myth," the "myths of patriarchal culture," and so on. We may find myth directly opposed (through conjunction) to some other term, leaving little doubt of myth's inferior status in the comparison: science and myth. We may find myth allocated the role of (sometimes revered, but always improved upon) forebear of more contemporary and more respectable human accomplishments: myth and religion. Myth has also been joined to other terms in a kind of uneasy alliance that connotes the shaky status of the pair in philosophic categories and concern: mythopoetic thought or language.

Generally speaking, philosophers see myths as primitive human constructions. Myths belong not only to the long-shadowed past (including societies that remain outside the progress of history) but to all archaic and un(der)developed manners of human understanding of the natural world, no matter when or where they occur. The mythical manner of interpretation, being so primitive and undeveloped, is essentially mistaken and merely masquerades as knowledge. The mistakes may be categorial, as in conflating the vegetal or animal with the human in totemic beliefs; or they may be causal, as in ascribing efficacy in the agricultural sphere to ritual dances and magical incantations. In either case, the assumption is that an increase in "real" knowledge about how the world "really" works will supersede and eventually eliminate the myths.

Of course there are exceptions to these assumptions about myth. Perhaps the most generous twentieth-century philosophic articulation of myth and its place in culture is that offered by Ernst Cassirer. He understands myth as a coherent symbolic formation organizing human experience, analogous but not equivalent to language, art, and science. For Cassirer, the specifically mythical organization of the welter of human experience is a necessary stage in the advance of human accomplishment. Myth gives *symbolic* structure to the unmediated organic give and take of an organism with its environment and thus allows for the inception of truly human, or cultural, life. Yet even by Cassirer's account, as we'll see in detail, there is something fundamentally mistaken in the mythical symbolic organization of experience, and myth must be superseded if there is to be human progress.

Philosophic discussions tend to present myth as something that human beings outgrow and leave behind as we become more knowledgeable or intellectually or technically or culturally sophisticated. Thus, human history, the processes of culture, and the advance of our understanding of the workings of the world are seen, in large part, as progressively divesting human life of myth.

Much work on myth has been going on outside of philosophic research. A good deal of this work has been in gathering together, organizing, and collating the wealth of material collected by missionaries and other fieldworkers during the latter half of the nineteenth century and into the first decades of the present century. The material amassed, the traditional stories and lore of non-Western, technologically unsophisticated societies, has formed the basis of various theoretical explanations for the origins, persuasive power, and continuing interest of myth. Anthropologists, such as Lévi-Strauss, offer complex models of interpreting myth based on a formalization of structuralist linguistics. Depth psychologists, following Jung's lead, chart the development of the individual psyche using the polestar of archetypal mythic patterns. Literary critics and analysts, such as Northrop Frye, have made wide use of recurring mythical themes in uncovering layers of meaning once buried in texts. Though myth has been addressed by a few philosophers in this century, it is a subject rare in comparison to the attention it's garnered in other fields. My work can be seen as an attempt to remedy this relative dearth of serious philosophical investigation into the nature of myth by bringing extraphilosophic scholarly concerns to the philosophic arena.

The present work belongs to what can be best characterized as philosophy of culture. Philosophy of culture is an investigation of those processes and products of the human endeavor that are both communicative and interpretive. That is, culture provides the "lenses," as it were, through which experience is viewed and recognized, and culture is the means by which these lenses are reground by those who use them, and culture is the process of passing the lenses from one to another. This is a notion of culture as the specific medium of human endeavor—an environment that at once shapes and is shaped by its inhabitants. There are certain generic features amidst the great variety of human interpretations of the world, and we can describe and investigate these. For example, it appears that every pocket of human cultural environment includes identification of a supernatural or extranatural force to which power of change in nature is ascribed. The generic features of cultural accomplishment can be discovered in specific kinds of cultural activity, as in investigating world religions. In investigating a particular sort of cultural process—mythmaking—I hope to articulate features of human communicative and interpretive activity that are the specific of traits found generically in culture. This will aid in developing a description of the generic traits of culture, a description that can then be tested against other specific types of cultural processes. This is not to say that "culture" is a mere abstraction from specific cultural accomplishment. In an essential way, human creatures are cultural creatures, regardless of particular kinds of cultural engagement, and this sense of culture must also be investigated.

There are any number of good reasons for beginning an examination of culture with culture's specific manifestation in myth and mythmaking. But, as with a great deal of intellectual work, my involvement in exploring myth and theories about myth as the road to a coherent philosophy of culture arose out of less likely research. My interest in this subject was fostered by the work of certain feminist aestheticians, notably Estella Lauter. These theories are primarily investigations into the ongoing relation of the dominant images of women that we find in our artistic heritage and in our contemporary milieu and the ways in which these images shape the lives of individual women. If it is the case that the images of women and the constellations of traits and attributes that we associate with women determine in some way or another our concepts of self, then changes in the dominant motifs offered in the publicly accessible arena of artistic production may be a positive way of reshaping the vicissitudes of gendered life in our culture.

Feminist aestheticians have been collecting enormous amounts of data on painting, poetry, sculpture, traditional fabricwork, and so on, done by women. There appear to be recurrent patterns in the variety of examples. This seems especially the case in artwork made or performed by self-identified feminists working within self-identified feminist communities. These recurrent patterns are often closely aligned, but not identical with, the "classic" myths of our culture. For example, Margaret Atwood, in "Circe/Mud Poems," transforms the journey of Odysseus and his seduction by the evil temptress Circe.[4] The transformation is effected by retelling the story through the eyes and voice of Circe. This seemingly slight alteration, a change in narrative perspective, radically alters the story, changes the way it affects the reader, and provides a powerful critique of the heroic (generally viewed as masculine) journey.[5] If it is true that we can find myth in the making in contemporary women's artistic and intellectual work, and if it is true that these myths have a continuing power to shape our lives, then we have a very important and exciting case study in our midst, an opportunity for directly observing a vigorous instance of this strand of cultural activity. But this project will bear ripe fruit only, it seems to me, if we know what a myth is and how myths function in human lives. And I am not satisfied that we know either of these.

For example, Catherine Keller has written a compelling version of process metaphysics, one that utilizes "mythic" images. She describes her own analysis:

Poetry and myth pull us toward a new religious sense that can be called arachnean, allowing us to articulate something like a feminist ontology of self. Here I shall propose four non-polar conceptual dyads: being one/being many, being public/being private, being body/being soul, being here/being now. These form a complex rhythm out of which connective and fluid selves compose themselves and their worlds.[6]

Keller offers a fascinating alternative to some traditional philosophic notions of the constitution of the self, and she does so through mythic images and narratives. She shows that reclamation of goddesses and heroines such as Athena, Arachne, Penelope, and Persephone, leads to a notion of the self in greater harmony with female experience and a notion of the self much more optimistic of the future of our human communities. But this is not yet to explain *why* the story of Arachne and her web is a myth, nor how this story is in a separate category from the story a mother may tell of her mother learning to crochet and making a beautiful afghan for her hopechest, nor how myths are perpetuated, and so forth. What counts as a myth in theories of myth or in theories that rely on mythical images? The intellectual proposals made by feminists and feminist aestheticians must be undergirded with a coherent account of the workings of culture and the processes and products of myth-making. At least in part, this is what I hope to add to the discussion.

The suggestiveness of the work in feminist aesthetics and feminist philosophy fanned the embers of a basic interest in mythmaking as an important form of cultural activity. (And as myth and mythmaking are important elements of these feminist theories and as myth and mythmaking seem to be prototypical cultural products and processes, my political and philosophical interests overlap in this area in a rather fortuitous way.) I have found an intellectually profitable avenue of action in formulating, as precisely as possible, answers to a fairly limited number of questions. Of course, the most obvious question is: What is myth? Important related questions are: What role does myth play in human life? Do myths continue to function in our lives? What relationship holds between myth and the broader cultural sphere? Sufficient degrees of precision and insight in answering these questions form the basis of other investigations, for example, in developing a general philosophy of culture or a specific theory in aesthetics or a feminist metaphysics. I will address the first of these at some length in the conclusion of the present work, while the other topics must await the future.

I begin the present examination of myth with a brief review of several philosophical and extraphilosophical theories about myth. I also include a discussion of the ways in which the term 'myth' is used in ordinary public discourse. A perusal of a wide range of material reveals *both* the lack of unanimity in conceptions of the structure and function of myth *and* a pervasive (though most often unacknowledged) judgment of the "otherness" of myth. In some senses, the latter is a simple observation—though one that has quite complex ramifications in a fully developed theory of myth. To say that myth marks what is "other" is *at least* to say that we reserve the term for beliefs or practices or claims of knowledge that are different from our own. The term 'myth' doesn't seem quite appropriate when applied to one's own beliefs, unless one has been forced to question these beliefs and found them to be an unreliable foundation. Even those who believe that myth may be a powerful force for personal and social transformation, view it as either something not yet attained or as something lying deep and unfathomable in the nether regions of the psyche. In chapter 1 I begin describing this function of myth—how we use it to define ourselves through difference, to identify what is other and hence, what is our "own." I take up the theme again in chapter 6 and the conclusion.

Fruitful as a review of a variety of conceptions of myth may be, we need to look carefully at one fully formed theory—in its entirety. This will serve as a kind of topographical map, a set of references to use in exploring the issue. We may find that the map is inadequate or incorrect from time to time, but to wander blind in this terrain seems foolish. Ernst Cassirer's careful work on myth is an opportune place to begin answering any philosophical questions on the nature of myth. I think it's fair to say that Cassirer's description of the mythical is the most complex, full, and generous treatment of the subject in the present century. But Cassirer is a German Idealist, in the tradition of Hegel and, to a lesser degree, Kant, while I find my intellectual home in American naturalism and pluralism. I heartily disagree with some of Cassirer's fundamental metaphysical, ontological, and epistemological assumptions. But his breadth of vision, the depth of his knowledge of a great variety of subjects, and his access to an extensive collection of material in the history of religion, ethnology, anthropology, and philology at the Warburg library, make him a most formidable figure in twentieth-century myth studies. In fact, we would probably have to go back as far as Giambattista Vico (whom Cassirer acknowledges as forebear) to find a theory of myth as broad in scope and as sensitive to the subtle workings of myth in culture as is Cassirer's.

My analysis of Cassirer's work is fairly lengthy and detailed, not only because his writing on the subject is so itself but also because understanding the place of myth in his general philosophy of culture demands some understanding of the general metaphysical scheme in which myth makes its appearance. In addition, my work on Cassirer forms a framework for a good deal of what follows it, and the framework must be substantial and reticulate in order to support a complex project.

One of the prominent aspects of Cassirer's project is the attempt to give full respect and full due to what we've come to call the mythical. Cassirer is committed to this for at least two reasons. The first is tied to his conception of consciousness, or Spirit, as the driving force in the progress made through human history. In this, Cassirer displays his Hegelian colors, and as Hegelian he sees Spirit as not my or your jot of consciousness, but as a great rolling wave of agency and efficacy, taking up, shaping, and making the material world a truly human, or spiritual, abode. Human history is thus the story of Spirit as it transforms its material environs into a spiritualized or symbolic universe. But Spirit is immaterial, and it cannot appear if not clothed in the "material," at least in Cassirer's view. Culture, or symbolic formation, is the means by which Spirit or consciousness forms its world. Through this formation, Spirit is able to come to see itself *as* Spirit when it recognizes symbolic products as of its own making. It is as if Spirit must construct a mirror in order to see itself and recognize its essence and power. If the history of the "reflections" of consciousness or Spirit is continuous or unified in some respect, then consciousness or Spirit must be understood as continuous and unified insofar as it is symbol making. If this is so, then myth, as symbolic or cultural activity, cannot be dismissed as merely a mistaken symbolic achievement, according to Cassirer. Nor, since mythical symbols are distinguishable from other cultural forms, can it be considered as either an incipient form (for example, classifying myth as protoscience) or as a degenerate symbolic form (for example, seeing myth as a corruption of an original religious experience).

The second reason for Cassirer's commitment to this task of investigating myth is political. Later in his life, Cassirer became convinced that myth hovers just beneath the surface of modern culture. Myth is far from being overcome by the gains we've made in rationally and humanistically determining our communal and political lives, or so Cassirer believed. Myth is able to reassert itself as a profound force in the public arena if enough uncertainty and instability infect the socioeconomic sphere. In particular, Cassirer could not make sense of the attraction to, and rise of, the National Socialist Party in Germany without recurring to his analysis of mythical consciousness and its word magic, appeal to emotion, and conservative force. Cassirer turned to his own earlier explanation of the persuasive power of myth to render explicable social and political phenomena that surpassed credulity. The atrocities of Nazi Germany seemed incomprehensible from a perspective based on an assumption of human development and progress, especially a perspective that includes the modern deep political belief in the efficacy of rational discourse. Only if the seemingly inexorable progress of human understanding is actually open to extremely anachronistic tendencies can we, according to this view, believe that humanistic progress is possible. Though if we admit the possibility of regression, we must deny the inevitability of progression, and rely only on *its* possibility.

Chapter 2 of the present work begins with a account of Cassirer's overall project, outlining his general methodological principles, his critical philosophy of culture, his description of the nature of the symbolic, and his analysis of its ontogenetic and phylogenetic development. Within this context, Cassirer formulates his understanding of the characteristics of consciousness as these traits are reflected in the variety of cultural or symbolic forms. The greater part of chapter 2 follows Cassirer's commitment to giving an accurate and even-handed description of mythical symbolic formation. This entails a close reading of the specific character of myth as well as the features of mythical formation that attest to the unity of all symbolic forms amidst the variety of specific differences.

After tracing the twists and turns of Cassirer's lifelong work on the question of myth, I suggest some features of his account that I find opaque and some I find problematic. A number of these features are inherent in Idealism. Cassirer takes as axiomatic the constitution of all symbolic forms (and therefore all of culture in its myriad aspects) as an accomplishment of Spirit or consciousness. This assumption is ameliorated by the correlative assertion that meaningful symbolic accomplishment is always, and can only be found as, an inextricable mixture of material and form. In this way, Cassirer avoids some of the difficulties endemic in conceiving of culture as a purely spiritual or ideal construction; but it remains the case that meaning is assumed to be constituted through symbolic formation under the agency of consciousness. Just as important to Cassirer's perspective, consciousness has a historical trajectory.

Spirit displays an evolutionary *progress* in its continuing symbolic or cultural accomplishments.

For Cassirer, the movement of consciousness through any one of the variety of symbolic forms is a movement toward freedom for consciousness.[7] However, if we examine closely Cassirer's understanding of mythical symbolic formation as the matrix or fundament out of which the other forms arise, we find two things. For Cassirer, myth is a cultural form that *must* be overturned if the other forms are to achieve their own particular flowering. And we find the vestiges of a dualist ontology underlying all of Cassirer's work.

Each symbolic form allows consciousness to understand itself as the progenitor of meaning. But, for Cassirer, when consciousness comes to understand its *mythical* symbols as products of its own making, mythical consciousness ceases and is replaced by another type of symbolic form, most often the religious or the scientific. The relative sophistication of any symbolic form other than myth can be gauged according to the apprehension consciousness has of itself as the symbolic formative power, a recognition that the product of symbolic activity is not merely a found feature of the world. An example of this would be changes in our understanding of "force." Consciousness (here in the mode of scientific symbolic formation) comes to recognize "force" as a symbol of its own making, as a conceptual item that is useful in organizing and understanding natural phenomena. Physicists no longer think of force as some active power exerted by material bodies. "Force" is a symbol that describes the relation between bodies, any bodies, and therefore it frees scientific ideation from a dependence on particular concrete bodies exerting force. In the most fully developed manifestations of a symbolic form, consciousness apprehends that the subjective features of the world (or what is included in the "realm" of the I), as well as the objective, are determined through symbolic formation. Though Cassirer, of course, does not use this example, we can use the work of poststructuralist semiological analysis to make the point. Lacanian and Derridian analyses are quite sophisticated manifestations of the symbolic formative activity of language.[8] This is language used to understand language. At the same time, this is a method of linguistic analysis that allows us to understand the "I" or the "self" as particularly pervasive symbols that organize experience around two poles—the objective, or world, and the subjective, or I. In other words, the self is not something essential or substantial, as in having a unique integrity and existence. Rather, the self is a residual symbolic product; it is the result, not the instigator, of linguistic activity. In this way, symbolic activity can be seen as organizing *both* the objective, or worldly features of existence *and* the subjective. According to Cassirer, consciousness is the progenitor of symbolic forms, and the most sophisticated symbolic work of consciousness (in scientific and linguistic formation) results in understanding that the truly meaningful aspects of the objective and the subjective are not intrinsic properties of either the world or the self, but are products of the activity of consciousness. Symbolic formation itself determines both the subjective and the objective, and symbolic formation is the accomplishment of Spirit or consciousness. For Cassirer, mythical symbolic formation is different from all other symbolic forms in that through myth, consciousness can never come to apprehend its own formative power in organizing experience. If consciousness does come to recognize its own handiwork as in, for example, seeing the Garden of Eden as a *symbol* of originary innocence rather than as a *real* event provided by nature, then myth ceases, and religion commences.

This activity of consciousness, its increasing recognition that *it* provides the forms into which the subjective and objective features of existence coalesce, attests to the increasing freedom of consciousness as the symbolic forms develop. In effect, according to Cassirer's analysis, consciousness gradually frees itself from dependence on material nature. Consciousness becomes more and more free as it understands that the world is not necessarily as it is given to a passive spectator. The world appears as it does because consciousness has transformed the "found" into the "created." But the mythical form, even in its most developed products, offers no hint of such freedom. Mythical consciousness, in Cassirer's view, remains tied to biological, organic, material nature. Mythical consciousness's own symbolic forms—of powers and deities and sacred events—are apprehended as given by Nature, not as formed by Spirit. The theme of freedom is an important one in the present work; it will appear again and again. In fact, I will bring to light a "myth of freedom" that plays itself out in many theories *about* myth.

I find certain of Cassirer's primary tenets problematic and offer detailed criticism of these later in the work, especially in the concluding chapter. For the moment, it will suffice to say that for Cassirer the implied *telos* of all truly human (that is, cultural or symbolic) activity is the achievement and maintenance of the greatest possible distinction between Spirit and Nature. Seen from the perspective of pluralistic naturalism, Cassirer's metaphysical claims cannot be supported. A good deal of his argument may be sound, but his conclusions do not necessarily follow. I will suggest ways of interpreting the same phenomena that will not end in a radical onto-logical dualism between what we call the spiritual and the mate-rial; nor, for that matter, in a monism that reduces either of these to an epiphenomenon of the other.

☞

As is obvious, a significant portion of the present work concerns Cassirer's analysis of myth and culture. Why should this be, from an author in deep disagreement on fundamental assumptions held by Cassirer? Whatever problems appear in Cassirer's work, he offers a grand and powerful description of myth. For him, myths are not merely stories or rituals. Myth shapes the world. Myth determines the very forms of space and time. Myth organizes experience into the antithetical regions of the self and the not-self. For Cassirer, there is a mythical world that human symbolic activity creates out of the raw matter of Nature. Furthermore, Cassirer's analysis of myth assumes a continuity between this form and other forms of sym-bolic activity. This means that we need not disparage the accom-plishments of mythical consciousness. Lastly, Cassirer's analysis of myth as a strand of culture is part of an overarching metaphysical theory. Cassirer does not believe that we can make sense of myth, or of culture, without explaining the ontological and existential condi-tions of human being set within a broader context. He offers us a synoptic and systematic account of the major features of existence, as they appear in human life, and as interconnected within a larger arena. On all of this, I must agree with Cassirer. But from my per-spective, it appears that he explored new territory and drew a map of the terrain, but did so without benefit of a compass and without the concepts of latitude and longitude.

Using this image, my work can be seen as an attempt to explore more fully certain areas that remain relatively obscure on Cassirer's map and an attempt to reorient the map itself. In spite of, or perhaps because of, the grand scope of Cassirer's work on cultural forms in general and on the mythical in particular, there are spots in his argu-ment that seem weak or sketchily drawn. These particular weak spots in his analysis are not necessarily products of any intrinsic shortcomings in the larger metaphysical scheme, and can be clarified using the work of other theorists of myth. To do this, I examine some of the most important aspects of the mythical world, as mapped by Cassirer, in light of the discoveries of three other authors—in chapter 3, Roland Barthes, in chapter 4, Mircea Eliade, and in chapter 5, James Hillman. Once we've drawn as complete a map as possible, a fair critique of the metaphysical assumptions underlying the analyses can be offered.

I use Roland Barthes' account of the structure of mythical signification to extend and deepen our understanding of the general traits of signifying or symbol-making activity and its relation to mythmaking. According to Cassirer, mythical symbolic form is a system whereby experience is organized or made meaningful, analogous to, or functionally isomorphic with, other symbolic systems. This is quite similar to the claims made by structuralist semiologists; and Barthes is an admirable exponent of these claims. Barthes deals specifically with the question of mythical systems of signification and draws precise parallels between the various modes of meaning production. Barthes' work is also pertinent in that he as well understands the political arena of the twentieth century as being infected by the mythical, though Barthes sees myth aligned not with fascism, but with bourgeois/capitalist ideology. Examination of the political implications of mythical signification sheds further light on the relationship of myth and freedom.

I follow consideration of Barthes' work on mythical signification with a closer look at the two most important accomplishments of mythical symbolic formation as "mapped" in Cassirer's theory. These are the constitution or articulation of the spatial and temporal, that is objective, features of existence, and the constitution or articulation of the subjective sphere or the self, each as construed through mythical symbols.

Mircea Eliade gives a detailed description of mythical spatiotemporality. He finds that space and time in the mythically or religiously oriented world of human experience are founded on an originary place or moment where the sacred breaks through into the profane or mundane world. Eliade calls this breakthrough the "hierophany." His explication of the salient characteristics of mythical space and mythical time bears striking similarities to Cassirer's explication of these. However, Eliade articulates a view in which the hierophantic moment is the originary and irreducible feature of human experience in the world, while Cassirer brings to bear a commitment to the originary formative power of consciousness. The structural similarities of their descriptions of mythical spatiotemporality are offset by this profound difference in perspective. Eliade's valorization of the mythical as a means of achieving true creative freedom for human being is also markedly different from Cassirer's implicit denigration of the mythical as a means of consciousness achieving a truly free condition. Eliade's appraisal of the state of freedom inherent in the mythical organization of the cosmos can be seen as the fulfillment of Cassirer's (unkept) promise of giving mythical form its full due as a legitimate cultural production.

James Hillman's work on myth is a chronicle of the constitution of the subjective, as opposed to the objective, features of existence. Hillman radicalizes Jung's insights into the archetypal determinations of the individual human psyche and places Jung within the historical tradition of psychology (the speech or *logos* of the soul), itself archetypally determined. *The Myth of Analysis* offers a complex account of the evolution of this archetypal determination. Hillman describes his project as an elucidation of the process of freeing the psyche from the categories imposed through the analytic paradigm. He takes as axiomatic the constitution of a coherent self through the confluence of archetypal patterns. These belong to an imaginal field, and are integrated as a unique self through a variety of historical, social, and instinctual forces. Psychoanalysis, embedded in its own archetypal fantasies, misunderstands the necessary pain suffered by the soul in the soul's quest for completion (the union of Psyche and Eros). Psychoanalysis sees this necessary pain as illness, as pathology, as that which must be excised, or at least cured. For Hillman, to deny the soul its suffering is to hinder the evolutionary development of the soul as it aligns itself with mythical archetypes; and it is this development that offers the possibility of the soul's transcending the particularities of embodied existence. As with Eliade's work, we can discover certain underlying structural similarities between Hillman's and Cassirer's understanding of the constitutive function of myth; and again, Hillman's embrace of mythical formation provides an illuminating counterpoint to Cassirer's implicit disparagement of such formation.

☙❦❧

The four main theories of myth that I outline could hardly be more different in terms of fundamental assumptions. Cassirer is a German Idealist, Barthes a neo-Marxist structuralist, Eliade a deeply religious thinker, and Hillman a Jungian depth psychologist. While we do find that the tremendous differences in fundamental assumptions lead to quite different theories about the way myth functions, we also find deep and abiding similarities. Chapters 2 through 5 of this work examine myth as a powerful symbol system organizing experience, describe the structure of mythical space and mythical time, and imagine what the self might be like when formed in a mythical world. Chapter 6 realigns the variety of opinions about myth and mythmaking into as coherent a pattern as possible. Put briefly, there are three primary characteristics of myth that appear in each of these disparate theories. First, myth serves to demarcate antithetical ontological regions; for example, myth identifies what is sacred and what is profane. Second, myths serve as a kind of threshold between these antithetical regions; for example, by reciting certain creation myths the speaker is transported from mundane to sacred time. Third, myth functions to determine the distinction between what properly belongs to the human sphere and what does not; for example, totem myths include certain other animal species within the sphere of the human clan, while stories of the origin of human beings serve to demarcate the human from the nonhuman.

Something rather surprising appears at this point in our analysis. What becomes apparent is that the concept of myth functions in each theory in precisely the same manner in which myth itself is described as functioning. This can easily be found in Barthes' analysis of myth, in which mythical signs or symbols obscure the distinction between Nature and History. Barthes' concept of what exactly a myth is places the *concept* of myth precisely between two antithetical ontological regions, one of which—History—belongs to what's properly human.

I am, perhaps, making a contentious claim in asserting that theories *about* myth and mythmaking can themselves be examined for important clues regarding the role that myth plays in the larger cultural context. This is similar to saying that texts on the structure of linguistics can themselves be used as evidence of the theories propounded in the texts or that the tools used by physicists can themselves be analyzed into their component gluons and skewed quarks. To make the same sorts of claim about myth and theories of myth seems strange. Myth is most often conceived as shadowy, as mistaken, as somewhat irrational—the very antithesis of what makes for pride in theoretical work. Even theories of myth that embrace myth, like Eliade's or Hillman's, do not present themselves as *exhibiting* myths. Nonetheless, there are certain important aspects of mythical signification and mythical constitution of the subjective and objective, as described in the theories of myth, that are at work in the theories themselves. We see some of the same significatory and constitutive functions in the theories that the theorists ascribe to the workings of myth in nontheoretical or non-self-reflective spheres of human activity.

Intellectual culture of the late twentieth century prides itself on being "mythless." Even those who feel a reverence for myth feel it as a kind of nostalgia for something lost. In fact, with the description of culture that I put forward in the concluding chapter, we see that myth and theories about myth are on a par; they serve the same cultural function. What I will suggest is that our theories *about* myth have come to play the roles of myth. Theories of myth function mythically.

Whatever value a particular theory assigns myth, myths (and the concepts of myth) remain a kind of permeable limit between two antithetical realms of existence, one of which is considered the "truly" human and one of which is "other than." This creates a clear distinction of the truly human from, in each case, a nemesis that threatens the *telos* implicit in human being and human cultural activity. For each of the four authors under close consideration, myth marks the boundary of the human condition that must be breached if human being is to be free. Strangely enough, freedom for human being is conceived in precisely the same way in each of these accounts of the mythical. Freedom is the absolute, unbounded creative power of constitution of both the subjective, and obversely, the objective features of existence. Furthermore, the locus of creative freedom is found to reside, ultimately, in the ontological region demarcated through myth as the truly human sphere. This conception of freedom entails the elimination of any constraints, conditions, or limits on this creative power. For example, for Eliade this means the freedom of human being to participate in the creation of the cosmos, including the creation of human being, by participating in the cosmogonic moment. Whatever is deemed mythical, whatever the value assigned to the mythical, and whatever the character of the ontological regions delimited through the mythical, unbridled creativity is the *telos* toward which human being strives—at least according to these thinkers. This *telos* is the unconditioned and unlimited power to create whatever is considered to be the true locus of humanity and through this creation positing that which exists only in contradistinction to the ontologically, logically, valuationally, and constitutively prior ontological realm. This, I believe, is the "myth" fostered by twentieth-century theories of myth (as well as other intellectual projects of our time): that the *telos* of human existence is absolute and unbounded creative freedom, that achievement of this *telos* is possible, and that this achievement would be good.

I draw a number of conclusions from these considerations, detailed in the final chapter of this work. I propose that the mythical is not only typical of cultural formation, but prototypical and necessary. I understand myth as a continuing and powerful feature of our lives, whether we are "primitives" telling fantastic stories around a fire or intellectual "sophisticates" explaining those fantastic stories. The power of myth is such that it must be understood and respected, and in this I follow the implications we find in Plato's *Republic*. If it is the case that the *polis* cannot, in the end, exist without myth, then it is our duty to discover and create the best myths for organizing our public and private lives. And, I believe, the myth of unbounded freedom as the *telos* of human existence is not among the best. I find it to be metaphysically untenable, and morally and aesthetically repugnant. The Conclusion outlines an alternative myth of human creation (in both senses: how human being creates and how human being is created). This alternative myth is one that depends on assuming a radical continuity of the human and nonhuman spheres, rather than the assumption of ontological discontinuity that's found in the theories under examination. This alternative conception of creation or creative freedom also depends on a description of the "nature" of culture.

Culture is the means by which human being interprets itself and its environment, though we must not think of interpretation only in the sense of translation or specifically conceptual acts. Culture, the general case of which myth is a specific, is also the arena of interaction of the human organism and its larger natural environment. Myth is an essential strand of cultural production; it is the means by which human being determines, discovers, and delimits its own range, its own boundaries. Mythmaking is the backbone of culture, the fundamental means by which human beings demarcate, that is to say, create, human being.

So myth *is*, in an important sense, the means by which the subjective as well as (through difference) the objective features of existence are constituted. But if this is the case, we cannot also adhere to a notion of the *telos* of the truly human as unbounded creative power or activity. This notion of freedom for the truly human condition cannot be held at the same time as we hold that human being is *self*-creative. The act of creation necessarily includes determination, delimitation, demarcation. Human creation (creation or constitution of the boundaries of the truly human) can be no different in this respect. If freedom for human being is the freedom to constitute both the subjective and objective spheres of existence, it cannot be unbounded; it must be constrained or conditioned. Creation is a giving shape, and giving shape is discovering and determining limits within the means provided by the creative context. I believe that we must abjure the notion of complete unbounded freedom of creation while embracing the activity of human being construing and interpreting itself; creating within the context or setting of the indefinitely complex environment we call our home.

In his essay, "Historical Naturalism," John Herman Randall, Jr. wrote,

> Not only are poetry, self-sacrifice, and religious adoration facts to be understood; nature lends herself to lyrical expression, to moral devotion, and to idealizing worship as well as to understanding, and all these activities of men have definite implications for the character of the nature that sustains them.[9]

This insight has sustained me in my examination of myth and theories of myth. These as well tell us about nature—human nature and the natural world in which human nature finds and construes itself; and discussions of culture, of myth, of human being must acknowledge the setting in which such processes occur.

1

What Is Myth?

This chapter could as well serve as an appendix to *The Magic Mirror*. It provides a brief overview of some important theories of myth without offering detailed analyses or criticism. Though the theories outlined here are interesting, they play little part in what follows in this book. This cursory review does show us two things about theories of myth, however. The first point is a critical one: most theories of myth are remarkably lacking in a definition of myth. Much may be said about the role of myth, or the power of myth, or the pervasiveness of myth without making clear what is under consideration. The second point is a more analytical one: by and large, theories of myth specify or exhibit category distinctions that demarcate what is truly human from what is other than this. These two points are taken up in much greater detail in chapters 2–6, and the reader may wish to move on quickly to the sustained arguments presented in those chapters.

⊛

What is (a) myth? It seems our inquiry must begin with the most basic question. What are we investigating? This simple question is really quite difficult to answer.

At times it seems as if anthropologists, ethnologists, folklorists, classicists, philosophers of culture, and all others studying myth are working in the manner of botanists or zoologists who have not yet clearly defined the difference between flora and fauna and the differences between varieties of these while investigating a world of constantly and wildly mutating forms of life. The study of myth is an exemplary instance of a science in the throes of defining itself and its objects at one and the same time. This may seem odd, but it is to be expected in a field whose original boundaries are shrinking alarmingly fast, as truly "virgin" societies have all but vanished from the face of the earth, due, at least in part, to our efforts to explore, examine, and understand them. At the same time as the boundaries of the field are shrinking, they also seem to be becoming more porous. We can observe this in the extension of the concept of myth in the popular media (as in the newspaper article titled, "More Myths about Seatbelts"). But we also see its extension in serious scholarly work explaining aspects of contemporary painting, the history of literature, economic practices, and so on. For example, a recent reviewer of Garry Wills' *Lincoln at Gettysburg: The Words That Remade America* claims that, "A rich mythology has grown up around this mythic moment in American history" and that, "Wills dispels some of the curiously persistent myths about the occasion."[1]

I would like to suggest that there is an implicit consensus in the way that the concept of myth is used, but this pervasive usage is both more and less what individual theorists and writers ascribe to myth. 'Myth' is a term used to describe what is "other," what does not belong to the existential, intellectual, cultural, or historical position of the person applying the label "mythical." This is a very general initial formulation of a functional property of the term 'myth'. Myth functions or works to identify and classify aspects of human existence that are foreign to the observer. There is nothing radical about this claim. However, we will see as we go along that there are a number of quite interesting ramifications of this feature of myth. 'Myth' is also functional in that it is a strictly relative term— like the shift in the center of the solar system in the Copernican Revolution in astronomy. What is other, what is mythical, depends on what one takes as the point of reference. The difference between the intellectual revolution in astronomy and the way that investigators of myth view their subject is that the mythologist seems to have great difficulty imagining the focal point of analysis as any other than his or her own. The astronomer can picture the movement of the planets from the perspective of the sun. The mythologist appears locked in to her/his own vantage point as the point of arbitration of what belongs to the other, and, therefore, the mythical is always a function or correlate or complement of the observer's position. A simple example of this comes from listening to the ways that people name narratives. To the Okanogan teller, the "Creation of the Animal People" is a story or a tale.[2] To the observer, standing outside the culture from which the story springs, it is a myth. The same observer would be hard pressed to see the story of the evolution of myriad plant life as a myth, though s/he may be willing to say that life arising out of nonliving, primal soup charged by bolts of lightening is the best story we've developed to explain biodiversity.

The closest myth comes to being acknowledged as part of the world of the analyst of myth is in the conception of myths as underlying, inarticulate assumptions about the world and human existence. These assumptions may be seen as misapprehensions, at best quaint and at worst dangerous, needing only the light of rational thought to expose and wither them. Analysts of myth may also understand schematic narratives that can be reproduced under new auspices, in new settings, as mythical. Northrup Frye uses this notion of the mythical to great advantage in *Anatomy of Criticism* and other works.[3] So, we may be able to identify the Oedipal myth in contemporary films or novels. Of course, the identification of the mythical narrative patterns often forces the myth out of its shadowy recesses in artistic (or psychic) processes. The mythical story's power to sway and persuade loses a great deal of efficacy when it is identified and analyzed; it may lose precisely those characteristics that earned it the title "mythical" in the first place.

In any case, it appears that the mythical "object" is unstable, relative, and inconsistent. Anything whatever may be called mythical—as long as "it" lies outside the realm identified as the analyst's own. It is the function of myth that remains the same; myth demarcates what is other, whatever that may be.

STRUCTURAL ACCOUNTS OF MYTH

Regardless of what seem to be problems in clearly articulating the object of inquiry in research on myth and mythmaking, most of the authors examined in researching the present work take for granted that there is some sort of consensus as to what constitutes the object of study for mythologists and related theoreticians. The mythologist tends to give many examples of myth without ever defining the term, as if we're all agreed as to what counts as a myth. This is quite clear in some of the classic works. For example, Edith Hamilton's *Mythology* is a straightforward paean to the transformation of the condition of human life from an earlier, more brutal form to the much more civilized (and much more like our own) later Greek culture. She writes that, "of course the Greeks too had their roots in the primeval slime. Of course they too once lived a savage life, ugly and brutal. But what the myths show is how high they had risen above the ancient filth and fierceness."[4] Hamilton makes no attempt to define myth, but catalogues the divinities spoken of in pre-Christian, though non-Judaic, accounts of the Greek, Roman, and Norse pantheons.

Sir James Frazer's work, *The Golden Bough*, is a "contribution to that still youthful science that seeks to trace the growth of human thought and institutions in those dark ages which lie beyond the range of history."[5] Frazer thought of his work as a chronicle of the human imagination as it grappled with the tenuous relation between thought and the vagaries of nature. He concluded that "the movement of the higher thought, as far as we can trace it, has on the whole been from magic through religion to science."[6] In Frazer's scheme, myth appears as the narratives that accompany ritual activity, by way of explaining the activity. Myth may also be stories, primarily in oral traditions, of various deities or of persons of heroic stature who cannot be located in a definite historical period. In either case, for Frazer, myth lies in a dark, prehistoric time, distinct from enlightened, historical, scientific life. Myth is a once necessary, but no longer viable, way of understanding the world.

Much of the data utilized in the study of myth are collections made by nineteenth-century white men in their quest to ferret out the unusual or the quaint and to bring Christianity and fealty to Empire to the heathens. This means that a certain skepticism must be brought to bear, performing a theoretical balancing act in interpreting texts (themselves primarily transcriptions made by the collectors of the data, translating from unusual languages) that may very well be the only accounts of societies now extinct or radically transformed by their acquaintance with the rest of the world. The evidence gathered as the myths of non-European societies included the following: any stories or descriptions of the various members of divine pantheons; accounts of the creation of the cosmos, the earth, society, plants and animals, subsistence-related rituals, and so on; notions of causal efficacy that depend on inserting a "non"-natural element into the causal series (what we call "miracles" in the Judeo-Christian-Islamic tradition); and stories attending ritual activity of any sort. It is on material of this sort that we've based our theories about myth, though there might be some dispute about where certain lines are to be drawn. Those with strong religious beliefs might, for example, exempt the creation accounts of their own tradition from the qualifier "myth." Some theorists, like Ernst Cassirer, distinguish between mythical practices and religious accomplishments, regardless of geographical or historical origin of the narratives and practices; while other thinkers, like Mircea Eliade, make no distinction at all between religious and mythical beliefs.

As twentieth-century classicists, folklorists, and ethnologists sifted through the accumulation of raw data, the various rituals, transcribed and translated narratives, etymological configurations, and so forth, were sorted into categories. This led to a number of quite succinct definitions of myth, primarily in terms of the structural properties of a story or ritual. These properties are then used to distinguish the truly mythical from the merely entertaining or the morally edifying. G. S. Kirk, a noted classicist, frowns upon defining myth either too broadly (as we'd find in such "universal theories" as those offered by Frazer and Cassirer) or too narrowly (as in defining myth as "sacred tales"). Kirk opts for the definition of myth as a "traditional oral tale," and claims that, "generally speaking a tale is . . . a dramatic construction with a denouement."[7] L. Honko offers a slightly more elaborate definition of myth, one that depends on the fulfillment of four criteria: form, content, function, and context. Simply put, this means that a myth is (1) in form, a narrative account of sacred origins; (2) in content, "contains information about decisive, creative events in the beginning of time"; (3) in function, serves as an exemplar or model in terms of which a "static" ontology is determined; and (4) in context, recited with a ritual pattern, making sacred events repeatable by the human participants.[8]

William Bascom, a folklorist, summarizes the state of his discipline's understanding of the formal features of prose narratives (generally gleaned from oral traditions), differentiating between myth, legend, and folktale. Bascom offers a chart consisting of seven categories, from the presence or absence of a conventional opening to the narrative (as in "Once upon a time . . .") to the inclusion of human or nonhuman agents as the principle characters in the narrative. He uses this chart to distinguish the three kinds of prose narratives on formal grounds. Under these headings, myth is classified as the kind of prose narrative in which there is no conventional opening, no restrictions on whether or not it must be told after dark, concerns something that happened in the remote past in an earlier or other world, has nonhuman principle characters, is believed within the particular society as fact rather than fancy, and can be described as sacred rather than secular.[9]

These definitions, along with the catalogues of myth offered by Hamilton, Frazer, and others, are structural or formal descriptions allowing for distinctions to be made within a wide spectrum of stories. Those who collected the data were predisposed to regard some rather than other narratives and rites as instances of myth, and refining the notion of myth meant collating similarities and differences *within* the mass of data collected. Given these considerations, the conception of myth exhibited in these theories is fundamentally that 'myth' is applicable only to cultural traits or forms not closely related to the traits and forms of modern technologically oriented, western Judeo-Christian societies.

FUNCTIONAL ACCOUNTS OF MYTH

While the definitions recounted above depend on particular forms of locution or recital (such as absence of conventional opening or ritualized enactment), functional definitions of myth depend on articulating how myths work, what myths do, or what affects myths have on human lives. Certain important conceptions of myth imply that it cannot be restricted to archaic or primitive societies, even if we were to expand the scope of the conception to include as vestiges of myth the most "primitive" manifestations in modern societies, such as fairytales, superstitions, and folk remedies. Some anthropologists attempt a specification of the notions of rational, prerational, and irrational activity. This classification can then be used, for example, to distinguish healing rituals and practices that are merely incipient, unsophisticated, but logical precursors to modern, scientific medicine from those practices that are based on myth.[10] We can consider this way of understanding myth as functional, rather than structural. In this case, myth is defined by way of functions of cognition rather than by way of the function of the ritual or story within broader cultural practices. Either way, defining myth functionally rather than formally opens up the possibility of applying the concept of myth to any social group, including the group to which the theorist belongs.

Both Joseph Campbell and Bronislaw Malinowski offer functional definitions of myth in terms of the service performed within a larger arena rather than in terms of myth's function in reflecting the developmental stages of cognition or rationality. Campbell claims that myths function "to bring the human order into accord with the celestial. . . . The myths and rites constitute a mesocosm— a mediating, middle cosmos through which the microcosm of the individual is brought into relation to the macrocosm of the all."[11] Furthermore, he claims, there are "psychological problems inherent in the very biology of our species"—the lengthy period of dependence of the extremely immature human neonate and the later recognition of the limited tenure of one's own existence on earth. These psychological difficulties can only be assuaged, says Campbell, through the medium of myth. He maintains that these two biological facts must be addressed, and that "both the great and the lesser mythologies of mankind have, up to the present, always served simultaneously, both to lead the young from their estate in nature, and to bear the aging back to nature and on through the last dark door."[12]

Where Campbell understands the function of myth as a kind of calibrating system that fits together the exigencies and vicissitudes of the human biological organism with an intuition of an utterly other, universal order, Malinowski describes the function of myth as the "dogmatic backbone of primitive civilization."[13] He denies that myth can be adequately explained or accounted for as primitive methods of understanding natural occurrences. He also disagrees with the notion that myth is a substitution of a concrete exemplar for a more difficult and abstract concept; that is, he denies that mythical symbols must be interpreted in order to discover the "real" referent. In fact, for Malinowski, myth cannot be understood as *any* sort of explanation or "intellectual effort." He writes,

> Studied alive, myth . . . is . . . a direct expression of its subject matter; . . . a narrative resurrection of a primeval reality, told in satisfaction of deep religious wants, moral cravings, social submissions, assertions, even practical requirements. Myth fulfills in primitive culture an indispensable function: it expresses, enhances, and codifies belief; it safeguards and enforces morality; it vouches for the efficiency of ritual and contains practical rules for the guidance of man. . . . It is not an idle tale, but a hard-worked active force; . . . a pragmatic charter of primitive faith and moral wisdom.[14]

Whatever stories or narratives fulfill these functions deserve the title of myth or sacred tale. Malinowski is quite happy to extend the field of myth to any contemporary society, including his own. He is, however, cognizant of the difficulties of doing such work within one's own social group.

Claude Lévi-Strauss applies the tenets of Ferdinand de Saussure's work in linguistics to myth studies. De Saussure and his followers developed a system of semiological analysis that charts the construction of meaning through the interplay of language. Very simply put (for a more complete description, please see chapter 3), semiology shows that there can be no essential or inherent meanings in the words and concepts we use. Rather, the meaning of a word depends on its juxtaposition with, or difference from, other words. In this view, language is not static, is not a passive carrier of meaning, but is active in constructing or constituting meaning. One might guess that a theory of myth derived from semiology would offer the most functional analysis or definition of myth and mythmaking. However, this is not the case. While he certainly gives us a detailed and fascinating account of the permutations wrought on the themes and mythemes of traditional narratives, Levi-Strauss's method of deciding which narratives will count as the objects of his inquiry is quite pedestrian.

In his introduction (called the "Overture") to *The Raw and the Cooked*, a work subtitled *Introduction to a Science of Mythology*, Lévi-Strauss provocatively likens his work to a piece of music. He regards his method of analysis as a method of composition, a layering of themes and images, expressive tensions, varying tempos and rhythms, alternating densities of analyses, contrasting and harmonious patterns of exposition. Lévi-Strauss also contends that this method of composition is particularly apt in an explication of myth, because of the close similarities between myth and music. He writes that both are "instruments for the obliteration of time." Both music and myth induce an experience of a "synchronic totality," resulting in "a kind of immortality."[15] Lévi-Strauss also makes trenchant comparisons between myth and music in regard to the relation between historical temporality and psychophysiological time, aesthetic experience and aesthetic production, and so on. His remarks are often startling and evocative, and his analyses fresh and inviting. But just *what* is it that he is writing about? That is, what counts as myth for Lévi-Strauss?

The closest that Lévi-Strauss comes, in *The Raw and the Cooked*, to defining what it is that he is analyzing as a structuralist, is an aside concerning possible criticism that he chose only those myths that lend support to his thesis. Lévi-Strauss rebuts this anticipated criticism by noting that he delayed publication of the work in order to examine the first volume of *Enciclopedia Bororo*, a compendium of traditions and traditional lore. His suggestion is that, as myths form a kind of web of signification, that the addition of more examples will not substantially alter any theoretical insight or scientific progress we might enjoy using the material already at hand, whether taken from the journals of missionaries or from contemporary ethnological and anthropological studies. He likens this to the fact that "experience proves that a linguist can work out the grammar of a given language from a remarkably small number of sentences, compared to all those he might in theory have collected."[16] I would suggest that this is true *only if* the linguist already knows which sounds, which symbols, which facial expressions, and which hand and body movements belong to the system of communication, and which are irrelevant. It would seem that only the meagerest linguistic analysis, one that ought not be quite trusted, can be developed if the linguist has included only those examples most familiar, or only those that fit the linguist's conception of what counts as a sentence, for consideration as relevant exemplars.

Lévi-Strauss analyzes 187 "myths" in the course of *The Raw and the Cooked*, but comes no closer to explaining the principles by which we must consider these stories as myths. In neither *The Elementary Structures of Kinship* nor in *Tristes Tropique* does he offer a more satisfying definition of myth.[17] The essay, "The Structural Study of Myth," in *Structural Anthropology*,[18] gives us a somewhat clearer notion of the meaning of the term 'myth', though still not sufficient for our purpose of deciding precisely what belongs to the investigative category in the first place, before we begin our explanatory calisthenics. In the essay, Lévi-Strauss recounts certain themes from de Saussure's work in linguistics, distinguishing *langue* and *parole* in terms of the diachronic and synchronic dimensions of language. He adds,

> we may notice that myth uses a third referent which combines the properties of the first two. On the one hand, a myth always refers to events alleged to have taken place long ago. But what gives myth an operational value is that the specific pattern described is timeless; it explains the present and the past as well as the future.[19]

Later in the same essay, Lévi-Strauss recurs to the relationship between *langue* and *parole* and claims that "myth is an intermediary entity between a statistical aggregate of molecules and the molecular structure itself." This analogy to chemical processes does not really help in *defining* myth. Lévi-Strauss is honest, no doubt, in denying that he has chosen particular myths to buttress his structural analysis. However, the pool of data from which he draws has a selection mechanism already built-in and this mechanism is not investigated by Lévi-Strauss in his most important works on myth. I would suggest that Lévi-Strauss has given us a theory of "myth" based only on stories that anthropologists, ethnologists, and missionaries have found to be unfamiliar, alien, fantastic, and other.

Hans Blumenberg offers another interesting and complex account of myth and mythmaking, one that defines myth in terms of its function in human life. His approach combines theories of human physiological and biological evolution with phenomenology. According to Blumenberg, in his *Work on Myth*, the best way to make sense of myth is to examine the purposes that myth must have served in the very beginnings of human existence.[20] Mythmaking holds the peculiar status of being, in a sense, *pre*-intentional, in the phenomenological sense of intentionality. Blumenberg's claim is that as the human creature (or perhaps we must consider this a prehuman creature) gained a bipedal, increasingly upright position and at the same time migrated from the sheltered rainforest habitat to the open savanna, there occurred a qualitative change in the human organism. The "sudden" leap to an environment dominated by a vast, inaccessible horizon and an increasing dependence on far-reaching visual acuity engendered an "absolutism of reality." This is a phrase Blumenberg uses to describe that state of being in which the very indefiniteness of the situation, the inability to discover or encounter any boundaries (as the new horizon of the world is, effectively, limitless and unbounded) overwhelms any sense of mastery on the part of the creature over its world. There is nothing to be mastered. Blumenberg writes that this is equivalent to a state of total anxiety; it is "intentionality of consciousness without an object . . . the whole horizon becomes equivalent to the totality of the directions from which '[danger] can come at one.'"[21]

The generalized, constant state of excitement and fear engendered by this new environment cannot be maintained indefinitely. The human organism cannot survive long in such a state of anxiety. However, Blumenberg suggests that this situation, extended for a certain period of time, contributes to the greater sense of anticipation and curiosity in the human animal, prerequisites for later intellectual development. Whatever the positive results of this indefinitely extended excitement and fear, the sense of overwhelming anxiety in the face of an environment that offers no opportunity for piecemeal mastery forces the human creature to transform unspecified anxiety into specific fears. Blumenberg writes, "Something is 'put forward,' so as to make what is not present into an object of averting, conjuring up, mollifying, or power-depleting action."[22] This process most likely begins with the attribution of names to some features of that which threatens to overwhelm. Here Blumenberg is in agreement with Ernst Cassirer (as we'll see in the next chapter), at least in terms of mythical language development, though the former adds that "by means of names, the identity of such factors is demonstrated and made approachable, and an equivalent of dealings with them is generated." The mere attribution of names, followed by the development of practices meant to placate, direct, subvert or otherwise manipulate these once overpowering experiences (the absolutism of reality) alleviates "*Lebenangst*," the "pathological" condition of human being in its transition from earlier evolutionary forms.

The power of myth lies in its function of making determinate the indeterminate, and, in this, "Myth is a piece of high-carat 'work of logos.'"[23] Furthermore, when the "work" of myth has managed to both demarcate the originally unbounded and constitute features of the world that can be met with the specific affect of fear rather than the unspecified state of anxiety, true intentionality can arise. Blumenberg claims that,

> Even when it is still a matter of being on one's guard for the invisible and evading it by observing its rules, affect is the inclusive bracket that unites partial actions that work against the absolutism of reality. Intentionality—the coordination of parts into a whole, of qualities into an object, of things into a world—may be the "cooled-off" aggregate condition of such earlier accomplishments of consciousness, accomplishments that had led the way out of the bracketing together of the stimulus and response and that were at the same time the outcome of this exodus.[24]

Blumenberg's contention is that this mode of accomplishment, as an accomplishment of *logos* as well as of *mythos*, does not end with the rise of science, of philosophy, or of monotheistic religious systems. Rather, the mythmaking mode of consciousness is able to "push back" the indefinite, indeterminate horizon until this threat is safely ensconced as absolutely "Other," effectively clearing the scene for the constitution of a human world. Mythmaking does not end at this juncture, but turns its energy toward a full reversal of the absolutism of reality into the absolutism of the subject. Blumenberg traces this progression through versions of the Faust "myth" as found in Lessing, Goethe, and Valéry, as well as the philosophic analogue to the myth in the work of the German Idealists. The implication is that the working of myth, in stretching itself toward the possibility of inverting the absolute sway of reality and installing the subject as complete master, would end itself. However, Blumenberg sees the absolutism of the subject as a limit-case that cannot be achieved. Myth cannot end itself. It continues to spin its variations, though eventually only on the single theme of the subject as self and world constituting.[25]

I am in sympathy with Blumenberg's project of discovering a functional definition of myth, a definition that is not confined to describing the peculiar stories of societies different from our own. His description of the mechanics of mythical constitution (especially in terms of demarcating certain boundary conditions holding between the human organism and its environment) is an important contribution to theories of myth. In fact, this conception of the function of myth plays an important role in the theory of myth developed in the present work. But the problem of what counts as a myth is not solved by Blumenberg. He relies on Old Testament stories, Hesiod's catalogue of the doings of the gods, the tragedies and comedies of classical Greek theater, and the historical variations wrought on the themes and characters found in these sources. Though Blumenberg uses a wide variety of sources for the "myths" he investigates, his method of determining precisely what counts as a myth suffers from the same kinds of problems we find in the work of Lévi-Strauss. What counts as a myth, for Blumenberg? He writes, "Myths are stories that are distinguished by a high degree of constancy in their narrative core and by an equally pronounced capacity for marginal variation."[26] This may indeed be the case, at least insofar as we're speaking of the means of cultural transmission of myths through history. But Blumenberg seems only to have gathered up a large collection of religious and literary artifacts and described the recurrent "theme[s] and variations." He analyzes these as myths, without making clear precisely why *these* recurrent patterns ought to be considered myths.

There are many other important and interesting theoretical accounts of the mythical and the function of myth, though I believe the sample offered here is representative of late nineteenth- and twentieth-century conceptions. However, there are two other contemporary theories of myth that deserve at least passing mention. As noted in the introduction, there has been some fascinating work done on myth in feminist aesthetics and feminist metaphysics. Much of this work is done through radically transforming Jungian and Freudian insights, reviewing these through the lens of female experience. Estella Lauter offers an explication of the changing mythic themes in contemporary women's poetry and painting, suggesting ways in which our cultural fund (especially as it is being transformed by women in the feminist movement) works in reciprocal relation in changing women's images and identifications.[27]

Paul Ricouer's work on myth ranks in complexity and interest with the work of Cassirer, Barthes, Eliade, and Hillman. However, Ricouer's concept of myth is quite similar to that of Eliade's, though Ricouer's emphasis is on the phenomenological aspects of Christian mythical symbolism, particularly that of the "Fall" of human being into sin. In fact, Ricouer refers to Eliade in the introduction to *The Symbolism of Evil*. He writes,

> Man first reads the sacred *on* the world, *on* some elements or aspects of the world, on the heavens, on the sun and moon, on the waters and vegetation. Spoken symbolism thus refers back to manifestations of the sacred, to hierophanies, where the sacred is shown in a fragment of the cosmos, which, in turn, loses its concrete limits, gets charged with innumerable meanings, integrates and unifies the greatest possible number of the sectors of anthropocosmic experience.[28]

Ricouer also shows his kinship with Eliade when he describes the relation of myth to history, and the possibilities for salvation in each mode of existence.[29] Given the similarity of perspective between Ricouer and Eliade, at least on what they understand as belonging to the mythical, I think it unnecessary to do a close explication of both in the present work.

CASUAL USAGES OF 'MYTH'

One more arena of the use of the term 'myth' should be explored, though we can't elevate these uses to the level of theory. 'Myth' is used widely in the public sphere outside of technical or academic treatments. Though in this sphere little attempt is made to define myth precisely, we can glean something of the notions underlying the use of the term. We hear and read of myth in casual conversations, newscasts, movie and book reviews, histories of cooking, newspaper editorials, and so on.[30] 'Myth' is often used as a synonym for mistaken beliefs: "Contrary to childhood myth, nails do not grow after death"; "the image of the scientist as an antisocial loner is a myth [as] the better scientists tend to be quite social." 'Myth' is used as a term of derision, as a curt dismissal of something as worthless: "new myths about cholesterol"; "the 'student-athlete' myth." 'Myth' may connote a larger-than-life status: "It's a mini-movie in the company of a mythic figure"; "it's really a mythical place, a supercharged symbol of all-American dreams"; "he takes on hugely popular subjects, busily pumps up their mythic status, then sets about deflating the legends." There is also a contemporary version of the euhemeristic notion of myth: "the difficulty of grasping the 'real' Katherine Mansfield was compounded after her death . . . by the mythmaking of her husband, who wanted her image everlastingly to be that of . . . a mystic in search of Truth and Love"; "The Museum of Modern Mythology [in San Francisco] includes the late Clara Peller of 'Where's the beef?' fame and the character of Mrs. Olsen, the Swedish lady who constantly shows everyone how to make coffee."

The use of the term 'myth' is quite pervasive in American culture. For a society that prides itself (or at least sees itself) as being scientific, technological, efficient, fact-oriented, and reality-based, we certainly speak and write often of myth, finding it all around us. But of course, "we" are cognizant of the myths *as* myths, "we" are not taken in, though we may occasionally give a barely audible sigh of nostalgia for something irretrievably lost.

Generally speaking, we can categorize the more casual use of 'myth' into three types. A myth is a falsehood—either a deliberate attempt to sway the unwary or a mistaken belief, quite unfounded, but a belief that has become persuasive through its mere pervasiveness. Myths are the products of stripping away all particularities, a presentation of a highly abstract caricature of a person or event that evokes strong resonance in large part because of its abstractness; this is really myth as stereotype. (Larry McMurtry is said to have "de-mythologized" the cowboy myth, in *Lonesome Dove* and *Anything for Billy*, by showing life on the American frontier as dirty, dangerous, and short, and the cowboy as brutish or naive.) Lastly, a myth can be a story, or more precisely, a narrative scheme, that through constant reiteration has come to seem prototypical of our fantasies—the myths of the self-made man and the peculiar spinster aunt.

MYTH AS *OTHER*

We can gain an important insight into how 'myth' functions, in general terms, by recognizing a feature that pervades all these uses of the term, from most to least technical, from formal to structural, to merely implicit definitions. Whether myth is valorized or dishonored, castigated or revered, or merely catalogued as interesting artifact, to call something a myth always marks it as the property of the "other." Myth belongs to some other culture, some other time, some other cosmology. Of course, the sense in which myth is other varies from theory to theory, from conception to conception. But there is always a sense in which whatever is mythical does not belong to "us," to "our" experience, to "our" ways of understanding the world, to "our" cultural accomplishments. The statement can be reversed and the sense of it remains: whatever does not belong to "our own" existential, historical, or intellectual position is mythical. It doesn't appear to matter exactly what constitutes the perspective of the analysis, what position "ours" is. In fact, even those who revere myth see it as characteristic of some culture or time other than their own.

Myth is what is other. Myth may be historically distinct or other, what belongs to another time or era—ancient Greek narratives are called myths. Myth may be what is sociologically distinct or other—aboriginal hunting rituals to ensure success at food acquisition are called mythical. Myth may be what is ontologically distinct or other—existence directed toward the sacred is called mythical to distinguish it from our own secular, historicized existence. Myth may be what is politically distinct or other—the products of ideological commitments not our own are called myths. Myth may be what is epistemologically distinct or other—to those who are rational, scientific, and logical, whatever is prerational, prescientific, or prelogical is mythical. Myth may be whatever is psychologically distinct or other—archetypal images or unconscious patterns that transcend individual existence are called myths. Myth may be whatever is developmentally distinct or other—primitives and children have myths, the more sophisticated mythologist does not.

The closest that myth comes to being intrinsically associated with our "own" sphere of accomplishment (whatever that might be) is in the conception of myth as underlying, inarticulate assumptions about the world and human existence, assumptions even "we" may have. These hidden beliefs are conceived as misapprehensions that should be rooted out, and that will be eradicated once exposed as the faulty premises they are. Even a conception of the mythical as schematic narratives that can be reproduced under fresh auspices, in new settings, in contemporary art or literature, is an instance of this feeling of the "otherness" of myth. In identifying such narrative patterns, we generally deny any continuing power of the pattern to sway us. Once the patterns are identified as mythical, they seem old, dated, holding at most a kind of nostalgic interest.

SUMMARY

Obviously, there are many ways of answering the question: what is (a) myth? But there is a common thread we've identified that runs through the more theoretical definitions and descriptions and the more casual uses of the term. We call myth those human, cultural accomplishments that identify what is other, and obversely, what is the same. The next question is: other than what? My contention is that myths function to demarcate what belongs to the truly human sphere and what does not. (This is certainly not a complete description of myth—we'll examine other conditions in chapter 6 and in the conclusion.)

Myths are the means by which we indicate to ourselves the range and scope of human being proper. Myths are human creations that, in effect, create the boundaries of human nature. The outline of human being is not set, is not static. One group of humans may create stories and rituals and artifacts that exemplify human continuity with the timber wolf, but not with the black bear. They describe themselves, they *create* themselves, in such a way that the range of the truly human extends so far, but no farther. Another group tells the tale and performs the rites that crystalize and create the belief that being human is consciousness reflecting on its own existence, that all else lies outside, all else is other than truly human. Stories of the origin of human being construct a boundary between the non- or pre-human world and the home of human being. Extreme Unction, a ritual attending death, draws the line between the corporeal body and the immortal soul, claiming the latter only for true human existence.

It is not only that we usually identify as mythical those cultural achievements that serve to delineate human being proper, though this function of myth is certainly implied in all the theories and manners of use under consideration, including those of Cassirer, Barthes, Eliade, and Hillman. Theories of myth themselves perform the function of indicating what belongs to human being properly understood and what does not. For example, we'll see that Roland Barthes defines myth as a particular kind of speech, one that obscures the distinction between what is natural and inevitable and what is historical and contingent. And it is the latter that belongs to human being in its least alienated, most real form, in Barthes' view.

We will see that the notions of myth at work in our theoretical accounts of myth themselves give us further clues to the nature of myth and its role in human life and cultural activity. Perhaps an analogy would be helpful. The building of houses, a pictorial history of human-made habitation, and various architectural theories can be brought together to understand more fully the place and role of shelter in human existence. And this is especially the case when we consider the theories themselves as cultural artifacts with deeply embedded assumptions, quite unable to give us the unvarnished "truth" about shelter, only another version of shelter's role. For example, we read Walter Gropius' essay, "The New Architecture and the Bauhaus,"[31] and find its greatest interest not in what it tells us of architecture per se but in expectation that the theoretical articulation of the building practices will tell us much the same thing, though in a different way, that the buildings themselves do. So, the repetition of mythic narratives, the compilation of narratives in anthropological studies, and various theories of the role of myth in cultural life can be brought together to understand more fully the ways that myth and mythmaking, as subject of inquiry and as activity, shape our existence.

It is not only that we tell ourselves stories and perform particular rituals, and through these delineate what we come to claim as the range and scope of human being. Our explanations of the stories—our stories about our stories—perform the same creative work. In either case, myths or theories about myth, our cultural activity is directed toward discovering and creating the boundary of human being.

The next four chapters examine four theories of myth in some detail. In chapter 6, we will see precisely how each theory, according to its own description of myth, serves the same function as does myth, though without admission of the fact. Furthermore, we'll see that these four quite disparate accounts of myth tell us the same, peculiarly modern, story of what human being *really* is. Our new myth, promulgated through intellectual endeavors, is twofold. The first is of our mythless condition, that "we" do not have myths. This is so even for Mircea Eliade, who valorizes myth as the path to full freedom for human being. Second, our modern myth portrays truly human existence as the unbounded or limitless creative freedom to constitute the boundary between the human and the non-human, the sphere of the subject and the sphere of the world. I will argue that this is a myth that bankrupts itself. It is also particularly unsuited for our human future.

2

Ernst Cassirer's Theory of Mythical Symbols

PHILOSOPHY AND MYTH

Ernst Cassirer chides philosophers, from Parmenides on, for relegating myth to the "realm of non-being,"[1] for ignoring myth, for treating it as mere illusion or error. When philosophers *have* turned their attention to the question of myth, it has most often been to demonstrate "its objective nullity," the "wholly 'subjective' illusion to which it owes its existence."[2] Cassirer takes myth and mythical consciousness seriously, applying great energy and acumen to solving this problem. And myth is a *problem* for Cassirer, one that must be solved or overcome if scientific knowledge is to achieve its full flowering.

Ignoring myth, or treating it as merely erroneous, is a mistake, a form of philosophical myopia, and Cassirer sees two "grave" dangers that follow from this. The first is that a disparaging attitude toward myth throws all philosophic analyses of culture into jeopardy. If there is some sort of unity in the variety of specific cultural forms (such as art, technological production, law, economics, ethics, and so on), then to posit one of these as error or illusion is to cast doubt on the others. The fabric of cultural forms is so closely woven with the threads of mythical thought, according to Cassirer, that to discard myth is to unravel the unity of the whole. If it excludes myth from the cultural domain, implying that some human activities are worthy of consideration and others not, philosophy seriously impedes and undercuts its inquiry into the "universal domain of problems which Hegel designated as 'phenomenology of spirit.'"[3]

The unity of cultural achievements is not simply a genetic relationship of more "sophisticated" and more "correct" cultural accomplishments arising out of an undifferentiated, chaotic, primal mythical (mis)apprehension. There are, according to Cassirer, affinities
between and among cultural forms that can only be accounted for if
we view myth as a fully formed cultural accomplishment, analogous but antecedent to other cultural forms. In fact, for Cassirer,
even empirical sensory experience can be fully understood only with
an adequate appreciation of the mythical. Perception itself is an
abstraction from a yet more primary world, that of mythical consciousness, "a world not of 'things' and their 'attributes' but of mythical potencies and powers, of demons and gods."[4]

If the first "grave" danger in our philosophical myopia regarding
myth is that it impedes our understanding of the history of culture's
accomplishments, the second is that it imperils the future of knowledge. Cassirer believes that the shade of mythical thinking continues
to haunt scientific endeavor. Myth taints the content of scientific
thought, for example, in our inability to fully transform the concept of
"force" into a "pure concept of function," devoid of mechanical pushes
and pulls. This indicates a lingering animistic or mythical component in our most sophisticated intellectual endeavors.[5] The surreptitious encroachment of mythical thought into the bounds of critical
inquiry cannot be halted merely by fiat. For Cassirer, the progress of
knowledge demands *conquering* mythical consciousness. The eradication of myth is possible only through understanding myth in "its
own specific meaning and essence."[6] Only through fully understanding
myth can we discover its potencies and finally render these inactive.

A serious examination of myth is essential for philosophy. On
the one hand, the unity of cultural forms can be articulated only by
tracing human accomplishments back through the common and primary cultural achievement of the mythical world. On the other
hand, the investigation of mythical form is not an analysis of a
benign, though interesting, mode of cultural formation. According to
Cassirer, myth is dangerous and must be prevented from further
infecting the slow and hard-fought development of human culture
and the human spirit. Only through serious and careful examination will we be able to eliminate this threat.

MYTH AND POLITICS

These more theoretical considerations in no way exhaust Cassirer's
concern with myth and mythical consciousness. Near the end of

his life, Cassirer devoted himself to understanding the forces tearing Western culture from its moorings, trying to fathom the conditions for the possibility of two world wars and the barbarism of the Nazi regime. He believed that a reinvigorated philosophy (especially a critical philosophy of culture) might aid in stanching the flood of irrational forces surging across Europe. Cassirer became more and more alarmed by the excesses of irrational thought and behavior in the twentieth century, irrationality that was not restricted to the thought and behavior of individuals, but encompassed large social groups and whole nations. He was convinced that a deep chasm had opened between theoretical, or critical, forms of knowledge and discourse and what seemed new rules and justifications for political action. No longer did the modern enlightened tradition of rational discussion hold sway in the arena of political and social activity. Cassirer felt that contemporary political norms demanded the *revocation* of all rational and scientific thought, and represented a return to the most rudimentary stages of culture.[7]

In Cassirer's eyes, this irrational, regressive force was eerily reminiscent of mythical thought. Hero worship, highly ritualized activity, incantatory slogans, stylized images and symbols evoking massive displays of raw emotion: all these signaled a return of the power of myth. But perhaps most telling, the justifications for the (at best) absurd, and (at worst) unspeakable, political activities were unassailable by reason. Whatever, if any, justification given for such actions and attitudes was invulnerable to the sort of reasoning that Western culture had carefully developed and husbanded through centuries of painstaking labor. Cassirer lamented,

> What we have learned in the hard school of our modern political life is the fact that human culture is by no means the firmly established thing that we once supposed it to be[; w]e must always be prepared for violent concussions that may shake our cultural world and our social order to its very foundations.[8]

How can we prevent a recurrence of this "violent concussion"? Cassirer's recommendation is the same, though more impassioned, that he called for in guarding against the encroachment of mythical thought into the home of theoretical or scientific endeavor. We must take myth seriously, we must not ignore its power and potency—we must include serious investigation of myth in philosophic inquiry. "In order to fight an enemy you must know him . . . not only his defects and weaknesses . . . [but] know his strengths."[9] Cassirer's last works were devoted to this task, applying his philosophic knowledge of the workings of mythical thought to the modern political arena. His self-professed philosophic idealism[10] was no hindrance in his commitment to eradicating particular social and political evils.

CASSIRER'S CRITICAL PHILOSOPHY OF CULTURE

A great deal of Cassirer's work on myth is contained in *Mythical Thought,* volume 2 of the monumental *The Philosophy of Symbolic Forms.* His analysis moves in a stately, beautifully reasoned manner, organizing a wide array of empirical data and theoretical hypotheses into a grand theory of the workings of mythical thought. *Mythical Thought* paints the picture of the emergence of consciousness in nature and its movement out of an immediate, barely formed world. Cassirer imagines the human creature confronting a welter of impressions and forming an organized and meaningful "world" out of this. The world as constituted of discrete entities is not *given* to the human creature, it is *created,* and is created as organized and meaningful through the symbolic. Symbols, for Cassirer, are the result of the formative activity of consciousness; symbols are forms achieved through the work of spiritual functioning in the material world. Symbols, as non-material, can appear only when enforming the material. A symbol is, in fact, an indissoluble union of the spiritual and the material, the forming and the enformed. As we'll see, the "matter" enformed is wide-ranging. Sensible experience may be enformed through the forms of empirical consciousness, mathematical "material" may be enformed through scientific consciousness, and so on. Mythical consciousness arises and develops through the construction of a symbol system peculiar to what seems the most rudimentary kind of human interaction with the world. Indeed, according to Cassirer, this symbol system is so primitive that it is the stage at which the human self and the world first become organized and distinguished.

To understand the full breadth of Cassirer's analysis of myth and mythical consciousness, we must understand something of the complex tapestry of his critical philosophy of culture.[11] We must locate his work on myth within the broader project of analysis of symbolic formation. Cassirer identifies the unifying thread in the tremendous variety of human spiritual accomplishment as symbol formation. He claims his task as the formulation of the universal conditions and principles of all symbolic activity, and describes his project in the following way:

Instead of dogmatic metaphysics, which seeks absolute unity in a substance to which all the particulars of existence are reducible, such a philosophical critique [as my own] seeks after a rule governing the concrete diversity of the functions of cognition, a rule which, without negating and destroying them, will gather them into a unity of deed, the unity of a self-contained human endeavor.[12]

Cassirer broadens what can be understood as the Kantian project, or critique of reason, to a critique of cultural or symbolic activity in all its forms. When we closely examine the typical modes of human symbol-making, we are one step further on the road to understanding the world as "pure *expression* of the human spirit."[13] Cassirer elsewhere writes,

It is this work, it is the system of human activities, which defines and determines the circle of "humanity." Language, myth, religion, art, science, history are the constituents, the various sectors of this circle. A "philosophy of man" would therefore be a philosophy which would give us insight into the fundamental structure of each of these human activities, and which at the same time would enable us to understand them as an organic whole.[14]

Culture, the accumulation of the products of symbolic formation, must be understood as the totality of the imprints of human work in and on the world.

Cassirer's notion of a critical philosophy of culture can be likened to the study of fossils. In the latter, we examine remains that at first glance seem extensions of inanimate rock. Yet, on closer scrutiny, these bits of rock appear to be not only part of the inanimate rock formation but expressions of an organization and regularity different from geological formation. The fossils then truly become remains, what is left over from a living form. None of that life remains, but an imprint of its peculiar organization of materiality can be read as a memorial to that life. The scientific task is to reconstruct what the activities of that life must have been to engender these particular configurations of ridges and whorls in stone.

The analogy with fossils is apt, for the investigator of culture must also take into account the material conditions that surrounded the life-form as well as the historical conditions that render the remains available to scrutiny today. The paleontologist is reading back from traces in rock to the life that created the forms leaving these traces. What were the activities (of organism and environment) that determined the shapes of living material to which these marks in rock are testament? The heterogeneity of forms is linked to a unity of function: life working its transformations on and in the material of the world. The paleontologist cannot study life apart from the particular manifestations of forms wrought, yet must not lose sight of the singular force, life, that gave expression to these particular and diverse forms.

So, for Cassirer, one cannot study "Spirit" or consciousness apart from the symbolic or cultural forms wrought. The traces left in the world by human activity give testimony to a unity expressing itself through myriad particular forms. The essence of human nature is symbolic activity, the products of which constitute the totality of culture. But whatever the variety of cultural or symbolic forms we discover, as with fossils, we are able to trace back to the singular origin of the variety of manifestations. With fossil remains, we trace back to organic life expressed through many forms; with cultural products, we trace back to Spirit expressed through its many symbolic forms. Cassirer has teased out a number of strands of symbolic work, each characterized by specific types of organizational forms. These are, at least, science (theoretical activity that includes critical philosophy), language, art, and myth, as well as the related subfields of biology, history, and so forth. The character of each strand depends on a number of factors: the material that is manipulated or articulated in the symbolic form, the particular types of unities exhibited in these forms, and the corresponding aspect of human being that finds expression in the form.

Cassirer examines the gamut of cultural forms and finds each a legitimate means of exploring the formative activity of consciousness. Each symbolic function is coherent and self-sufficient, and each can be investigated for its specific ordering of the world of human being. But Cassirer also posits a hierarchical arrangement within the variety of cultural forms. The lowest rung of the hierarchy is a most primitive mixture of protolinguistic and mythical activity giving rise to a rudimentary distinction between self and world. At the apex of the formal hierarchy is a purely theoretical apprehension of function, untainted by any reference to a world independent of concept formation.

Theoretical consciousness (including critical philosophy) not only builds on mythical and primitive linguistic forms, it must overturn them. As "Spirit" comes to recognize itself as distinct from

"Life," it begins to understand that the vehicles of meaning—symbols—are its own constructions, subject to the control of consciousness and reason.[15] Spirit comes to recognize symbols *as* symbols and not as aspects of the natural world. For example, in its primitive functioning, consciousness assigns names (a kind of linguistic symbol) to aspects of the world. These protolinguistic symbols bring together features of experience into unified and quasi-objective forms, and aid in distinguishing the self, or the subjective, from the world. But these symbols are not apprehended by consciousness as originating in consciousness. A name is construed as an essential feature of the thing named, a property of the thing, not a creation of consciousness.

At the same time as Spirit comes to recognize its symbolic accomplishments as its own, Spirit gradually purifies itself of dependence on "substance." That is, consciousness begins to distinguish between the spiritual and the material, and comes to align itself with the nonsubstantial. Also, as consciousness comes to recognize the formal or formed aspect of the world as its own creation, it begins to be able to separate the forms from the matter enformed. This allows consciousness a much greater advantage in gaining knowledge. For example, physics has seen the transformation of the concept of matter from that of inert mass to merely a different way of conceiving of energy. The scientific symbol, "matter," lost its dependence on substance, and came to be recognized as just another symbolic way of organizing experience and knowledge in a coherent fashion. When the symbol can be freely lifted from the material to which it is engaged and understood as a means of organizing disparate impressions, then the symbol can be applied to other aspects of the world. If matter is merely another way of conceiving of energy, then those aspects of the world that appeared as inert and irreducible can now be understood as dynamic and part of a larger and more coherent energetic universe.

According to Cassirer, as symbol formation becomes more sophisticated and as consciousness comes to see itself as the progenitor of the symbolic forms organizing experience, the world and the self lose the mantle of substantiality. This crutch for understanding gives way to relational concepts of functional determination, as for example, in consciousness coming to understand the "self" as the relation between the various activities and behaviors of the human organism, or in "matter" being understood as energy in one of its forms.[16] In Cassirer's eloquent account of the fundamental similarities of the various symbolic forms—from the earliest accomplishments to the most contemporary—we discover generic features of all human interaction in and with the world. Every symbolic form constitutes unities amidst multiplicity and organizes experience into spatial and temporal dimensions, though, of course, each form does so in a unique way. But the broader implication of his analysis is that the historically earlier forms of cultural activity exhibit a more primitive human engagement with the world. Mythical consciousness is less removed from strict biological embeddedness in the natural order than are art and religion, for example.

According to Cassirer, as consciousness grows out of its mythical formative activity, it is gaining freedom from immersion in the natural, substantially determined world. Cassirer's understanding of freedom is similar to Kant's in that under nature there can be, by definition, no freedom, and hence, no truly human position. If nature is absolutely determined through its own mechanical laws, then human nature conceived as merely part of the natural scheme is determined as well. Cassirer is emphatic when he claims that embeddedness in the natural world, or the world seen as self-subsisting substance, is a kind of passivity.[17] An underlying premise of Cassirer's work is that consciousness moves from a state of passivity—taking the world as given by the world, as brute substance—to a state of activity. This activity is consciousness constructing symbols, forming a meaningful world out of a substantial world, taking the world not as given, but recognizing it as created or spiritually formed.

This activity is always a movement toward freedom, freedom understood as much as an ethical and political ideal as a metaphysical condition. For Cassirer, the peculiarity of consciousness lies in its ability to fashion a symbolic ladder. With symbol formation, consciousness can raise itself from the necessities of the biological and physical world. The ladder is constructed, rung by rung, as consciousness discovers (and creates) new materials that are constituted by its own formative activity. The progress of consciousness toward greater and greater degrees of freedom is the progress of consciousness in its development toward knowing itself as a purely spiritual principle with no reliance on substance; even substance as a category of thought eventually disappears. Consciousness is, and gradually comes to understand itself as, function in action; the realm of being for human being is act*ing*, form*ing*, symbol construct*ing*.

For Cassirer, whatever consciousness may be in its more fully developed functions, the development itself can be monitored and mapped according to degrees of freedom from the blind, mechanical interaction of any organism with its environment. As consciousness wrests itself from its embeddedness in nature, its fundamental act of unification is applied to objects of greater and greater remove from the absolute particularity of non- or pre-conscious life. For example, as the linguistic symbolic form develops, class names are utilized, and a wide variety of particulars can be brought together or unified under the term 'fruit.' This unified "object" is nowhere found in presymbolic experience, but once developed it functions to organize human activity in food-gathering. The beauty of Cassirer's system of explanation is that it assumes the priority of human work in the world. Interaction with the world is requisite for the human biological organism in transcending the genetic limits of the species, as well as for transcending the limits inherent in certain categories of thought. But, as we shall see, the world in which humans work itself changes in this process, in the movement toward freedom.

⊚⇞⊚

Where must Cassirer begin in his critical philosophy if it is to be broader in scope than the Kantian critique of reason? His account must be amenable to the historically bound character of both consciousness and the world, as well as allow for the increasing freedom of consciousness from its natural and original constraints. Cassirer claims that a critique of pure theoretical consciousness, exemplified in a critical philosophy of science, is an unfortunate starting point for an adequate philosophical explication of symbolic formation. An analysis of scientific consciousness is hard pressed to obviate all traces of naive realism. A concept of "nature" as an independent, substantial existence to which knowledge must be related is almost always implied in scientific reasoning. For Cassirer, this assumption impedes the free construction of abstract symbols, and thus impedes the progress of scientific knowledge. It also obscures the fact that the categories and concepts applied to nature are furnished by consciousness, not essential features of the object. It can be quite difficult to see the creative power of consciousness in symbols such as "gravity," "force," and "energy," though these are purely symbolic constructions. If we insist on assuming that these qualities are inherent in the objects of ascription rather than symbolic means of organizing the objective features of the world, we are hard pressed to understand the essential role of consciousness in organizing a world of objects and attributes. Though science itself is a symbolic or cultural form, and as such offers as legitimate and fruitful an entrance into critical philosophy as any other symbolic form, for Cassirer, its problems outweigh its merits as a starting point of the analysis of human activity.

A critique of the concept of culture in general, on the other hand, obviously having the products of human fashioning as its objects, can much more clearly correlate the functions of Spirit with the concrete expressions of these functions. Language, artwork, architecture, literature, and so on, are obviously expressions of the human spirit, obviously not "given" by nature. As the objects of a critical philosophy of culture seem unquestionably the products of spiritual fashioning, the implicit material realism infecting scientific thought is obviated. However, even cultural forms other than the scientific may evidence a kind of naive realism. Art, for example, may continue to be judged in terms of faithful "reproduction" of a natural world that exists independently of the artwork. Only by overcoming this bias toward the mimetic function of art, can painting and sculpture come into their own, recognized as fully symbolic.[18] The appeal of a critique of *mythical* forms is that insofar as the analyst has overcome the perspective of mythical consciousness, s/he is not tempted to impute an independent existence to the objects of mythical consciousness. Though one might slip into a reliance on the concept of independent substance as underlying the functions described by contemporary physics, or expect that great works of art function mimetically, it seems impossible, for the critical philosopher, to regard the gods and goddesses, stories of origin, fears and delights of the mythically oriented world as anything but humanly or culturally constituted.

THE EMERGENCE OF THE SYMBOLIC
OUT OF THE BIOLOGIC

If mythical consciousness is closely tied to the unmediated biological interaction of the human organism and its environment, but is yet a fully fledged symbolic system, then an understanding of the rudiments of the symbolic in general, in its original departure from the strictly biological, should reveal important characteristics of the mythical form of consciousness. Cassirer outlines the first stirrings of the symbolic out of the biologic in his late work *An Essay on Man*. The general characteristics of all living forms, as we learn from biology, are found in the relation of stimulus to response and adaptation to an environment that in turn accommodates these activities in an overall ecological system. Human organisms certainly follow the same general pattern. But we also understand that each life-form has its own particular organization within the general framework. Corresponding to the particular structures or forms are myriad "worlds" inhabited by the forms. Following the biologist Jacob von Uexküll, Cassirer comments: "In the world of a fly, . . . we find only 'fly things'; in the world of a sea urchin we find only 'sea urchin things.'"[19] In the world of the human, then, we find only "human things." The human world of human things can be demarcated by its specific differences from the general traits of all animal life. Cassirer articulates the difference between human beings and other sentient creatures as a qualitative change in the stimulus-response system. The human animal adds a third link to this chain, inserting a symbolic system between the two poles of adaptation. With this change in the functioning of the organism, there arises a delay, an interruption of the immediate response to stimuli. This loosening of the causal series marks a qualitative change in the biological world. According to Cassirer, this is not merely a broadening of the world, nor a mere increase in the breadth of activity of the human animal. The *animal symbolicum* "lives, so to speak, in a new *dimension* of reality."[20] The specific difference of the human animal is not rationality, though that seems an inherent feature of human activity at many levels. The specific difference of human functioning is symbolic formation. Rationality is too restricted a concept to account for the range and richness of human behavior.

The symbolic understood as delay in the straightforward stimulus-response sequence is not yet a sharp enough tool for distinguishing the human animal from some others. Pavlov's dogs, for example, were able to incorporate the sound of a bell into the feeding situation as an integral part of the activity. Some animals are capable of incorporating many extraneous elements into their behavior, and the presence of these elements seems to allow for an interruption of straightforward and immediate stimulus-response. Cassirer makes his description of the *animal symbolicum* more precise by contrasting its activities with the seeming symbolic work of other creatures. To effect this contrast, we can look to the symbolic character of language, which appears to be the only cultural or symbolic form that we might share with other creatures.

Cassirer distinguishes between propositional language and emotional language. Animal language may indeed express certain "subjective" states—of hunger, need for affection, terror, and so on. But, in animal language "we find no signs which have an objective reference or meaning."[21] This difference allows for distinguishing between signs and symbols, attributing the latter to human communication only, never to animal behavior. Furthermore,

> [s]ignals and symbols belong to two different universes of discourse: a signal is part of the physical world of being; a symbol is part of the human world of meaning. . . . Signals . . . have . . . a sort of physical or substantial being; symbols have only a functional value.[22]

We can also distinguish between practical imagination or intelligence and symbolic imagination or intelligence. The former can be characterized as the learned combination of events and signs. This is a strictly particular relation, not transferable to widely divergent things or events. Thus, some animals learn to associate a word or other cue with a specific situation, as a ringing bell and feeding. But this is not yet symbolic intelligence. That entails the transformation of the particular cue situation into the understanding of the possible universality of signs; the "symbolic function is not restricted to particular cases but is a principle of *universal* applicability."[23]

The universal applicability of symbols, that everything has a name, is not to be confused with uniformity of applicability, that there is a fixed relation between a name and a thing. Universal applicability must exhibit variability or versatility of the symbol in order for the sign to have a truly symbolic function. A child who has not yet grasped the variability of a name will not understand that "not every name of an object is a 'proper name,' that the thing may have quite different names in different languages."[24] (We shall see that mythical consciousness borders on the nonsymbolic in this respect.)

Cassirer examines the case of Helen Keller's admission to the symbolic world. This case is interesting to Cassirer for a number of reasons. One is that Keller's case adds fuel to his refutations of "sensationalism"; that Keller lived with a paucity of sensible experience in no way denied her access to a rich intellectual and cultural life. Keller's case also allows Cassirer to broaden his concept of the symbolic beyond vocal signs. The spoken word is typical, but not prototypical, of the symbolic. He writes:

> If the child has succeeded in grasping the meaning of human language, it does not matter in what particular material this meaning is accessible to it[;] . . . man can construct his sym-

bolic world out of the poorest and scantiest materials. The
thing of vital importance is not the individual bricks and stones
but their general *function* as architectural form. In the realm of
speech it is their general symbolic function which vivifies the
material signs and "makes them speak."[25]

That the symbolic is understood as a much broader category than the
linguistic paves the way for many of the later steps in Cassirer's
analysis of cultural forms.

The development of this symbolic intelligence allows for the
further specification of the peculiarly human. Modern Gestalt psychology and sophisticated animal studies seem to show that the perception or awareness of relations (such as spatial or optical relations)
does not depend on any sort of "objectifying" symbolic activity. The
nonsymbolically structured world of a nonhuman creature may yet
be relationally structured in terms of size, distance, brightness of
hue, and so forth. The simplest acts of perceptions "imply fundamental structural elements, certain patterns or configurations."[26]
But the human animal, building on the preliminary acquisition of
the symbolic, is able to "isolate relations, to consider them in their
abstract meaning." The relations themselves can be designated symbolically and therefore as divorced from concrete particulars exhibiting the relations. We can see this symbolic achievement quite clearly
in the earliest formulations of geometric relations. Even in its most
rudimentary expression, geometrical speculation must attend to the
relations between forms, unmoored from any connection to particular physical or perceptual objects.

These considerations highlight the general features of symbolic
activity. Any cultural or symbolic form must display the following
traits: (1) discontinuity in the biological organization of stimulus to
response, which allows for or demands the inclusion of alternate
links in the series—these are signs; (2) transformation of sign activity from emotional language or expressions of immediate subjective
states to the protosymbolic activity of referring to objects—this is
naming; (3) universal application of naming—that everything has a
name or a symbol; (4) versatility of the symbol—that the name is not
invariably fixed to any particular object; and (5) that a name or symbol can designate relations between things as well as the things
themselves.

The emergence of symbolic activity changes the human world
irrevocably. "Man cannot escape from his own achievement," Cassirer writes,

[h]e cannot but adopt the conditions of his own life. No longer in a merely physical universe, man lives in a symbolic universe. Language, myth, art, and religion are parts of this universe. They are the varied threads which form the symbolic net, the tangled web of human experience. All human progress in thought and experience refines upon and strengthens this net. No longer can man confront reality immediately; he cannot see it, as it were, face to face. Physical reality seems to recede in proportion as man's symbolic activity advances. Instead of dealing with the things themselves, man is in a sense constantly conversing with himself.[27]

Symbolic formation allows isolation of features of the ever-changing flux of biological, organic existence. These isolated features may then be held constant in the form, providing access to an "ideal" world articulated through symbols. Only in this way can the human animal overcome the "limits of his biological needs and practical interests."[28]

POSSIBILITY OF A CRITICAL ANALYSIS
OF MYTHICAL SYMBOLS

We have traveled from Cassirer's specific motives in dealing with the subject of myth, through his general metaphysical stance and his method of a critical philosophy of culture, to the teleology of freedom exhibited in his work. This led to a description of the first stirrings of consciousness out of organic life and toward freedom from embeddedness in natural or substantial existence. We charted this through Cassirer's articulation of the generic traits of symbolic activity, and finally, to his contention that the human world is a symbolically wrought universe. It is only at this point that we can begin a fruitful examination of Cassirer's understanding of the place of myth and mythical thought within the larger arena of symbolic or cultural activity.

Cassirer, of course, uses the perspective of a critical philosophy of culture in dissecting mythical consciousness. This affords us access to a world that is otherwise mostly hidden from us. But the critical perspective itself obscures certain essential features of the mythical world. This problem pervades Cassirer's work, and try as he might, he cannot completely avoid it. The very language adopted by critical philosophy depends on distinctions Cassirer claims have no place in the mythical world. The categories of thing (relative permanence) and attribute (relative flux), subject and object, I and world, abstract and concrete, general and particular, part-to-whole and fore-ground-to-background relations, all are facets of empirical or scientific symbolic formation, and not the mythical. And as the scientific is developed and expressed in the *break* from the mythical, in direct opposition to it, a scientific/theoretical account of the properties of the mythical is a project of heroic measure. The very processes of subsuming particular instances under general laws that accommodate such instances, and the reverse (the intrinsically dialectical movement of analysis and synthesis), which Cassirer understands as the form of theoretical knowledge,[29] is an imposition of the perspective of scientific consciousness on the mythical world. The difficulty is certainly greater than the difficulties inherent in, for example, trying to describe a piece of music adequately in words. The music is not a window into an entirely other cosmos, as the mythical forms appear to be. A better analogy, though still a less difficult task, would be gaining an adequate aesthetic appreciation of a symphony performance using a computer readout of the vibratory frequencies in the concert hall.

The very act of articulating the mythical world linguistically effaces certain features of the object of inquiry. In myth, the word has not yet become separate from the world; signifier/signified is an opposition foreign to mythical consciousness. To speak about, or write about, the mythical world is to divorce oneself irrevocably from it. We can see this in an act as simple as calling stories of gods and goddesses "myths." Such classification immediately divorces the analyst from the experience of a form of belief in these stories, certainly an intrinsic aspect of the mythical world. This makes mythical symbolic activity particularly resistant to theoretical analysis.

This would especially be the case if "philosophy were nothing but the critique of knowledge, and if it were allowed to limit the concept of knowledge so as to encompass only 'exact' science," claims Cassirer. As a matter of fact,

> All theoretical explanation finds itself in opposition to another spiritual force—the force of myth. In order to protect themselves against this force, philosophy and science are obligated not only to replace particular mythical explanations but to do battle with the whole mythical interpretation of existence and to reject it *in toto*. It must not only attack the products and configurations of myth but must attack its root.[30]

This deadly confrontation does not bode well for a fair and accurate philosophical analysis of myth.

Cassirer's notion of a critical philosophy of culture allows for certain features of the mythical world to escape extirpation. He believes that mythical consciousness and powerful mythical symbols cannot be completely destroyed, but that a severe pruning of these is necessary. In a lecture given at Princeton, Cassirer said,

> We cannot entirely suppress or quell [myth]; it always recurs in a new shape. . . . It is not destroyed or annihilated; it has only changed its form. But this very change is of paramount importance. The organism of human culture does not eliminate the mythical elements root and branch, but it learns to control them. It develops new constructive powers of logical and scientific thought, new ethical forces and new creative energies of artistic imagination. By the appearance of these new forces myth is not entirely vanquished, but it is counterbalanced and brought under control. It is true that this equilibrium is rather a labile than a static equilibrium; it is not firmly established but liable to all sorts of disturbances.[31]

There is an obvious tension between the drive of theoretical consciousness to eliminate all vestiges of the mythical and Cassirer's own commitment to examining each cultural form as part of a rigorous critical philosophical anthropology. It is as if a zoologist were to try to understand the ecological niche of a newly discovered predator while at the same time work to eliminate the predator as a danger to other species. Cassirer sees the project of understanding the mythical world as essential to an adequate appreciation of the scope of symbolic formation. Yet his examination is intended to domesticate or eradicate the power of myth. Cassirer treats mythical consciousness as a respected enemy. Myth may indeed be part of human experience, but it must be kept within clearly proscribed bounds in order to prevent it from deflecting consciousness as it wends its symbolic way toward freedom.

Given these considerations, is it possible for critical philosophy to give a fair and adequate account of myth? Cassirer uses at least three different methods for obviating these difficulties. The first is a tried and true intellectual device of keeping a dangerous, perhaps irrational, subject in its place. That is, we range opposition forces around the mythical to hem it in, to delimit and define it in terms of what it is not. Cassirer describes the beginnings of the true philosophic spirit in its confrontation with and disavowal of the mythical. He outlines the triumph of the religious unifying function of Spirit over the dispersed forces of mythical power. He traces the gradual refinement of scientific-theoretical consciousness in its paring away irrelevant assumptions tainted with mythical thought. Language and art are followed as word and image divorce themselves from an inarticulate immersion in the world of myth, finally attaining the status of pure representation for consciousness.

The second method Cassirer uses in describing the mythical is to display the vestiges of myth in the contemporary scene. As we've seen, Cassirer considers the most virulent of these the eruptions of the mythical into the political sphere, culminating in the barbarisms and atrocities of the twentieth century. But the continuing presence of mythical consciousness can be seen in less extreme examples. Certain aphasic conditions can best be understood, according to Cassirer, as a degeneration into an absolute particularity of perception and conception characteristic of mythical consciousness.[32] The language of children exhibits certain traits akin to the magical or mythical properties of words, as well as to the nondifferentiation of signifier and signified inherent in the mythical use of words.[33] And the "expressive" character of the mythical world breaks through into our ordinary experience from to time:

> for even in the life of civilized man [myth] has by no means lost its original power. If we are under the strain of a violent emotion we still have this dramatic conception of things. They no longer wear their usual face; they abruptly change their physiognomy; they are tinged with the specific color of our passions, of love or hate, of fear or hope.[34]

These contemporary vestiges of mythical consciousness suggest the flavor of the archaic form of human experience.

Thirdly, Cassirer handles some aspects of his analysis of myth in a manner similar to that used by, among others, Descartes and Freud. Descartes subjugates (by reducing) the unruly qualities of sensible experience to the precision of the clear and distinct ideas of mathematics and geometry. Freud uncovers the logical structure of the ideas in the unconscious and finds them identical to those of rational thought. Cassirer finds certain activities of consciousness to be constant regardless of symbolic form. Mythical consciousness, like scientific consciousness, articulates the objective features of the world as space, time, and number. But, as we'll see shortly in more detail, mythical thought lacks the category of the "ideal," and so myth's articulation of the objective features of existence structures the world in ways quite foreign to us. Cassirer writes that the structure of mythical thought may appear peculiar,

> but it never lacks a definite logical structure. . . . [The processes of mythical thought] express the same desire of human nature to come to terms with reality, to live in an ordered universe, and to overcome the chaotic state in which things and thoughts have not yet assumed a definite shape and structure.[35]

While Descartes and Freud try to explain away the seeming absolute "otherness" of extended nature and the unconscious by showing such alterity to be merely what is not yet encompassed and clarified by science (mathematical physics or psychoanalysis), Cassirer allows for a real incommensurability between the worlds articulated through different symbolic systems.

PERCEPTION AND CONCEPTION
IN THE MYTHICAL WORLD

Given the difficulties inherent in evoking the mythical world and given the strategies used by Cassirer in analyzing the features of the mythical world, his description of the mythical is an impressive accomplishment. What follows is a picture of the mythical world, pieced together from clues and directions scattered throughout Cassirer's life's work.

The mythical is the symbolic matrix out of which all other truly human worlds and selves arise. It is the formative activity that is closest to purely biological existence.

> It is only in these [mythic] activities as a whole that is effected that progressive differentiation of "subject" and "object," "I" and "world," through which consciousness issues from its stupor, its captivity in mere material existence, in sensory impression and affectivity.[36]

What is this power that wrests itself from nature, gradually constituting a subject and a world? Cassirer, in arguing with Max Scheler, writes of the formative energy of "Spirit" over against the efficient energy of "Life."[37] Life, according to this argument, is the untrammeled transaction of organism and environment, an equilibrium of stimulus-response, an equivalence of energy transformations. Spirit enters the equation as a doubling-back of this force on itself. This doubling-back is an "act of self-generation," a division of Spirit that both allows and necessitates symbolic activity. Allows, because the doubling-back generates an opening in the world where meaning can occur and accrue. Necessitates, because as Spirit falls back upon itself, its unimpeded commerce in Life becomes displaced, and a mediated path back to the world must be found.

It is important to note that when Cassirer writes of "mythical consciousness" (or the shorthand, "myth"), he is not referring to any individual human being in some state of self-reflection or self-identification. It is only in and through the mediation of the mythical form that the "I" becomes distinguished from a world that is "not-I." In this, myth is much like the other symbolic forms. Cassirer writes,

> The crucial achievement of every symbolic form lies precisely in the fact that it does not *have* the limit between I and reality as pre-existent and established for all time but must itself create this limit—and that each fundamental form creates it *in a different way*.[38]

But the I that is a product of mythical formation is foreign to us. Inasmuch as we have abandoned the mythical perspective, we have taken up the I as developed in other symbolic systems. As a matter of fact, the dissolution of mythical thought occurs "when the soul ceases to be considered as the mere vehicle or cause of vital phenomena [as it is in myth] and is taken rather as the subject of ethical consciousness."[39]

The most general feature of the mythical is one that Cassirer characterizes as a lack. Mythical consciousness does not include the dialectical movement of thought.[40] This movement, which can be clearly discerned in the more developed features of empirical or theoretical consciousness, entails the reflective grasp of some feature of the flux of biologic or natural existence. This feature is held, as it were, in consciousness, and used as a guidepost amidst the ever-changing background of the world. Further impressions can be measured against this less fluid form, and a sort of triangulation occurs. Certain features of the world (those that resemble this more stable nexus) begin to appear as typical, thereby adding force and perseverance to the grasped form. Other features of the world flow by as transient, and finally as accidental, as opposed to essential, features.

Such are the conditions, according to Cassirer, of the differentiations and distinctions implicit in objective empirical perception. This differs only in degree of complexity from the logical form of analysis-synthesis in scientific knowledge subsuming particular occurrences under general laws.

This organization is entirely absent from the mythical. This is not to say that the mythical world is an utter chaos of undifferentiated impressions. But, claims Cassirer, given the absence of any means of measuring present experience against something that is not itself immediately present in perception or conception, the "resultant picture of reality lacks the dimension of depth." The relative shallowness or flatness of the mythical world distinguishes it from the empirical-scientific at every turn of Cassirer's analysis. Perception in the mode of the latter, a "process of selection and differentiation which consciousness applies to the chaotic mass of 'impressions,'" lays the groundwork for any measuring of the fluctuating against the relatively enduring.[41] Empirical-scientific perception allows for accretion of the relatively stable features of the world into objects and for sloughing off the relatively transient features, demoting these to attributes. The world that is built up through this process is a world that has depth in the sense of areas of solidity that act as anchors amidst the more fluid. The distinctions between reality and appearance, truth and error, laws of identity and transformation, and so on, are developed only through this process of constituting conceptual unities. As the accidental are shorn from the essential features, a core of essentiality, held in consciousness, becomes the mark of truth, reality, and identity. (Cassirer is careful to acknowledge that this core will itself be measured against further articulations of typicality.) Again, in its most primitive forms, the empirical has not yet distinguished individual centers of self-reflective consciousness holding or apprehending these cores of essentiality as ideal. The organization of centers of self-reflective consciousness can develop only as this sort of objectifying and unifying dialectical activity turns to the task of forming the I.

Cassirer claims that it would be a mistake to try to understand the mythical world as arising out of even the most undeveloped *empirical* perception. He writes, "If this were the case, myth would transgress at every step not only the laws of logic but also against the elementary facts of perception." It is necessary to unearth the *mythical* perception that would have allowed for the articulated world of myth to arise.

Without such a grounding in an original mode of perception, myth would hover in the void; instead of being a universal form of spiritual manifestation, it would be a kind of spiritual disease; however widely distributed, it would still be an accidental and pathological condition.[42]

Only by discovering an original mythical mode of *perception* can Cassirer rescue mythical *conception* and symbol formation from the charge of error and illusion.

Cassirer does not use this image, but it may help to picture the primitive state of the world of mythical perception as like (to our eyes) a two-dimensional surface of some lightweight fabric, covered with colors and shapes, moving in a breeze. As it billows and recedes, ripples and curves, certain colors and figures and bits of figures approach and others fall away. Mythical perception captures the crest of the fabric as it billows. As nothing can be held in consciousness that is not immediately present in perception, what is perceived is constantly sliding over into new perceptions; there is no ideal or constant as background to the foreground of continual flux. There cannot be an image of what the moving "fabric" might look like if it ceased billowing. There is no category of stable reality to which the particular perceptions are related as instances of momentary appearance.

For Cassirer, this fluidity is characteristic not only of mythical perception, but also of mythical understanding of causality. Perception of physical objects with a solid core of essential features is possible only when (empirical) thought holds these features constant in reflection. This allows general laws of causality (including those of cause *to* effect) to be adduced from particular and nonrepeatable events. Causality in the mythical mode, on the other hand, built out of mythical perception, can only proceed *across* phenomena, as it were. "Here [in mythical thinking] every simultaneity, every spatial co-existence and contact, provide a real 'sequence.'" Cassirer reminds the reader of Hume's claim that the concept of necessary causal relation arises out of conjunction and contiguity of perceptions. Cassirer implies that Hume's description, while inadequate to the forms of theoretical symbolic accomplishment, if taken very broadly is an apt description of the conception of causal relations in the mythical world.[43]

The characteristic "metamorphoses" that occur in the mythical world are also structured by the form of mythical perception. As with "identity" in the empirically ordered world, two things cannot occupy the same space at the same time in the mythically ordered world. In the flat plane of the mythical, the "law of metamorphosis" demands and involves radical transformations quite foreign to empirical consciousness. Cassirer comments, "Anything can *come from* anything, because anything can stand in temporal or spatial contact with anything."[44] The rat *can* be begotten from a rag and a few seeds. The mythical world is not inhabited by the sorts of things that retain a core of identity through change of inessential aspects. Change of appearance *is* change of identity. Temporal succession of particular appearances surrounding a core of stable traits does not seem to occur in the mythical world. Temporal succession of wildly divergent events are grasped by myth as transformations of identity, as metamorphoses. A bird flies so high it disappears, but not merely from sight. It may become the star that is next to appear in the spot where the bird was last seen. Initiation rituals in the mythical world mark the literal transformation of one entity, a child, into another, an adult. For myth, this seems not to be a developmental transition of a "core" self changing in important, though inessential ways (inessential in regards to identity, not to social role). Rather, one sort of being metamorphoses into another.

Cassirer understands the law of metamorphosis to be the most general law governing the structure of the mythical world. Empirical thought, with its abstractive, formalizing character, understands the world according to certain principles of classification, systematization, and organization—exhibited in differentiation of classes of phenomena into species, genera, families, and so on. He claims that in myth, however, the "limits between the different spheres are not insurmountable barriers; they are fluent and fluctuating. There is no specific difference between the various realms of life. Nothing has a definite, invariable, static shape."[45] The division of the world into antithetical classes such as animate/inanimate, flora/fauna, human/nonhuman, is, for empirical-scientific consciousness, "fundamental and ineffaceable." According to Cassirer, the mythic mind has no such inescapable boundaries.

It would be a mistake to assume that the fluidity of the mythical world is any impediment to the development or implementation of practical living skills. Cassirer reminds us several times of the acuity of perception and thought exhibited in primitive hunting and tracking, cave paintings, and so on. This world is certainly not utterly chaotic and undifferentiated. Rather, it is a world that is not first and foremost a world of "pragmatic or technical interest"; it is neither "a mere object of knowledge nor the field of . . . immediate practical needs."[46] Cassirer maintains that the division of life into the spheres of practical *or* theoretical activity is itself a consequence of empirical thought.

THE "SYMPATHETIC" IN MYTH

Prior to such division of life activities, and prior to the mapping of the world according to nonpermeable categories and classes, there is a "lower original stratum." The practical understanding and manipulation of the world is always secondary for mythical consciousness. The primary form of understanding is neither analytic nor synthetic, but "sympathetic." The original grasp of the world is of the world as a kind of living totality. There is the "deep conviction of a fundamental and indelible *solidarity of life* that bridges over the multiplicity and variety of its single forms." However, the world viewed as a "society of life" is yet another expression of the relative flatness or shallowness of the mythical world.[47] There is no hierarchy of forms in the mythical world, no understanding of a privileged position for the human species, for sentient life in general, or even for the biotic as opposed to the inorganic. In fact, there appears to be no nonliving sphere in the mythical world. Mortality is never a fact for myth, and is certainly not a universal law. "A" life is never "lost" in this system, though it may be radically transformed. The lack of differentiation between the nonliving and living spheres, as well as the lack of hierarchically arranged subclasses within the latter, is mirrored in a kind of temporal nondifferentiation. The individual does not cease to be at any time, but reoccurs in metamorphosed form, generation after generation. The history of a clan or family is never an unbroken sequence of unique individuals, it is a recycling of the same lives again and again.

Mythical perception and mythical thought never disclose a world of indifferent things. Mythical consciousness inhabits a world alive in every nook and cranny. This living world pulsates with its own rhythms and desires and motives. The human animal relates to this world as it would to the faces of those it loves or hates. Cassirer sometimes calls this the "physiognomic" world.[48] In the earliest stages of the mythical world, the physiognomic character is not yet apprehended as particular loci of living form; it is a "universal character of reality."[49] Only later do independent centers of expressiveness begin to be discerned. With the further development of language, the names of individual gods and demons appear to label these loci of expressiveness, and certain rocks or trees, for example, experienced as threatening or provident, come to have sacred status.

Mythical perception is not entirely unavailable to the critical philosopher working in the mode of theoretical consciousness. Again using animal studies and psychological analyses of the development of children, we find the rudiments of a kind of perception that could afford access to the mythical world. The most primitive units of perception for the human infant do not seem to be stable object forms, but rather quite complex configurations of what Cassirer calls the "expressive" features of the world. The *smiling* or *anxious* parental face is composed (according to empirical perception) of extremely mobile, variable aspects, that appear (again according to the empirical) as inessential over against the more stable features, perhaps hair or eye color. But for the infant, the mobile aspects—the expressive mouth or the wiggling eyebrows—are the anchors or focal points of the perceptual world. The perceptible world for the child, as well as for (at least) the higher primates, is a world of alluringness, repulsiveness, friendliness. The sky may indeed be threatening, the flowers cheerful, the darkness dangerous. These seem to be "objective" features of a quite primitive perception. In fact, this appears to be more primitive than perception construed as simple objects built out of discrete or simple sense data. Cassirer claims that this primitive perceptual organization can best be described as a world in which the "thou" is always prior to the "it."[50] Again, "thou" and "it" are not to be understood as standing over against a well-formed "I," but rather as characteristics of the perspective in which both the I and the world of mythical consciousness become articulate. We also cannot account for the expressive character of the mythical world as being a projection of subjective attributes or qualities, because the subject as a unified locus of experience is formed in and through the symbolic form itself, in interaction with an expressive world.

MYTH AND LANGUAGE

These peculiarities in the mythical world, of perception, causality, transformation, and identity, and the experience of the world as alive, all attest to the characteristic flatness of the mythical perspective. Of course, this in no way means that the mythical world is empty or devoid of perceptual or emotional richness—quite the contrary. But, at least according to Cassirer, the mythical world would be quite foreign to us because mythical consciousness is not in the business of constituting abstract terms or generalized categories or perceptual typicalities to which the particulars of experience may be

relegated. Rather, much of mythical experience could be characterized, if Cassirer is correct, by the tremendous singularity and particularity of experiences and events. These unique particulars are
related, in mythical experience, in complex patterns unfamiliar to us.
For example, if there are no relatively fixed categories of inanimate
and animate (general and abstract conceptual unities that have no
objective correlate in experience, though whatever appears in experience can be assigned to either one or the other category), then
observing an animal in relation to its environment would be quite
different than it is for us. Any animal would appear as the necessary
result of just this *present* confluence of living forces, as a living part
of a much larger living whole. Of course, neither the part nor the
whole would be thought of as alive, for that necessitates an opposition between animate an inanimate, an opposition foreign to myth.

The lack of any reflective measure of typicality, the inability to
hold any feature of experience as constant over against the flux
imposed on the human animal by omnipresent nature, is also
described by Cassirer as the absence of any representative function in
mythical consciousness. Representation demands, at the very least,
the relation of (presented) part to (nonpresent) whole. For example,
we may represent the natural number series as "1, 2, 3, . . ." Representation may extend to extraordinarily attenuated aspects of experience and quite complex states, as in a "smiley face" representing
"Pollyanna happiness." The representative function of an image or a
selected element of a larger context depends on the recognition of
something "standing for" something else that it is not. According to
Cassirer, the representative function is altogether lacking in the
mythical symbolic form. Pins stuck in a doll do not represent doing
harm to someone. The doll is not a representation, it *is* that person.
Toenail clippings and fallen hairs do not represent, they *are* the person. A mask does not represent the totem animal, it *is* that animal.[51]
The inability of mythical consciousness to apprehend or construct
representations is not only a mark of unidimensionality in the mythical world. It is also marks the entrapment of consciousness in
nature. In a different context, Cassirer writes that "the images in
which [myth] lives are not *known* as images. They are not regarded
as symbols but as realities. This reality cannot be rejected or criti-
cized; it has to be accepted in a passive way."[52] The making of images
is certainly one escape from embeddedness in nature. If the image of
the bear *is* the bear, then supplications may be made to the image,
and one need not wait for the world to provide the opportune
moment for mitigating the threat posed by the bear. But until the

images are recognized as images, as the products of consciousness, the images remain traits of the world impinging on and determining the human animal.

If it is the case that mythical consciousness, at least in its more primitive manifestations, lacks even a rudimentary representational function, then the question of the role of language becomes quite important. Cassirer has written almost as much on language as a symbolic form as he has on myth, analyses much too complex to be given an adequate accounting here. Language has its own pattern of development, its own objectifying function, its own dialectical processes, its own paths toward freedom for consciousness. But it also seems to be the case that language in some form or another is as archaic as myth, and in its earliest manifestations reflects more the form of myth than the form that will become its own coherent, self-sufficient symbolic activity. Insofar as mythical consciousness lacks the representative function, the spoken word in the mythical world lacks this function, and cannot be understood as belonging to the fully linguistic.

In its later manifestations, language follows its own line of development and achieves what Cassirer calls the "versatility" of the symbol or the name; that is, the symbol is not invariably attached to the named as one of the named's possessions. Prior to the achievement of symbol versatility by linguistic consciousness, we find "universality" of name; that is, that everything *has* a name in the sense of an essential possession of the named. The mythical world may indeed exhibit universality of name, but, according to Cassirer, cannot attain the variability or mobility of true linguistic symbolic activity. Cassirer compares this to a stage of linguistic development in children as well as to retrogressions exhibited in certain aphasic conditions. The comparison is to an inability to distinguish the name of something from the intrinsic properties of the thing. He comments, "children are often greatly confused when they first learn that not every name of an object is a 'proper name,' . . . they tend to think that a thing 'is' what it is called."[53] For mythical consciousness as well, the name belongs to the named as one of its irrefrangible aspects. This appears to be a condition for certain word taboos and for word magic. As the name belongs to the named, and as the representative function of the part-to-whole relation is absent, then the name is the named, and to pronounce the name is to produce the named.

In the mythical world, to "say the name" is not yet an activity of a subject, for the subject does not yet exist as a discrete locus of action. The word, the name, speaking, all belong to the natural order of determination, as much as food, defecation, and running do. As long as the linguistic symbol is not known *as* symbol, it remains a link in the chain that binds human being to the world of nature and mechanical causality. In its earliest manifestations, language belongs to myth. Language takes up its function of freeing consciousness from the confines of nature only as it begins to assume its identity as representative, and finally, as fully symbolic.

MYTH AS GROUNDED IN FEELING AND EMOTION

We cannot restrict our analysis of myth to its forms of perception, thought, and language. To do so would be to offer an adumbrated picture of mythical consciousness and the world mythical symbolic formation produces. As well, if we look only at these cognitive operations of myth, then it is still possible to read myth's categories of space and time, number, causality, and so on, as merely mistaken efforts at what can be accomplished much more adequately in scientific-theoretical symbolic formation. Cassirer reminds us that "myth does not arise solely from intellectual processes; it sprouts forth from deep human emotions."[54] Our analysis of the formative activity of mythical consciousness must include both the intellectual and the emotional spheres of human experience.

In *The Myth of the State*, Cassirer distinguishes between rites or rituals, on the one hand, and myth or mythical narratives, on the other. He calls these, respectively, the dramatic and the epic elements of the symbolic activity of mythical consciousness. The dramatic is prior to the epic, both temporally and logically. The distinction drawn is analogous, though not equivalent, to the distinction between practice and theory in the empirical-scientific symbolic activity. Mythical narrative develops as an oral accompaniment or explanation of the originary rites and rituals. This is a rather neat distinction for Cassirer to draw, for it allows the inclusion of the bodily and physiological aspects of human activity in the constructions of the mythical.

Cassirer understands emotion in physical terms,[55] and uses "feeling" and "emotion" interchangeably. Humans share the fact of feeling states with many other animals, some of whom exhibit quite complex emotional states (such as blushing), more primitive ones (such as crouching in fear), while even the simplest organism can be attracted or repelled by its environment. Feeling states appear to be the more primitive of the possible human responses to the environment. Cassirer writes, "it is indeed obvious that, biologically speaking, feeling is a much more general fact and belongs to an earlier and more elementary stratum than all other cognitive states."[56] But bare emotional response is a passive act, a reaction called out by the world; it testifies to continued immersion in the biological sphere.[57] Mythical consciousness transforms this passive state into an active *expression* of emotion. Cassirer claims that,

> The expression of a feeling is not the feeling itself—it is emotion turned into an image. This very fact implies a radical change. What hitherto was dimly and vaguely felt assumes a definite shape; what was a passive state becomes an active process.[58]

In part, mythical symbolic activity is an objectification of feeling, an active process of manipulation of a natural state of affairs into a form that can carry meaning.

The "image" that Cassirer mentions in this passage is certainly not a pictorial or verbal image. It is, rather, a bodily image. Ritual reenactments use the body itself as vehicle of meaning. However, mythical consciousness does not differentiate between the abstract and concrete, and the rituals of the mythical world are not representations in the full sense of standing for something other. Rites and rituals, according to Cassirer, are the "motor manifestations" of appetites, desires, and needs as "translated into movements—into rhythmical solemn movements or wild dances, into orderly and regular actions, or violent orgiastic outbursts."[59] But once in the world, once added to the plethora of phenomena that are "there" for mythical consciousness to apprehend, ritual action becomes the occasion for understanding the world in human terms. The repetition of the hunting posture, for example, where or when no prey is to be found, can become the moment of discovery of something new in the world. The actors and observers stumble upon an objectification performed by Spirit. When the inhabitant of the mythical world begins to ask the question of what such ritual activity *means*, the physical action becomes symbolic. The material transformed in the act is the living body, now become meaningful. Various answers may be given to the question of meaning, and these answers are myths or mythical narratives. But the decisive step for mythical consciousness is in posing the question.

Cassirer maintains that an essential feature of consciousness in any of its symbolic modes is its unifying function; that is, that disparate elements of experience are brought into relation with one

another. In more fully developed religious systems, the unifying function may play itself out in the identification or unification of the soul
with some supernatural realm or force or Being. In myth, it appears as
a fervent desire "of the individuals to identify themselves with the life
of the community and with the life of nature."⁶⁰ We can also see the
unifying function in the mythical world in ritual activity, or a "unity
of feeling." Myth begins with the "awareness of the universality and
fundamental identity of life."⁶¹ The rites and rituals of primitive cultures satisfy this urge to unification by erasing the individual agent and
substituting for it a role or a part in the ritual activity. The ritual act
makes firm the sense of being an integral part of the larger whole, a
part that can have no meaning or existence except as part of this social
whole. Totemistic rituals exemplify the felt identification with other
animal and plant life, while certain agricultural rites exhibit the felt
unity of human procreativity with the fecundity of the earth. Such ritual activity is an expression of the unifying function of mythical consciousness. The rites also give further credence to the notion of the
"sympathetic" nature of mythical consciousness.

A second essential trait of consciousness exhibited in any symbolic form is its objectifying function. Linguistic symbolic formation
objectifies sense-impressions. It does this through naming, through
the subsumption of particulars under more general class terms.
Objectification also plays itself out in the emotional sphere for mythical consciousness, but mythical symbolic formation objectifies feelings, not sense-impressions. As with unification, objectification
through myth is expressed in ritual activity. The *ritual* display of
emotion is more than the straightforward discharge of physiological
or neurological states. Though Cassirer does not use this example,
we can think of ritualized mourning behavior in *keening.* Discharge
(of grief, for example) tends to dissipate the emotion, loosing the
energy outward and leaving the organism empty and quiescent. Emotions expressed through symbolic form "have, as it were, a double
power: the power to bind and unbind." Emotions expressed through
symbolic form are not only attenuated and dispersed, but condensed
and intensified through repetition. This doubling-back of force solid-
ifies the emotional state, transforming the raw material of nature
into something capable of carrying meaning.⁶²

MYTHICAL SPACE

Mythical consciousness organizes the world primarily through objectifying feeling and emotion as in ritual activity organizing the world

around certain nodes of condensed and intensified emotional states. But mythical consciousness also organizes the world as spatial and temporal. This occurs through objectification of bodily conditions or feeling states. Cassirer does not make the distinction between emotion and feeling very clear, and in fact uses them synonymously in *The Myth of the State*. However, his analysis of space and time in the mythical world, especially in volume 2 of *The Philosophy of Symbolic Forms* and in *An Essay on Man*, focuses on kinesthetic orientation of the body, and the felt rhythms and periodicities of biological existence, rather than on what we are more likely to call emotions—fear, awe, and so on.

The organization of space around these human experiences is less primitive than, for example space as experienced by a newborn chick. The chick, though able to discern and follow a path of grain within minutes of hatching, exists only in "organic space." Activity in organic space does not seem to depend on any learned responses to the environment, but consists of quite delicate instinctual stimulus-response of the organism in its environment. "Higher" animals occupy a "perceptual space," composed of a variety of optical, tactile, olfactory, and other sensory factors. In concert, these factors organize the world around sensible experience of the organism. The human animal appears to be deficient in both organic and perceptual space. But the human organism is able to compensate for the deficiencies "by another gift which he alone develops and which bears no analogy to anything in organic nature." Through a long process of development, human beings come to understand "abstract" or "symbolic" space.[63]

Cassirer understands mythical space as lying somewhere between symbolic space (with its possibility of understanding a cosmic order independent of sensible particulars and having general laws of constitution) and a "space of action" (dependent on visual acuity, repetition of encounter, and habitual responses, and closely aligned with organic and perceptual space). Cassirer understands the space of action to be much more developed in "primitive" life, but it cannot ground empirical-scientific constructions. There is no way of generating geometric space, for example, out of the absolute particularity of the contents of the space of action.

Cassirer writes that in mythical space the "distinction between *position* and *content*, underlying the construction of 'pure' geometric space, has not yet been made and cannot be made." This distinction demands, at least, the ability to detach a "here" and a "there" from all sensible particular content. This abstraction is unavailable to mythical consciousness. As a thing's name belongs to the thing as an essential feature, so a thing's place belongs to it as an inherent possession.[64]

Cassirer clarifies this distinction by using the example of astrological explanation, a relatively late and well-formed product of mythical consciousness. Events in a mythical astrologically ordered cosmos are *not* understood as determined through the causal efficacy of the heavenly bodies. That is, there is no causal mechanism imputed to the stars and the planets as somehow effecting results, action at a distance, on earth. Rather, myth apprehends an *identity* of events in the earthly and heavenly spheres, just as we might view the branching of a tree's limbs, twigs, leaf veins, and root system as all expressions of the singular, essential form of the tree. For myth, the same structures that are writ large in the heavens are writ small on the earth. Astrology is the most systematic refinement of the spatial determination underlying all mythic thought and organization. Yet even in it, space is delimited and arranged according to concrete, particular bodies.

Mythical space has no contentless form-in-itself. In its most primitive manifestations, mythical space is organized around specific kinesthetic states and bodily orientations (such as left and right, above and below). In its most developed manifestation, mythical space is organized around concrete heavenly bodies or astrological zones. Whatever the level of sophistication of spatial organization in the mythical world, the categories of space function to unify the diversity of experience into an articulated, structured whole, relating macrocosm and microcosm in a coherent pattern. All symbolic forms share this function. Mythical space differs from other spatial orderings in that it is essentially and necessarily bound to concrete particulars. Mythical consciousness can never perform the abstraction or idealization that would allow for transcending the particulars of bodily existence.

MYTHICAL TIME

We have seen that mythical space has more primitive and more sophisticated manifestations. Cassirer finds this to be true of mythical time as well. In its more primitive form, the temporal unity of the world is apprehended as a "kind of biological time, a rhythmic ebb and flow of life." All natural phenomena appear as life processes. Again we find a bridge between the microcosm and the macrocosm. Mythical time structures all events, ordering the entirety according to a principle of unification akin to the pulse of felt biological existence. While diverse phenomena are unified in mythical time, the abstraction of a specific temporal dimension of existence has no place in the mythical world. Each "sector" of the world seems to have its own time. For example, harvest rituals belong to the end of summer as an essential possession of the season. Such events are natural expressions of the "essence and efficacy" of the rhythm and pulse of the annual cyclic process. In the mythical world, there is no conception of an overarching, single, successive, sequential temporal order to which all events can be related. Rather, to mythical temporal intervals "there belongs an intensive content which makes them similar or dissimilar, corresponding or contrasting, friendly or hostile to one another." As temporal intervals or phases are constituted by this "intensive" content rather than by a fixed chronology of nonreversible sequence, the relations between various processes can take on magical properties. Divination is, literally, seeing the future in the present. Rituals do not commemorate past events, but create those events in the present. The sun, as it rises and sets, is not following its own immutable laws, but is amenable to human influence or the intervention of demons and divinities.[65]

Mythical time, according to Cassirer, proceeds from the strict identification of human being with natural processes. This identification is combined with the lack of ideal categories—just as we've found in all other mythical organizational patterns. In the most primitive experience of time, temporality is not apprehended as a unique, specific form of experience. Time is not understood as a contentless form amenable to subsuming particular events under its general rule of past/present/future ordering. Mythical time is, rather, a possession of the ever-changing appearances in the world; as the name and the space of a thing or event belong specifically to it, so the time of a thing or event belongs to it. Mythical time appears to be the reverse of empirical time; in the latter, things and events are subsumed under a general temporal order, in the former, time is subsumed under the things and events themselves. In the advanced stages of empirical-theoretical consciousness we discover time as a functional ordering process dependent only on conceptions of nonreversible serial sequence. This temporal form has the past as something that can be recollected; that is, the past is identified and recognized as not-present, as re-presented, but never as repeatable or reliveable. The temporal schema of the empirical world holds the future as an ideal, as an imperative, as a task to be envisaged and accomplished.[66] The temporal organization of the mythical world, far from the universalized, relational organization manifested in empirical-theoretical consciousness, is more closely allied with sheer biological, organic existence.

The more sophisticated manifestation of mythical time borders on truly religious significance. In fact, this temporal structure is one way out of the matrix of mythical consciousness and toward the fully symbolic. Insofar as mythical consciousness begins to comprehend a cosmic temporal process, an "eternal cycle of events," to which particular aspects of experience can be related, "contemplation is directed not toward the mere content of change but toward its pure form." Contemplation remains mythical if it locates the source of temporal rhythms in the emanations of particular concrete planetary bodies, for example. But the seeds of a "fundamentally different and more profound view of the world" are sown in the prospect of the "temporal order as a universal order of destiny, governing all reality and change, . . . a truly cosmic potency." At its least concrete, subtlest limit, mythical consciousness constitutes a universal temporal process "endowed with divine and demonic, creative and destructive forces." But this universal temporal process cannot be understood by mythical consciousness, as it can be by religious or scientific consciousness, as a purely ideal or purely spiritual ordering principle under which all particulars can be subsumed.[67]

THE SACRED AND THE PROFANE

Though the mythical world is never organized according to abstract, ideal laws, there is a most general division ordering the mythical world, claims Cassirer. The mythical world is divisible into the antithetical realms of the sacred and the profane. The mythical world, through its peculiar spatial schema, organizes and relates diverse elements, as the spatial schema of any symbolic form must. The fundamental distinction in mythical space appears to be that between the space that is readily accessible to human action and the space that is not. The former is the profane arena, a sphere of possible physical accomplishment. It is organized around the body's position and the body's relation to its environment. The sacred sphere, inaccessible to the efficacy of action, is a "precinct which seems to be raised out of its surroundings, hedged around and guarded against them." The spatial schema of sacred-or-profane structures the entire mythical world. As empirical spatiality subsumes the various sensuous phenomena under categories belonging to homogeneous, geometric space, so mythical spatiality organizes various phenomena according to its particular distinction.[68]

Cassirer claims that the originary distinction between the sacred and the profane permeates all features of the mythically ordered cosmos, that "all reality and all events are projected into [this] fundamental opposition,"[69] and that "mythical consciousness arrives at an articulation of space and time . . . not by stabilizing the fluctuations of sensible phenomena but by introducing its specific opposition . . . into spatial and temporal reality."[70] The opposition between the sacred and the profane in spatial organization appears to hinge on the apprehension and construction of limits, impositions of mythical consciousness on an otherwise undifferentiated surface of the world. Mythical space is generated outward from a "foundation in feeling," as we saw above, an articulation proceeding from a central zone of personal embodied orientation or modeled on the body and its parts writ (cosmically) large. Yet that does not answer the following questions: "How, in mythical space as a whole, do particular 'regions' and directions come to be singled out—how does it come about that one region and direction is opposed to the others, 'stressed' over against them, and endowed with a particular distinguishing mark?"[71] Such questions must be answered for Cassirer to make good his claims concerning the function of any symbolic form. Space must be organized, in some manner or another, an organization peculiar to each symbolic form, in order for spirit to make itself at home in the form. And space is the "universal medium in which spiritual productivity can first establish itself, in which it can produce its first structures and formations."[72]

Consciousness, regardless of what symbolic form is utilized, must introduce inviolable distinctions into the undifferentiated and chaotic plethora of presymbolic experience in order to reappropriate a spiritually articulated world. Mythical consciousness, in its inability to transcend the material, substantial order of nature, introduces a distinction that assures the continuation of its passive role vis-à-vis nature. Mythical consciousness, in determining zones of the sacred, zones that take on an active, demonic power of their own, constructs the conditions for its own enslavement by powers it itself has symbolically spawned.

Sacred zones, or sacred spaces, in the less primitive mythical organization of the cosmos, are stringently delimited areas at once hallowed and taboo, both attracting and repelling. These zones are sometimes identified as particular demonic forces. Whatever the "intensive content" of the zone, it is enclosed by distinct boundaries and unbreachable limits. This sets apart certain features of the world as imbued with the sacred, an accent of special value "distributed" by mythical consciousness as it structures its habitation "objectively." This limit-setting is a necessary step in consciousness overcoming its bondage to a world not of its own fashioning; it is a step out of passivity and toward activity. (Cassirer remarks several times on the etymological roots of "contemplate" in a most primitive sense of "to cut" or "to divide." This sense then becomes that of "time" and "space" [*tempus* and *templum*], then as "temple," a region set apart from profane time and space. The transformation process culminates in a "spiritual frame of reference, toward which all being and all change are oriented."[73])

The organization of mythical space into the antithetical regions of the sacred and the profane is never determined, according to Cassirer, by any constant objective or substantive content. *Any* part of the world may become imbued with the sacred. What determines a region as sacred is a function of the necessity for mythical consciousness to raise some feature or features of the world, whatever these may be, as absolutely distinct from the undifferentiated continuum of natural, organic existence. This seems the closest that mythical consciousness can approach the construction of truly ideal (nonparticular and abstract) symbolic formation. But sacred spaces, as mythical, remain a trap for continued passivity of consciousness, and must be eliminated if consciousness is to advance toward freedom from passive, natural existence.

For Cassirer, all features of the mythical world are shot through with the differential values of the sacred and the profane. Thus we expect to find specific forms of sacred time in his description of the mythical world. Cassirer explicates at least three different sorts of sacred time. The first of these is the time of origins. This sacred time is determined by a "rigid barrier" separating the mundane experience of becoming and change in the "empirical present" from an almost timeless, "absolute past, which neither requires nor is susceptible of any further explanation." Mythical consciousness then explains mundane events in terms of their foundation in sacred time. The cyclical, repetitious phases and intervals of particular temporal processes thus find anchor in a primordial time that does not partake of cyclical nature. Coming into being, or the origin of any particular, is sacred, and this sanctity of origin *qua* origin marks a truly mythical conception of the cosmos. Cassirer writes, "By being thrust back into temporal distance, by being situated in the depths of the past, a particular content is . . . established as sacred, as mythically . . . significant."[74]

Another type of mythical sacred time, according to Cassirer, can be identified as the transitional rhythms that break up the course of the otherwise mundane, "mere 'flow' of time," the regular rhythms of biological existence. Sacred significance is accorded to felt differences in the onset and/or cessation of particular phases of life. Rituals often attend such interruptions of the normal ebb and flow of organic life, furthering raising the transitional periods out of the mundane and into the sacred.[75] All rites of passage, for example, exemplify this type of sacred time.

As mythical consciousness progresses from its most primitive determinations, those that exhibit the least independence from physical, organic existence, the determinations of sacred time assume greater abstractness and generality. In the third arena of sacred time we find the most well-developed manifestation of the temporal that is possible for mythical consciousness. Cassirer explains that when consciousness "orients itself toward being and becoming as a whole . . . it gradually frees itself from immediate confinement in sensory impression and momentary sensory emotion." This orientation has not yet achieved a strictly conceptual formulation, but remains more as a "feeling" of universal temporal order. The highest degree of abstraction in mythical temporality, as in mythical spatiality, can still be apprehended only "concretely, only through a definite physical process." In the development of mythical spatiality, the organization of the world moves from a center located in the efficacy of the human body to the astral bodies as loci of power determining zones or sectors of space. In the development of mythical temporality, time is first apprehended as extensions of the rhythms of personal biological existence, then moves to understanding the rhythms of astral bodies determining time as "a universal order of destiny, governing all reality and all change." *Cosmic* temporal ordering, proceeding from centers of existence transcending the sphere of human efficacy, is sacred time. Here mythical consciousness, in its articulation of the world through its symbolic form, reaches an internal crisis marking the final moments of mythic thought and heralds a truly religious orientation. When particular, substantial bodies, biological or astral, "become a medium through which the idea of lawful [temporal] order . . . is apprehended," myth has reached its furthest limits. At this moment, mythical consciousness is on the verge of understanding concrete, particular existences as representing, or being instances of, a sacred, universal order. But, insofar as sacred time depends on concrete, particular bodily rhythms as loci of temporal organization, it remains within the mythical, however great the expansion of the felt identity of human biological existence and the cosmos.[76]

THE MYTHICAL SELF

There is one last constitutive act performed by consciousness in its mythical symbolic form that needs to be examined before we move to more general conclusions and observations about Cassirer's treatment of myth. As myth must constitute the objective features of existence (as spatiality and temporality), so it must constitute the subjective features of existence. Cassirer claims that neither the soul, nor the I, nor the ego exists in the first stirring of Spirit out of its immersion in biologically determined nature. Myth is the most primitive mode of symbolic formation, and it constructs the primordial self.

As with the constitution of space and time, the division of the world into the sacred and the profane, and all other accomplishments of mythical consciousness, it is "action which constitutes the center from which man undertakes the spiritual organization of reality." And it is through the progressive "consciousness of action" that the I and the world, the subjective opposed to the objective, become more and more sharply delineated as separate provinces. Human action in the world, when driven by desire and necessity, belongs to the peculiar fluidity of undifferentiated, untrammeled organic, biotic existence. One can imagine, for example, that for a human infant or a cat there is no such thing as "my" hunger needing to be satisfied by something "outside" my self. Rather, "feeding" would be, literally, a global experience of undifferentiated parts, with the bottle or the mouse at the furthest reaches of the "hungry world." In fact, this undifferentiated experience is available to the adult human—especially in terms of hunger or sex drive. The trance that one may fall into when satisfying great hunger seems an example of untrammeled biological existence. There is merely the transformation of hunger into satiation; the "I" and the "world" do not exist as antithetical, but only feeding occurs. Insofar as action has not yet been symbolically organized, the distinction between stimulus and response has not yet been marked. This also means that efficacy has not yet been attributed to various loci of independent action. Cassirer writes that, in the mythical world, there "is only a single undivided sphere of efficacy, within which a continuous exchange takes place."[77]

Cassirer, as we've seen, maintains that mythical conscious-ness is embedded in biological, material nature. He also maintains that the self or I is the end product of the development of mythical configuration. Furthermore, as end product of mythical formation, the I or the self cannot itself be the source of the formative activity of myth. Cassirer argues against any explanation of myth that depends on a preexisting core of self-reflective subjectivity. Insofar as the human animal is a symbolic animal, then the self as unified cluster of attributes is a product of symbolic formation. Myth is the original symbolic form and the form is the progenitor of the self, not the reverse. Cassirer also argues against explanations that export a notion of the soul as a personal possession "with immutable attributes"[78] into the primordial organization of the mythical self/world constellation. He is careful to discount accounts of myth that assume some sort of projection of an already constituted inner content of self onto the world.

How then does the mythical self arise? According to Cassirer, the "willing and acting subject" is determined through limits imposed in an "immediate relation to reality." The immediate rela-tion seems to be sheer uninterrupted biological, physiological, and sensuous interaction between the human organism and its natural environment. When such interaction, based on "immediate impres-sion," is disrupted by an impression of overpowering, "irresistible force," that impression is removed from the "mere series of uni-form being and uniform recurrence." According to Cassirer, the first manifestation of Spirit in the mythical world is as an objectifica-tion of extreme emotional states, and it is here that the mythical self begins its development. It appears that mythical consciousness does make a rudimentary distinction between the spiritual and substan-tial, but first "locates" the power of spiritual efficacy in the *objective* features of existence. Only later does consciousness reappropriate the spiritual as belonging to the *subjective* realm.

Any aspect of nature that happens to provoke an extraordinary sense of wonder or fear or joy becomes imbued with a tone of over-whelming efficacy and objective reality. Mythical consciousness is unable to subsume this overwhelming impression under any gen-eral causal laws, and the impression remains "incomparable and unique." The isolated moments of sheer overpowering intensity of impression have as their only common trait their absolute particu-larity or "egregiousness." This imparts a certain common tonality to a variety of impressions. This differential introduces a rift into "indistinct, 'indifferent reality,' by dividing it into different spheres of meaning" effecting a "purely qualitative" difference in the cosmos. Out of this arises what Cassirer calls the "momentary gods." As he recounts in *Language and Myth*, momentary gods first appear to mythical consciousness when excitement becomes compressed, splits off from internal experience, and presents itself as an overpowering feature of the objective world. *Any* feature of the world may acquire the value or accent of the sacred, "provided only that instead of remaining within the accustomed sphere of actions and events it captures mythical interest and enthusiasm from one angle or another." The momentary gods are symbolic expressions of the emotional experience of "the extraordinary, the unusual, the uncommon."[79]

The momentary god, or the overwhelming impression, blots out the remainder of the world and any sense of the subjective sphere is swallowed up by the overpowering immediacy of the impression. This concentration of the self and world in a particular moment results in a compression of experience "of fear or hope, terror or wish fulfillment" so volatile that the "spark jumps somehow across, the tension finds release, as the subjective excitement becomes objectified." Cassirer seems to be describing a sort of detonation performed by mythical consciousness. When the dust clears, so to speak, momentary gods have appeared in the world, loci of active power over against a human self which is passive in relation to its own creation. The formation of the momentary gods shows precisely the inadequacy of mythical consciousness as it construes the world and the self. Once again, as we saw in the mythical constitution of space and time, it is the body and its states that are the basis of the formation of the objective features of the world. But there is a difference when the objective features so construed, the momentary gods, are identified as *spiritual* power. There is a confluence of the spiritual and the material, with the spiritual exhibited as an aspect of the material world.

The momentary god, determined by an entirely concrete, particular trait of human experience, such as fear or joy, may persist in its identity as an "independent being . . . [with] form and continuity, . . . as an objective and superior power." As momentary gods proliferate and as the rudiments of linguistic naming develop, the mythical world "undergoes a progressive organization and ever more definite articulation." The momentary gods, if they persist, may develop into "functional gods" more clearly related to the activities of farming, hunting, and so on.[80] The functional gods stand in closer relation to the actual agent of symbolic formation, because these gods are enmeshed with daily productive human labor. Still, both spiritual forms (momentary and functional gods) confront consciousness not as an expression of Spirit's own constitutive activity, but as alien force.

The spiritually efficacious principle moves to an even "closer, more intimate relation to the person" in the development of "tutelary" spirits. Tutelary spirits are not yet apprehended as part of the subject, "but as something objective, which dwells in man." This internal, but nonsubjective spiritual form finally is transformed into a nonsubstantial, subjective attribute. Cassirer reminds us of the Socratic daemon, and claims that it is at this point in the development of the subjective sphere that the "soul ceases to be a mere natural potency and apprehends itself as an ethical subject."[81] The evolution of the self through mythical symbolic formation leads to the destruction of the mythical form. When the soul is apprehended as a nonsubstantial entity, subject to general or universal ethical laws, the dependence of consciousness on the organic and biologic ceases, and the self becomes identified with the spiritual.

THE END OF MYTH

This final transformation in the form of Spirit, when the soul apprehends itself as an ethical, nonmaterial subject of action, really marks the end of mythical consciousness, at least insofar as the constitution of the subjective sphere is concerned. As long as Spirit gains form through mythical symbolic activity, it remains embedded in material existence. In the mythical, Spirit is unable to make a clear distinction between its own accomplishments and the exigencies of Nature. Mythical consciousness cannot achieve a true representative functioning; it is unable to constitute idealities separate from, but standing for, the particulars of experience. The formative activity of mythical consciousness cannot transcend the givenness of material, biological existence. It can only substitute reformulated material necessities (that it itself has fashioned) for those necessities originally determining human existence and action in the mythical world.

With the constitution of tutelary spirits, mythical consciousness verges on attaining the I as an ideal unity capable of self-engendered ethical action. It has reached the crisis point in the dialectical progression impelling myth's development; this signals the end of mythical consciousness and the commencement of a new form. Within the mythical mode, the subjective shows itself first as entirely indistinguishable from bodily existence and emotional states. Only by stages does the soul, as spiritual principle, become disengaged from materiality. Cassirer traces the development of an independent, spiritual principle as it separates itself from the material. This is the soul's journey toward its *telos*, freedom from identification with organic existence. This freedom also implies the self-apprehension of consciousness or Spirit as the productive agent of the ideal formations that makes possible these movements toward freedom.

If Spirit forms itself as an ideal, nonmaterial unity, identifies itself as the subjective features of existence, and demarcates itself strictly from the objective features of existence, then it has broken the shackles of physical, biological exigencies. Symbolic formation accomplishes the identification of Spirit with self, and sets this new unity over against the brute necessities of Nature.

Cassirer's characterization of the mythical as the matrix out of which all other symbolic forms arise through a struggle to overcome their origins and allow for the development of freedom for consciousness has a corollary proposition. He characterizes mythical consciousness as that which can never make the distinction between the real and the ideal, the image and the imaged, the signifier and the signified, the particular and the universal, the concrete and the abstract. It is only in mythical form that consciousness recognizing itself as the generative power of the symbolic constructions spells an absolute doom for the form. In the moment that consciousness apprehends the image as a self-created representation, and not as a repetition of the imaged itself, myth and magic are overcome, and art is born. When the name ceases to inhere in the named as its natural possession, or when speech and writing lose an entirely mimetic function, language proper erases myth. As reflection grasps a feature of the perceptible world and holds it as a measure of typicality against which further impressions can be judged as essential or inessential, mythical perception disappears and empirical perception comes into the world.

MYTH AND FREEDOM

In Cassirer's account, the mythical is certainly a cultural form. Human mythical activity is a shaping of the self and world, the subjective and objective, by means of a coherent, self-sufficient order and logical necessity of structure. Myth is consciousness investing the world and the self with meaning, organizing experience through categories of "unity and multiplicity, coexistence, contiguity and succession."[82] These same categories are found in any developed symbolic form, with each form producing a unique articulation of the subjective and objective spheres. The particular unities and multiplicities, and so forth, that are constructed through each form differ enormously. This can easily be seen in comparing the products of scientific-theoretical consciousness with those of mythical consciousness. The predominant trait of human being that is expressed in each form differs as well. Art, for example, corresponds to direct intuitions of mobile, living forms,[83] while myth proceeds from emotion and other physiological states. The material manipulated in each form, that which becomes invested with meaning, also varies from form to form. In language, it is the word, once the original bond of language and myth is severed. The word or name then attains a status of universal variability and functions in the realm of representation, no longer tied to concrete particulars. Thus the "material" manipulated in linguistic symbolic formation is progressively divorced from the "stuff" of which the natural world is composed. This is true for all symbolic forms except the mythical.

Myth has the peculiar distinction of being a symbolic formative activity that does not transform the abode of consciousness or Spirit from the material, physical sphere into an ideal, nonsubstantial sphere. Myth does indeed hold the world at a distance by combating the "passive world of mere *impression*, in which the spirit seems at first imprisoned, [with] a world that is pure *expression* of the human spirit."[84] This is true of every symbolic form. In myth, what is immediately given to the *animal symbolicum* becomes the occasion for an attempted separation from this immediate reality. But mythical configuration, with its inability to differentiate signification and thing, merely remakes the world in physical, material terms. Myth cannot substitute meaning for being and therefore can only replace an original bondage to the world with physical, material chains of its own fashioning.[85]

In his analyses of mythical spatiality and temporality, in his discussion of the constitution of the mythical self or soul, as with the account of ritual, Cassirer is positing the unalterably embedded character of the mythical mode of Spirit in the materiality of Nature. Insofar as the material utilized symbolically is the body and its physiological and kinesthetic states, and insofar as the organization of the world into unities and discrete features proceed from the body and its states, just so far is consciousness shackled to biological nature and its brute mechanical laws. This is why Cassirer finds myth to be the most primitive cultural or symbolic form.

Myth marks the immersion of consciousness in the ontological nemesis of consciousness—nature. Myth must be overcome and eradicated if consciousness is to begin its arduous trek toward freedom. This is true, for Cassirer, not only because the mythical lacks even a rudimentary category of the ideal, and consequently has no mode of representation available to it. This might mean that humankind, stuck in the mythic mode, never knowing its symbols *as* symbols, could never advance far into what we understand as scientific or philosophical achievement. It does seem that the ability of empirical-scientific consciousness to refine its symbols and manipulate these in hypotheses, and the ability to hold as an ideal a future that is better than the present, has meant the eradication of certain diseases, a rise in the standard of living for many human beings, an increased understanding of the structure of the physical universe, and so on. This is not, however, Cassirer's primary motive in insisting that the mythical must be overturned and disavowed. The intimate and indiscerptible union of the mythical mode of consciousness and biological, physical existence means that consciousness, according to Cassirer, can never free itself from nature if the activity of consciousness is confined to mythic formation. Human being could never attain the "means of progressive self-liberation."[86]

Cassirer's reading of the mythical world and its place within a larger cultural and natural context draws us inevitably to questions of ethics and politics, each of which imply some sort of freedom. But with Cassirer's analysis, this is a freedom unavailable in the mythical world. There can be no ethics in the primitive mythical world, or so it appears, because that world is almost entirely one of mechanical, natural law. Whatever ethical proscriptions might belong to the mythical are construed as emanating from the structure of the world itself, commands of nature that must be obeyed. Mythical thought is completely conservative in that it serves to maintain what is understood as having been the case from the beginning of time. Mythical life is "enclosed in the narrow circle of positive and negative demands, of consecrations and prohibitions, of observances and taboos."[87] Any deviation from this constant reiteration of what is construed as founded in the origin of the world threatens to destroy the mythical altogether. As long as human being is completely passive, completely reactive, completely at the mercy of a world structured by the world and not liable to idealization into meaning, there can be no choice, no self-engendered possibility. There can be no more an ethical system than appears in the world of a cat or a cactus. Ethical principles demand, at the very least, a rudimentary freedom from absolute determination of human action by mechanical forces.[88]

Furthermore, for Cassirer, the apprehension of a distinction between the real and the ideal, the actual and the possible, is a kind of freedom. This sort of freedom is a necessary condition for knowledge in general and ethical understanding in particular. Through symbolic formation, dependence on concrete physical existence can be transcended, as the "symbol has no actual existence in the physical world," and the sphere of meaning can supersede the sphere of being. Only in this way can consciousness achieve truly ethical ideas and ideals, for it "follows from the very nature and character of ethical thought that it can never condescend to accept the 'given'; the ethical world is never given, it is forever in the making." The mythical world affords no access to the sphere of the ideal or to the sphere of the purely possible. Therefore it affords no access to the ethical, for it is barred from the realm of meaning. Cassirer writes: "In primitive thought it is still very difficult to differentiate between the two spheres of meaning and being. They are constantly being confused: a symbol is looked upon as if it were endowed with magical or physical powers." Only as consciousness moves out of its mythical matrix does this confusion cease, which allows for the "distinction between actuality and possibility," the necessary condition for apprehending a distinction between "is" and "ought."[89]

The same sorts of arguments can be used to deny the existence of a truly political formation in the mythical world. While remaining within the general framework of Cassirer's analysis (though he seems to say nothing in particular about this), we can suggest that mythical constitution, as it proceeds from the physical body outward, constructs a primitive (and nonmetaphorical) "body politic," but this is not enough for true political organization. At least from Plato on, an engagement with the hypothetical has been a necessary ingredient in devising political forms. Certainly this is true of all attempts at social and political reform; but any political state, organized according to an ideal, of whatever sort, depends on an apprehension of the distinction between possibility and actuality. This demands the same minimal freedom for consciousness demanded in the construction of ethical principles.

Even if we look at political organization with no eye for ideals implicit or explicit in the organization, the notion of freedom still comes to bear. Cassirer asks us to make a direct link between myth-ical consciousness and barbaric political consequences in the rise of fascism and National Socialism in the twentieth century. The rational organization of the political state is possible only during periods of relative freedom from conflict and insecurity. Faced with the threat of complete social and economic collapse, stymied at every turn, rational organization gives way to mythical organiza-tion. Along with what Cassirer calls the "mental rearmament" of Germany via the wholesale production of artificial myths having no connection to imaginative creativity, came the absolute con-striction of action into public, political rituals "as regular, as rigorous and inexorable as those rituals we find in primitive societies." The terrifying bondage of such a political organization as Nazi Germany was, in great part, a self-imposed bondage of those who chose slavish adherence to the newly generated myths. Cassirer writes that "if man were to follow his natural instincts he would not strive for freedom; he would rather choose dependence."[90]

Even if we could put these considerations aside, we in the mod-ern period are bound to equate politics and freedom, or the lack of freedom. Cassirer's impassioned exhortation in *The Myth of the State* shares this concern. But his other work as well, aimed at expli-cating the tentative (and perhaps faltering) steps of consciousness toward freedom, begs for a concomitant political analysis. Cassirer's analysis leads to the conclusion that true political freedom can only be achieved through the renunciation of the emotional and "natural" appeals of the mythical. These appeals always depend on primitive desires for unification and identification with the social group as a whole and on the physical and biological claims of existence. True political freedom, for Cassirer, can only occur through overcoming myth and adhering to the aim of creating rational, ideal cultural forms.

☙❧

We are still left with fundamental questions concerning freedom and its place in Cassirer's general metaphysical perspective. We can chronicle the advance of consciousness as it strives to evade the constrictions inherent in the mythical world. We can understand freedom as the end toward which rational ethics and rational politics strive. But ethical freedom and political freedom are *particular* ends, in *particular* (no matter how important) spheres of human activity. Freedom holds even greater sway in Cassirer's scheme of things than this. Freedom is a *telos* built into and directing the movement of consciousness in any and all of its endeavors from the very moment of the emergence of Spirit out of Life. The evolution of culture in general and of specific symbolic forms is an evolution toward the fulfillment of an implicit promise. Nature; Life; biological, physiological, emotional existence; these act to trap, to constrict, to constrain consciousness. They threaten to force consciousness into passivity, reaction, impression. The direst straits for consciousness, its least free state, is its primordial embeddedness in strict natural or biological causality. Only by rendering nature into culture can consciousness even begin its ascent toward the upper regions, the purity of freedom. This is so because culture, in its most advanced forms, is thoroughly understood by consciousness as the product of consciousness, as its *own* expression. Every symbol fashioned carries the possibility of holding Spirit's nemesis at bay. Cassirer's life work is a chronicle of the history of the struggle of consciousness to avoid falling back into the mire.

The question of freedom and freedom's relation to myth is a thread that runs through the entire present work. We will return to the conception of freedom in each of the following chapters, as Roland Barthes, Mircea Eliade, and James Hillman all find a *telos* of absolute, unbounded creative freedom as essential in understanding the positive and negative aspects of the mythical. In the conclusion of this work, I deal specifically with the notion of creative freedom, showing why this notion must be unmoored from the concept of freedom as absolute freedom from constraint and compulsion.

SOME PROBLEMS IN CASSIRER'S ANALYSIS

Cassirer's account of myth is certainly the most comprehensive, in detail and in scope, of any of the accounts we'll examine in this work. The complexity and comprehensiveness of his analysis is due to his commitment to allowing myth its deserved place in the spectrum of cultural achievement. Cassirer is determined to examine myth as an essential avenue of Spirit manifesting itself through symbolic activity, and he has embarked on an adventurous journey, a genuine philosophy of culture in its myriad forms. Nonetheless, there are a number of problems in Cassirer's analysis, some of which we'll examine here and others of which we'll examine in chapter 6.

Cassirer is quite explicit in pointing to the entire history of cultural activity as evidence for the unity of the project of Spirit. But he has left out an important feature of culture: the means by which cultural products or symbolic formations "travel" through history. If we take culture as merely the aggregation of symbolically wrought features of the world, a mass of symbolic products, then we have a hard time explaining the continued efficacy of these products over hundreds and thousands of years. Cassirer sees cultural artifacts as produced through the agency of consciousness coming to understand its own creative and active character. This happens by way of consciousness progressively abstracting the spiritual features it discovers in its own accomplishments in the world and appropriating these features as its own progeny. If this is the case, then the continuing fascination of these products, once their role in the freeing of consciousness from the constraints of substantiality has ended, can only be a commemorative or nostalgic act. If the products of the symbolic activity of consciousness have performed their roles well, they can only stand as markers to what consciousness has overcome and surpassed. The products of symbolic activity, having no "life" of their own in Cassirer's scheme of things, would have no more relevance to the ongoing activity of culture, once their role had ended, than the shed skin of the snake has in the ongoing life of the creature.

Of course, Cassirer's description of culture is quite complex. If it is the case that myth is anomalous in the field of cultural activity, and if the other forms, such as art, language, religion, and science, each have their own particular tempo and role in the progress of consciousness, then Cassirer's description can account for the variety of cultural activities in any given period of history. He is careful to abjure any notion of a linear configuration or progression of the *products* of consciousness (again, excluding the mythical); so it is not the case that religion is superseded by art, in its turn superseded by language, and so on. Each strand of symbolic activity expresses a particular feature of human experience. Each strand is also the means by which that feature of experience becomes symbolically articulate and appropriable as ideal rather than substantial, and comes to be apprehended as belonging to the spiritual rather than the material.

This description may account for the richness and diversity apparent in any particular historical period, but it does not explain the enduring and compelling interest we take in many cultural products. Cassirer's theory may well explain the synchronic aspects of culture, but it cannot account for the diachronic. The Egyptian pyramids, the Rosetta Stone, Mayan temple ruins, the mimetic use of language: all have a continuing power to arrest and dazzle. The efficacy of these products resides not only in their power to evoke the past conditions of symbolic activity now surpassed. These cultural products, countless in number, attest to the fact that they are more than merely commemorative, that their endurance and compelling nature are the result of more than a fond regard for the more primitive manifestations of consciousness marking its quest for freedom. Something needs to be added to Cassirer's explanation of the career of cultural products. They cannot be merely the residue of the agency of symbolic activity that is a progressive movement toward freedom. It seems there must be more to the propagation and endurance of cultural products, something more than the commemoration of the progress of Spirit.

A related, though perhaps deeper, problem in Cassirer's analysis of culture is his equation of cultural evolution with cultural progress. Cassirer understands the development of cultural forms along the lines of an evolutionary model, but his model depends on an ineradicable telic principle. He writes that the evolution of cultural forms is determined and directed by "an ideal progression toward a point where spirit not only is and lives in its own creations, its self-created symbols, but also knows them for what they are."[91] Cassirer's inviting promise of a thorough-going evolutionary model of accounting for the phenomena of culture is belied in several ways. He assumes a teleological principle determining the shape and fortune of culture; that is to say, consciousness is driven by its inexorable goal of completely free creative activity. This transforms the notion of evolution as dependent only on the interaction of repetitious structures and chance,[92] into a scheme of developmental *progress.*

Cassirer's analysis of cultural forms and of the specific role of mythical formation in their development rings true (to the precepts of contemporary evolutionary theory) only if we are able to draw out and hold as idiosyncratic his assumptions regarding an origin and aim of the cultural process. The elimination of an origin and aim that are not themselves features of the process to which they lend their finality is similar to that elimination in our understanding of evolutionary biology. We cannot, it seems, hold onto a notion of an inherent aim in the process of evolution. It is a mistake to think of this process as determined by an overarching principle, of survival of the fittest (in the long run), or the drive for the continuation of the species, or any other sort of principle. For example, organisms did not develop sexual reproduction *in order to* increase the available pool of genetic material and so secure better chances for adaptability. By chance, randomly, the transfer and mixing of genetic material occurred. The persistence of this trait in living organisms attests only to its persistence, its repetition, nothing more. The origin of evolutionary process is chance; the aim of the process is repetition. The process of evolution has no *archē* determining it, no *telos* directing it, though we certainly can discover local aims, local compulsions, local determinations of future activity.[93] What this all suggests is that Cassirer's outline of the development of culture cannot be described as an outline of an evolutionary process, unless we are willing to give up the results of recent work in the theory of evolution or reject the inclusion of the *archē* of consciousness and the *telos* of freedom as determining the ongoing process of culture.

We also need to ask what guides Cassirer to select certain of human activities as those appropriate for the critical philosophy of culture as an evolutionary process. He is certainly not claiming that *all* human action or work in the world is amenable to inclusion in the cultural sphere. It is important to notice that though Cassirer writes of defining human being in terms of activity in the world rather than in terms of essences or in terms of being, he has made methodological decisions that skew his investigation and the results of his investigation. He examines only those activities performed exclusively by human beings. Cassirer founds his analysis on what is *peculiarly* human rather than on the generic traits of human life— some of which are continuous, at least in analysis, with other organisms. For example, as we saw above, Cassirer distinguishes between propositional language and emotional language, predicating the former of human behavior only. Once making a clear and absolute distinction between human symbolic activity and the sign activity of our closest animal relatives, he follows the path of this purely idiosyncratic human trait through its cultural and historical permutations. In this way, Cassirer eliminates the possibility of maintaining a truly evolutionary or organicist account of human activity in its changing forms and manifestations.[94] He has circumscribed the definition of human in such a way that there seems to be no recourse but to postulate Spirit as a supervenient addition to the world. But this addition to the world maintains itself as not *of* the world. If what is "really" human is taken to be that which has no continuous relation with other features of the living world, then one is cut off from explaining the human as arising out of that world.

None of this is surprising in Cassirer's systematic account of culture. He is a critical idealist and we should not expect him to betray his metaphysical presuppositions or perspective. However, Cassirer relies on a notion of an actual, concrete, material substratum of nature with its own real causal necessities, lying in wait to trap unwary Spirit. His account is a juxtaposition of (subtle, functional) idealism with material realism. Given this, Cassirer must resort to the "fact of sudden mutation and of emergent evolution"[95] to explain the radical discontinuities he discovers between sign and symbol activity, that is, between the most "advanced" sector of non-human existence and the emergence of truly human activity. Relying on emergent evolution as a hypothesis does not necessarily present a great problem, and in fact, this is a hypothesis that I accept. But it presents no great problem only as long as what we are describing belongs to the arena of natural processes. Cassirer is using it as a principle to cover the emergence of cultural formation in the world. Consciousness and its attendant symbolic activities belong not to nature, but to Spirit, at least according to Cassirer. His explanatory vehicle creaks and groans along this artificial welding of the material and the ideal, nature and culture, "Life" and "Spirit," bondage and freedom, by means of evolutionary theory. It may be that these problems cannot be mitigated while remaining within the province of Cassirer's particular description of the relation of consciousness and nature.

Even if the above difficulties were resolved, the question remains: Is it necessary or desirable to define culture, as Cassirer does, as the accumulated remains of the process of *consciousness* in its symbolic activity? Cassirer's explanation of culture seems a promising one. He describes consciousness as gradually and progressively delimiting and determining the shape and configuration of the human world and the human self. This shaping leaves evidence of the fundamental acts of unification and objectification performed by human activity. Furthermore, forms always imply a content formed. Consciousness can only become apparent, can only show itself, as that which gives shape—to something; as that which forms—something.

Cassirer is quite careful in claiming that Spirit depends on some kind of material as the "that-which" is shaped by the activities of consciousness. The symbol, as an indiscerptible unity of the formed and the formative, always retains traces of its material origin. The world of natural processes, however this is construed and interpreted and represented through the various symbolic forms, provides the "matter" necessary for the formative activity of consciousness. But this is matter understood functionally; that is, not as having its own integrity, but only as the correlate of Spirit's objectifying action through its symbols. If we agree with Cassirer, we agree that culture is the residue of spiritual processes conceived as *antithetical* to natural processes. Cassirer opts for a subtle form of idealism based on a functional, rather than strictly metaphysical distinction between Spirit and Nature. But this functional distinction finally erases the reality or integrity of that which is opposed to Spirit or consciousness. Consciousness works over more and more of what it finds, and Nature as ontologically distinct from Spirit is, for all intents and purposes, effaced or absorbed through being spiritually articulated and appropriated.

As we'll see in detail in chapter 6, this leads necessarily to the conclusion that there is a real and absolute metaphysical distinction between Spirit and Nature (no matter how intimately these may be conjoined). This in turn means finding the formative activity rather than the formed to be of greater importance, significance, and value; that is, that consciousness holds the place of ontological priority in Cassirer's system. With these assumptions, it seems we must accept a *telos* of greatest distinction between the two metaphysically distinct regions, Spirit and Nature. We can see this very clearly in Cassirer's contentions regarding the goal manifested in each form, what provides the driving force behind the progressive elaboration of each cultural form. The goal, for consciousness, is to secure the conditions for its complete emancipation from its natural state.

Cassirer is willing to acknowledge that any and all products of human creative endeavor give equal evidence of the formative power of human being in concert with the world. But, he also insists on a pre- or trans-personal consciousness as the progenitor of culture, and he assumes that the *telos* of freedom from nature is what drives consciousness in its many accomplishments. Cassirer seems to be saying that human being, at its most free, *is* consciousness living in a world that has become entirely symbolically articulated, and that consciousness knows itself as the creative force behind the symbolically wrought world.

Underlying Cassirer's brilliant analysis of the history of scientific accomplishment, religious understanding, and linguistic naming of the world as all means utilized by consciousness in moving out of the mire of substance and recreating the world as an analogue of functional concepts, there is still the intellectual commitment to the notion of brute nature as an implacable but escapable fact or condition. The products and processes of culture (in whichever of its various forms) are overlaid on brute nature and insofar as we transform the surface of nature into the veneer of culture, we are at home in the world. Only so far can Spirit be truly master in its own house, when everything there is of its own making.

Finally, we come to what I believe to be the crux of the difficulties in both Cassirer's metaphysical scheme and his critical philosophy of culture. This is his concept of freedom as the aim of symbolic accomplishment. The notion of free creation of the forms of the self and world through the agency of consciousness in its symbolic activity necessitates a notion of freedom from (at least, natural) constraint and compulsion. This is an idea with a distinguished pedigree, of course. Cassirer's version is of consciousness, imbued with its own constructive and creative energy, wresting itself, pulling itself up by its own bootstraps, from the blind, mechanical compulsions imposed on human being by the organism's own material context. Yet freedom from constraint or compulsion finally seems no freedom at all. The severance of all ties to a compulsory world beyond our control implies only a freedom of isolation. And such isolation, an attempt at some sort of unrelatedness to the natural context, seems to rule out many of the possible relations we hold dear as the outcome of a free state of being. This seems to be the case in at least two ways. First, if true freedom is freedom from constraint, then in what way could freedom be the source of any hoped-for results? That is, if no constraint or compulsion is implied in our notion of freedom, then in what way could freedom be the necessary cause of any effect? Perhaps a greater difficulty with this notion of freedom as freedom from the natural context, is that freedom from constraint or compulsion is a freedom without responsibility.[96] If we forfeit the notion of responsibility as a necessary response to a compelling request or command, mustn't we also forfeit any political or ethical efficacy or righteousness we associate with freedom and responsibility?

Cassirer's description of the process and progress of consciousness symbolically articulating and then appropriating the world leads to the conclusion that the inevitable direction of consciousness is toward understanding itself as independent of all natural processes. This provides an imperative for all of us engaged in cultural production. It seems incumbent on us, according to the implications of Cassirer's work, to foster and further the goal of greater and greater freedom of consciousness from nature, of advancing the march of Spirit in its forward movement. But this leads me to conclude that Cassirer's assumptions and hypotheses are wrong, or at least very inadequate. Given recent developments in our understanding of the precarious balance of ecological forces making possible any life at all on our planet, we surely can't believe that true freedom lies in an increasing independence (at the conceptual or any other level) from our material and organic condition or environment. Many of the intractable problems faced by human beings today are the result of a blindness toward the fact that human being is inseparable from the conditions for the possibility for any organic existence. Such implied independence can also be used as a shield, a way of denying that our actions, as a species, are responsible for the very real possibility that the global ecosystem may become so damaged as to eliminate most forms of life on the planet.

Cassirer certainly does not advocate any of these dire results, nor does he predict them as consequences of his assumptions and hypotheses regarding the priority of consciousness over nature and the imperative of greatest separation between the two. But if an assumed independence of the human process from other natural processes, with a concomitant lack of responsibility in regard to these processes, leads to severe and life-threatening consequences when used as assumptions in the economic or technological arenas of human endeavor, can we hope they'll have a salutary effect on human life when used as metaphysical or ontological assumptions? This would only be the case, it seems, if we deny any cultural value to our philosophic projects.

☙❦❧

There are three basic strands of Cassirer's account of myth that we will follow in the next chapters. In chapter 3, his description of myth as symbolic in nature will be compared to Roland Barthes' analysis of myth as semiological or significatory. Chapter 4 examines the structure of mythically constituted objectivity as expressed in the spatio-temporal features of the world; Mircea Eliade provides a counter-point. Chapter 5 investigates the nature of subjectivity in the mythical world, outlining James Hillman's picture of the archetypally constituted soul as contrast to Cassirer's description of the mythical self.

3

Mythical Symbol, Mythical Sign

Roland Barthes'
Semiological Analysis

Roland Barthes offers a precise semiological analysis of contemporary myth in *Mythologies*.[1] This is a collection of essays written during the mid-fifties examining myth in areas as diverse as film, television, cooking, and photography. Barthes' work is an unabashed polemic against the practice of myth. He writes, "I resented seeing Nature and History confused at every turn, and I wanted to track down, in the decorative display of *what-goes-without-saying*, the ideological abuse which, in my view, is hidden there." Barthes understands mythmaking as the politically motivated displacement of the contingent origin of events or meanings with what appears to be inevitable. This theft of origin is accomplished by way of mythical "speech." What is left after myth's work is the "falsely obvious."[2] Barthes, like Cassirer, sees myth as a dangerous, insidious power that must be unmasked for the ignorance that it is, and that it fosters. Again, like Cassirer, Barthes believes that the power of myth will be destroyed only when we have come to understand its ways.

MYTH AS SEMIOLOGICAL SYSTEM

Barthes describes myth as a "mode of signification, a form";[3] myth is a language, or a type of speech, and must be analyzed as such. Anything whatsoever can be the "object" of this language, and each object is transformed through its place in the system of mythical signification. Neither the subjective motivations for the form of speech nor the objects "spoken" of can give us full insight into the structural and functional features of myth, though either may occasion our analysis. This means that in order to understand mythical speech, we must discover its properties of transformation, the way mythical speech works in constituting meaning.

Barthes does not claim that myth should be analyzed as if it were a discrete language, such as French, or Urdu, uncovering its grammar, origin, and so forth. Rather, "myth in fact belongs to the province of a general science, coextensive with linguistics." This is semiology, the "vast science of signs," a science not of bare facts but of meaning and signification.[4] Barthes' understanding of the type of analysis necessary in studying myth comes directly from Ferdinand de Saussure, who envisioned a general science "that studies the life of signs within society." De Saussure saw his own work in linguistics as an examination of a "special system within the mass of semiological data." He saw other systems within the general science: "the alphabet of deaf mutes, symbolic rites, polite formulas, military signals, . . . customs, etc."[5]

Barthes analyzes myth as a coherent semiological system, or system of signification. Semiology, following de Saussure, posits a relation between two terms, the signifier and the signified. The signifier and the signified belong to two different orders or categories (for example, a concept and an acoustic image) and may be correlated in a relation of equivalence, but not of identity. De Saussure compares the science of semiology to that of economics as both are composed of systems of differential valuations; "both sciences are concerned with *a system for equating things of different orders*—labor and wages in one and a signified and signifier in the other."[6] A semiological system involves the correlation of three distinct terms, adding "the associative total of the first two terms [the signifier and the signified]"; this is the sign.[7]

To use Barthes' example: I may give my sweetheart a dozen roses in order to express my passion. But this is not a simple substitution of the signified (my passion) by the signifier (the roses). In fact, I give my sweetheart "passionified roses," the sign or signifying act that is the correlation of the first two terms in the triad. In a sense, neither my passion nor the roses are meaningful until correlated in this act of signification; though of course each may be meaningful in another context. The object or signifier (an object in this case, though of course the signifier could be a word, a symbol, etc.)

remains what it is, as does that which is signified, prior to and following the act of signification. Only its position in this signifying triad demands the signifier function as the instantiation of this particular meaning. Barthes explains that it is only in semiological analysis that we could distinguish between the "passionified rose" and the roses. On the plane of nonanalytical experience, the sign and the signifier cannot be dissociated.[8]

De Saussure uses the following as an example of the significatory triad: We have the concept of a tree and the sound image "tree." The concept is the signified and the sound image is the signifier, and the relation of these in my saying "look at the tree" is the sign or signifying act.[9] For Barthes and de Saussure (as opposed to many other theorists in the field of linguistics), the *sign* is never empty, it is always a concrete particularization of some signifier/signified relation. On the plane of analysis, the *signifier* is always empty, altogether arbitrary, a token; *'arbor'* or *'Baum'* could just as easily be the signifier as *'tree'*. Only when the signifier is united with the signified does it become a meaning-full sign.

This semiological tridimensional pattern signifier/signified/sign is found in mythical signifying systems as it is found in any semiological system. But myth has the peculiar property of having as its signifiers only that which has already been fully initiated into some other signifying complex. That is, myth can only use already constituted signs as its signifiers. Barthes uses the following diagram (figure 3.1) to indicate the difference between mythical signifying acts and other semiological systems:

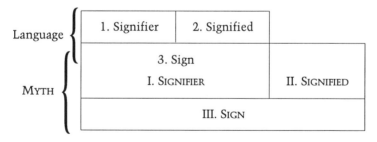

Figure 3.1

This shows the use that myth makes of already constituted signs. If the sign 'tree' is taken over as a signifier in another act of signification, we have an instance of mythical language. For example, the sign 'tree' (with its own already correlated signifier and signified) may be used in an advertisement, as in the slogan "beautifully land-scaped trees are the mark of the sophisticated homeowner." In this instance, the *sign* 'tree' becomes a *signifier* in a new semiological system, now conjoined with the concept of pride in ownership (the newly *signified*) in constituting a new level of signifying activity, here advertising. This peculiarity of mythical signification makes it a *"second-order semiological system."*[10]

As the same thing holds the position of sign in the first-order semiological system and signifier in the second-order system, Barthes expands his technical terminology to include "meaning" for the former and "form" for the latter. The signified in either the first- or second-order system is a "concept," but 'sign' is used only when describing the correlation of signifier and concept signified in first-order language. The position of the sign in the second-order system of myth is now designated "signification." We can emend Barthes' diagram in the following way (figure 3.2):

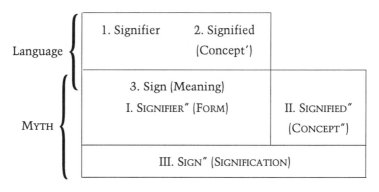

Figure 3.2

In the example used above, the sound image 'tree', conjoined with the signified concept (concept'), constitutes the *meaning* of 'tree' in the signifying act of indicating a particular object. The sign 'tree', constituted in this act becomes a form or a token as it functions as signifier in a second signifying act. The *form* 'tree', is conjoined with a second concept (concept"), pride in ownership, in a second-order sign or signification—buy our product.

The signs that are transformed into signifiers in mythical speech can be any sort of material, as myth utilizes this material only insofar as it has already been denuded of its concrete particu-larity. Images, words, foodstuffs (for example, "chicken soup" could function as a signifier to the signified, parental love), anything whatsoever can be stripped of its first-order, particular meaning, and reduced to the emptied form of signifier in the second-order system. The first-order semiological system (the triad signifier/signified/sign), "innocent" and "transparent" on its own, loses its fully concrete, particular meaning and becomes the "language-object" of myth, becomes one of the elements used by myth in constructing its own system, "a *meta-language*, . . . *in which* one speaks about the first."

It is important to note that Barthes' description of mythical speech, while quite precise, covers a tremendous amount of signifying activity. It appears that any instance of a metalanguage is an instance of myth. For example, Barthes uses a Latin grammar text as one of two primary illustrations of mythical speech. In this, the phrase "*quia ego nominor leo*" has a simple first-order meaning: "because my name is lion." However, as it is given as a grammatical example, it belongs to a more global semiological system. The meaning of the phrase is obscured as it is utilized as an object in a meta-language. Barthes writes, "Inasmuch as [the Latin phrase] is addressed to me, a pupil in the second form, it tells me clearly: I am a grammatical example meant to illustrate the rule about the agreement of the predicate." Mythical, or second-order, signification usurps the first-order sign, full of its own meaning, and empties it of particularity so that its form can be filled with a second-order concept, in this example, "grammatical exemplarity."[11]

MYTH AS DUPLICITOUS FORM

The work of myth occurs in the ambiguity and duplicity wrought in signifying acts insofar as the signifier of myth is *both* meaning and form. We can elaborate Barthes' example of the passionified roses: as sign correlating my passion and these flowers, the roses are "full"; they are, or have, meaning. The passionified roses are a sign in a first-order system of signification. We can trace the conditions under which I give them. We can ask, Why roses and not pansies? Could I really afford a dozen roses? Is it lust or is it Love? But, if the roses were to appear in a photo of two smiling people in an advertisement for diamond rings, for example, something very different happens. The roses are nearly emptied of their concrete, particularized meaning (as sign of *my* passion) and become ciphers to be filled. Myth takes an already constituted sign (passionified roses) and uses it as a signifier conjoined with yet another concept (a second-order signified), perhaps "Buy an engagement ring and passion will be yours."

We may view the ad as a photograph of *this* particular woman and *this* particular man gazing dreamily at each other while exchanging gifts of flowers and gems. We may wonder if they really love each other or if their seeming impending marriage will last or if they share equally in the household chores. If we look at the ad this way, we are analyzing the meaning of the photo in a first-order semiological system. Insofar as the image has not yet been appropriated by the concept in the mythical system of signification, it remains full and readable on its own terms. But when the first-order sign or meaning is transformed into a second-order signifier, or form, its own real history and contingency is glossed over. Myth turns the first-order sign into "an empty, parasitical form"; myth "impoverishes it, it puts it at a distance, it holds it at one's disposal."[12] In this, the meaning of the photo (having to do with a particular emotional relationship between particular people) is drained off, and it becomes an empty form utilized by an advertising myth in a second-order signifying act. The image of two people in love becomes *any* two people, and the love becomes completely sentimentalized; in fact, the image must be so devoid of specific content that the observer may see him or herself in it as the signified.

But myths are effective only when domesticating the meaning without altogether destroying the vitality of the first-order system of correlations. The consumer of myth must have available the reservoir of meaning that belongs to the first-order system, which then oscillates with the aridity of the form that belongs to the second-order system. The consumer of the myth alternately focuses on the first-order signification—a particular couple in love, and the second-order signification—the enticement to buy a diamond. The alternation is smooth, because the movement from one order to the other is performed through an object that is both meaning and form; the roses (or gems) are sign in one system and signifier in the other. As mythical signification holds sway, meaning and form are like two sides of a coin as it is being tossed; the sides cannot be dissociated, yet continually show their distinct faces. This ambiguity or forced alternation of a meaning that is full and a form that is empty gives the appearance of life to the mythical signifier.

The sign, as *meaning*, that is, in a first-order system, has a full historical determination, full contingency. Barthes explains that this history and contingency are drained off and finally absorbed by the concept of the second-order system, the second signified. But this second, mythic signified, the second concept, has its own historical determination and concrete situation—one that is obscured in the oscillation of meaning and form. It is this that flows back into the emptied form, dislocating the meaning's own history and substituting a counterfeit. To return to our elaboration of Barthes' example of the passionified roses: the second-order concept ("Buy a diamond ring and passion will be yours") has a certain economic and political history and intention tied to South Africa and its international relations and internal politics. The clarity of the concept becomes diffused, distorted, a "nebulous condensation," because that to which it is conjoined is unstable, alternating between meaning and form, fullness and emptiness. Barthes calls this relation one of "deformation"; the second-order concept "alienates" the meaning of the first-order signifying act.

MYTH'S ULTERIOR MOTIVE

In insisting on interrupting this dynamic and restoring proper order to the metalanguage and its objects, the consumer of myth ceases consuming and becomes a mythologist—a decidedly political act. Interrupting the oscillation of mythical meaning and form deprives myth of its primary power, the "naturalization" of the concept. Naturalization is the modus operandi of myth. For the myth consumer, the concept, mythicized, "is not read as a motive, but as a reason."[13] The driving force of mythical signification, its concept, is always "motivated." Barthes means this in two distinct but related ways. First, the relation between the signifier and the signified in the mythical system is never altogether arbitrary, though the signifier in first-order systems is quite arbitrary. There is no motivated or necessary connection between roses and passion. It is through convention only that I do not use pork chops as the signifier of my passion.

Mythical signification, on the other hand, always contains an element of motivation in this sense. We can see this in myth's analogical, as opposed to arbitrary, choice of a signifier. In our example: the image of love or passion in the ad for diamonds is analogous to what we hope for during our engagement. The analogy must always be there in mythical signification. If the signifier were merely a close-up of a diamond ring, there would be no mythical signification, only first-order discourse ("Buy a diamond ring"). But the analogy must always be partial. If the image were of a couple having sex at the jeweler's counter while clutching wads of cash and diamond rings, we would have a complete image of the concept ("Buy a diamond ring and passion will be yours") and there could be no mythical signification. For Barthes, myth is always driven or motivated obliquely via the power of partial analogy.

The second way of understanding the motivation residing in every mythical signification is that myth always acts to survive, to maintain itself in its parasitical life. If the meaning of the signifier is altogether obliterated, the sign becomes an "example" of the concept driving it. That is, if our photo-ad evokes no emotional reverberations in me, the ad is merely an example of advertising gimmickry. If the form is erased, none of the vitality and history of the image can leak out and feed the second-order concept. That is, I may never leave the "story" of the man and woman in love; and my buying diamonds is irrelevant and unnecessary to this narrative. Mythical signification must avoid both the erasure of the meaning and the erasure of the form of the first-order signifier usurped in the mythical signification. If either form or meaning is erased, the myth is doomed to fail.

Myth avoids its doom by transforming the "perfectly explicit," and contingently determined, intention of the concept or motive ("Buy diamonds!"). Instead, the intention or motive is "immediately frozen into something natural," as if there were an essential or necessary relation between passion and diamonds. This occurs in part because in myth there is only a partial analogy, and no more, of the signifier to the concept. This means that in myth there appears a "natural" connection between the signifier and the signified, as if the image "naturally conjured up the concept"; as if the signifier called out the signified. The mythical second-order system disguises its semiological structure. Every signification system is a system of *equivalence* or exchange, putting in relation items of distinct and causally unrelated categories (here, emotions and gems). But myth presents itself as a system of the *identical*. What appears in mythical "reading" is a counterfeit system of induction. Myth seems to be "a kind of causal process: the signifier and the signified have, in [the myth consumer's] eyes, a natural relationship." The mythical system is read as if it were a set of facts. But these facts can never be traced to their origin, as myth always provides an "alibi" for the missing links to reality. The second-order or mythical concept has, Barthes claims, the "perfect alibi: it is enough that its signifier has two sides for it always to have an 'elsewhere' at its disposal."[14] As long as the oscillation of meaning and form continues, myth cannot be pinned down and held culpable in its particular signification.

Mythical signification uses its sleight-of-hand to insert a signifier that acts as if it belonged to the concept signified. Myth offers an obvious but false foundation for the semiological system. As well, by concentrating our attention on the hypnotic alternation of meaning and form, myth magically erases the historically and contingently bound motive of both the first- and second-order signified. This ulterior motive is hidden and the consumer of myth is tricked into seeing an innocent natural causal relation in the signification. This provides "an historical intention [with] a natural justification, and [makes] contingency appear eternal."[15] If mythical signification is decomposed into its constituent significatory acts, with each a clearly contingently determined construction, it loses its power to mystify and alienate.

BOURGEOIS MYTHICAL SIGNIFICATION

Barthes' analysis of mythical signification indicts bourgeois/capitalist attempts to eliminate the dialectical force of revolutionary or truly political speech. Bourgeois mythical signification "organizes a world which is without contradictions because it is without depth, a world wide open and wallowing in the evident, it establishes a blissful clarity." This is possible because of the nature of mythical signification and the subsumption of such signification to the goals of the bourgeois/capitalist system. Mythical signification, in its oscillation of meaning and form, conceals the arbitrary character of all significatory functioning and substitutes for it a false (that is, perceived as natural or inevitable) foundation.

Barthes' specific concern is with mythical speech or signification in the contemporary scene. He aims at radically undercutting the insidious solidification of bourgeois and right-wing hegemony in today's mass culture. Hence, the myths he examines exemplify an inherent conservatism. This conservatism is fostered by the "naturalization" of the historical conditions of bourgeois ideology and capitalist economic practices. Barthes writes,

> Everything, in everyday life, is dependent on the representation which the bourgeoisie *has and makes us have* of the relations between man and world. These "normalized" forms attract little attention, by the very fact of their extension, in which their origin is easily lost. . . . [P]ractised on a national scale, bourgeois norms are experienced as the evident laws of a natural order—the further the bourgeois class propagates its representations, the more naturalized they become.[16]

Furthermore, according to Barthes, the structure of bourgeois ideology is precisely parallel to that of mythical signification—thus the double power of bourgeois mythmaking. Both bourgeois ideology and mythical signification aim at immobilizing the transient, contingent features of the world, offering the historically determined status quo as the inevitable result of inexorable natural processes. The amalgamation of these two forces, the mythical and the bourgeois, has as its outcome an indomitable control of the shape of culture.

> Just as the cuttlefish squirts its ink in order to protect itself, [bourgeois ideology] cannot rest until it has obscured the ceaseless making of the world into an object which can forever be possessed, catalogued its riches, embalmed it, and injected into reality some purifying essence which will stop its transformation, its flight towards other forms of existence. . . . [And] the very end of myths is to immobilize the world: they must suggest and mimic a universal order which has fixated once and for all the hierarchy of possessions.[17]

For Barthes, mythical signification finds its ultimate fulfillment and utility in serving the demands of the "bourgeoisization" of culture. And the primary demand of such organization and production is bourgeois conservation of the bourgeois world; the demand is to impede History. Thus myth in the contemporary world is absolutely conservative in its function.

For Barthes, bourgeois and right-wing ideologies so control and exploit the power of mythical signification that they have cut out the tongue of the oppressed and may succeed in bringing History to a halt. Barthes offers an account of mythical signification that in its very precision is made broad enough to fit as an explanation of bourgeois and petit-bourgeois usurpation of most areas of contemporary culture. The mechanics of mythmaking are quite specific in Barthes' model. Myth is the elision of the historically determined and determinable character of the motivated signified in a second-order semiological system or metalanguage. Barthes' explanation of why we find this mechanism in almost every contemporary cultural product is that this is the form of bourgeois ideology as well as the form of mythical signification. The bourgeois/capitalists have appropriated myth and in this doubly conservative and oppressive force, conquered culture. And of course, as bourgeois ideology comes to control more and more of the production of representations in modern culture—in theater, magazines, newspapers, fiction, T.V. programming, and commercial advertising—there is an ever-expanding network of mythical signification to bulwark the bourgeois world. We should remember, however, that though myth and bourgeois ideology have a particularly close affinity, myth can operate under any conditions whatsoever, except that of revolutionary language.[18]

LITERARY LABOR

For Barthes, the locus of unalienated, free human being can only be discovered in labor. Directly related to labor is true political language, co-efficient in the active transformation or manipulation of nature. Barthes writes of labor,

> If I am a woodcutter and I am led to name the tree which I am felling, whatever the form of my sentence, I "speak the tree," I do not speak about it. This means that my language is operational, transitively linked to its object; between the tree and myself, there is nothing but my labour, that is to say, an action. This is political language: it represents nature for me only insofar as I am going to transform it, it is a language thanks to which I *"act the object"*; the tree is . . . simply the meaning of my action. But if I am not a woodcutter, I can no longer "speak the tree," I can only speak *about* it, *on* it. . . . There is . . . one language which is not mythical, it is the language of man as a producer, . . . wherever he links his language to the making of things.[19]

The self and the world, the subjective sphere and the objective, are always determined through labor, according to Barthes' perspective. Barthes is a neo-Marxist, and obviously believes that capitalism has usurped most forms of free productive labor. The bonds of the bourgeois-capitalist organization of reality are particularly strong because such signification has enlisted mythical speech as its accomplice. Alienated labor produces an alienated self and a world of reified institutions that appear impervious to change, impervious to History. Myth further obscures the contingent origin of the forms of self and world we inhabit, thus adding its counterweight to historical progress; myth is the most insidious form of human entrapment.

Barthes investigates many types of cultural activity as providing information on the structure of signifying acts. Among these are the "garment system," the "food system," the "car system," the "furniture system," and so on.[20] However, again we find (as we did in examining Cassirer's work on symbolic forms) a "first among equals" in the array, in terms of offering a way out of the bondage that constrains human being. A certain kind of "literary work" provides the greatest possibility of freedom from the bad faith, alienation, and false Nature imposed by the bourgeois mythical organization of reality.

Modern literary work, insofar as it writes "*in the full awareness of what it is doing,*"[21] is the greatest force in contemporary culture against bondage to false Nature. Barthes envisions a radical literary politics, an acknowledged construction of the subject and object of discourse through the free play of literary/semiological labor. Barthes writes of literary work coming of age in the modern period, severing its ties to classicism and humanism. In this progression, literature has lost its traditional aim of somehow portraying or mimicking a material reality or an emotional or intellectual being that exists outside of the signifying act of writing. Literature has freed itself from such dependence, and Barthes claims (citing Roman Jakobson) that the truly literary work "refers to that type of message which takes as its object not its content but its own form." He continues, "it is only by its passage through language that literature can continue to shake loose the essential concepts of our culture, one of the chief among which is the 'real.'"[22]

Literature has come to understand itself not as a transparent instrument providing access to a nonlinguistically or nonpoetically structured reality, but as formal in the sense of pure linguistic or symbolic formative structuring of self and world. For Barthes, the literary text that acknowledges itself as a system of signs has dropped all pretense of writing "about" the world, and "knows" itself as writing or semiologically constituting the world, always within the borders of the literary sphere. Moreover, the subject (or author) is as well constituted through the semiological activity of the new literary work; the "subject is immediately contemporary with the writing, being effected and affected by it."[23] There is no extratextual agent somehow expressing an extratextual meaning about an extratextual world through the text. Such a work would merely reinstantiate the reifications of the particular social and economic context, it would not be free labor, but alienated; it would not constitute free human beings, but alienated ones.

The new mode of literary work no longer uses "to write" as a transitive verb, according to Barthes. It no longer writes *about*— either the world or the self as standing outside the text, outside the play of signifying acts. It transforms "to write": not into an intransitive verb, having no object, but into a "middle" verb, which corresponds to the diathetical middle voice, "to write itself,"[24] having as object that which it itself creates. This literature, exemplified in the work of Proust, Joyce, Mallarmé, and Robbe-Grillet, is the epitome of the struggle toward significatory emancipation.

Barthes claims that using structuralist semiology, "itself developed from a linguistic model," to understand literature, "which is the work of language," allows him to do away with a false dichotomy between the metalanguage of analysis and the language-object analyzed. He believes that the "logical continuation of structuralism can only be to rejoin literature, no longer as an 'object' of analysis but as an activity of writing."[25] Semiological analysis then, writing itself, would prove the most powerful tool for avoiding the snares of bad faith and alienation, even more powerful than the literary labor analyzed.

LITERATURE vs. SCIENCE

We must remember that Barthes claims that *any* metalanguage, including the discourse of scientific endeavor, can fall prey to mythical usurpation or encroachment. Any instance of a metalanguage, or second-order system of signification, must be held as mythical (or bourgeois) suspect, any semiological system divorced from its contingently determined language-object is prey for the transitive verb 'to write (about)'. Bad faith, alienation, and false Nature cannot be avoided by scientific discourse, says Barthes, because this signifying activity can never fully exercise itself as writing itself but must always understand itself as writing about. Unless, of course, scientific discourse is practiced as radical semiological or literary discourse, practiced "in the full awareness of what it is doing."

And what is it that science does? Science, as a semiological system (or, one could say, a collection of systems), constitutes subject and object through signifying activity, as does any semiological system. It is perhaps clear that scientific discourse constitutes certain objective features of the world as meaningful—"protons," "gravity," "mass," "energy," and so on, are signifiers belonging to scientific discourse. These signifiers are conjoined with particulars signified in science's signifying acts. With careful examination, we are able to discern the contingent and historical forces contributing to the particular (and changing) uses to which the signifier is put, and therefore, to the contingent and historical ground of the objects of scientific inquiry and discourse. The system of signification organizes the (scientific) world into particular objective features.

It is less clear how scientific discourse, driven by contingent historical processes, constructs the subject. In fact, scientific writing tends always to present itself as if there were no writer, as if there were no subject implied. The author, as historically located and contingently determined, is hidden. Barthes writes,

> Every utterance implies its own subject, whether this subject be expressed in an apparently direct fashion, by the use of 'I,' or indirectly, by being referred to as 'he,' or avoided altogether by means of impersonal constructions. These are merely grammatical decoys, which do no more than vary the way in which the subject is constituted within the discourse, that is, the way in which he gives himself to others, theatrically or as a phantasm; they all refer therefore to forms of the imaginary. The most specious of these forms is the privative, the very one normally practised in scientific discourse.[26]

(There are important echoes of Lacanian psychoanalytic concepts and practices here, especially concerning the "imaginary" and the "spectacle"/"specular."[27])

The apparent erasure of the contingent subject (the author or researcher) of scientific writing, in the name of neutrality and "objectivity," is fraught with political implications, perhaps because of the authoritative nature of scientific discourse in contemporary culture. Moreover, Barthes maintains that discourse becomes a kind of totalitarian code if it effaces or neglects to admit to itself that it is creating or positing the subject, as well as construing its object. He goes on to suggest that in discourse in which the attempt is made to erase the subject (as historically contingent agent), objectivity as well as subjectivity are imaginary constructs.

Barthes also suggests that emerging modes of writing-itself (including radical semiological analysis) serve as models for a kind of radical dispersion or decentralization of the power to constitute meaning, including the imputed organizational power of a centralized subject determining or construing meaning. Barthes writes of the efforts of this new literature that the "meaning or the goal of this effort is to substitute the instance of discourse for the instance of reality (or of the referent), which has been, and still is, a mythical 'alibi' dominating the idea of literature."[28]

Barthes implies that scientific discourse must be subjected to radical literary analysis, of the sort he practices on the products of the new, unalienated literary labor. If science does not submit to this, it maintains its role in the reifications performed by the particular economic processes at work, in the obfuscation of the contingent determinations of human existence. Barthes writes,

> Scientific discourse believes itself to be a superior code; writing[-itself] aims at being a total code, including its own forces of destruction. It follows that writing[-itself] alone can smash the idol set up by a paternalistic science, refuse to be terror-stricken by what is wrongly thought of as the "truth" of the content and of reasoning.[29]

The mythologist's critique, like "writing-itself," is the process of breaking the bonds of totalitarian signification, any system that purports a noncontingently or nonhistorically determined truth.

❧

If scientific literature is literature and subject to the same forms of critique as all other literary construction, then Barthes is indicting the mythical elements of scientific-theoretical discourse. This of course would include an indictment of the critical philosophic work accomplished by Cassirer. If what Barthes claims about scientific discourse is true, then Cassirer, never precisely examining the formative activity of his own methodological language (as part of scientific-theoretical discourse), remains dependent on concepts and categories, especially in relation to the subject, that are not yet fully functional. Cassirer has not found a method of analysis that is "completely aware of itself" as structuring the investigating subject as well as the field of investigation.

Outlining the sort of radical semiological analysis that Barthes might want to perform on Cassirer's work is only one way we can begin to draw out some implications for a comprehensive theory of myth. Indeed, a radical semiological analysis of Cassirer's theory of myth, an instance of scientific discourse, would show that the theory itself functions mythically. (In fact, I will argue, in chapter 6, that theories of myth *do* function as contemporary myths, though I argue on much different grounds than does Barthes.) However, this conclusion ought not be drawn quite yet, at least not by reducing Cassirer's analysis to an instance of what Barthes describes as scientific discourse. Doing this, it seems, obscures precisely those discoveries of Cassirer's that might bolster, as well as contradict, Barthes' contentions. In an important sense, Barthes' work is more global than

Cassirer's: Barthes analyzes semiological systems, Cassirer uses scientific discourse, a type of semiological system. But it seems we do not yet know enough to know that Barthes is *correct* in his claims; therefore we do not yet know that Cassirer's work ought to be stripped of its particular findings and seen merely as an instance of second-order discourse. There are many ways of comparing these very different theories of myth, and some of these tell us as much about what myth must be as about either Cassirer's or Barthes' idiosyncratic perspective. We will examine a few of these considerations in the remainder of this chapter. Other considerations will wait until chapter 6.

MYTH AND POLITICS

Barthes and Cassirer understand the mythical as inextricably bound up with political practices of the twentieth century. Cassirer interprets the atrocities of National Socialism and the seeming intractability (in the face of reason) of certain political forms as a resurgence of mythical consciousness, a reversal of the rational, humanistic gains achieved through history. Barthes claims a more pervasive, though perhaps less obvious role of mythical signification as a means by which bourgeois culture gains a stranglehold on the movement of History. Cassirer can only account for the appeal of fascism by offering as its rational explanation a watered down version of his more general characterization of mythical consciousness. Only certain features of his careful analysis of mythical symbolic organization—its wellspring in emotion, its conservative character, its expression of the primacy of social rather than individual experience, the important place of ritual in everyday life, word magic—are brought to bear in his discussion of fascism. The mythical organization of space and time, mythical perception, the "law of metamorphosis," the "sympathetic" understanding that assumes the solidarity of all life, the "physiognomic" expressiveness of the mythical world in its being apprehended as primarily a "thou" rather than an "it"—all these features of the mythical, so carefully described by Cassirer on other occasions, fall by the wayside in his analysis of the otherwise incomprehensible power of fascism.

For Cassirer, as for Barthes, myth is an absolute conservatism.[30] Myth is oriented to a misty past that cannot be investigated for the truth about origins. It is irrevocably bound to this past by the incessant repetition of ritual reenactment of events originating in the sacred past. Myth is unable to grasp the contingent character of human linguistic production, seeing words rather as an aspect of natural necessity. That myth understands language, gods and goddesses, and sacred narratives as part of the natural world means mythical consciousness remains embedded in the sphere of biological and physical laws. Myth is also absolutely conservative in having no category of the ideal. The "ideal" is necessary for envisioning a world that could be better and therefore for understanding the present world as mutable.

More to the point of this comparison of Barthes and Cassirer is the latter's explanation of trends in twentieth-century political life. Where Barthes sees the alliance of bourgeois ideology and mythical signification as the dominant cultural determinant in contemporary Western nations, Cassirer contends that the alliance of fascism and myth in our century is unprecedented in European history. This generates enormous political power, and has become possible only with certain technological achievements. The wholesale manufacture of myth ("Manufactured in the same sense and according to the same methods as any other modern weapon—as machine guns or airplanes"[31]) has entirely transformed modern political life. Cassirer explains that in our century, the deliberate manufacture of myth came on the scene as "one of the greatest triumphs of modern political warfare." Myth created solely for the purpose of furthering fascistic goals "was no longer an incalculable and uncontrollable thing. It could be made at pleasure; it became an artificial compound manufactured in the great laboratory of politics."[32] These newly created myths appeal to the deep emotional turmoil experienced in the threat of economic and social collapse. The new myths offer order and regularity in the face of chaos and acute uncertainty. The myths draw on a reservoir of irrationality lying close to the surface of modern human life with its sheen of rationality. These myths depend on a primitive desires for social solidarity and group-recognized norms. These desires have only been marginally exorcised in the modern period, as we've fostered individual determination and responsibility.

Cassirer warns against what he calls twentieth-century political myths. Barthes claims that his own work on myth is a "semioclasm" aimed at unmasking and undoing the "essential enemy (the bourgeois norm)."[33] These positions are alike in using a term or concept—myth—that has almost always been seen as the epitome of the irrational but altogether powerful and wickedly subversive force that attacks what we, as rational beings, hold dear. Cassirer and Barthes use the term 'myth' as the major weapon in attacking cultural and political conditions or events that do not, cannot, make sense on their own.

If it is through myth that dangerous political forces gain power and legitimacy, then adding the precision of Barthes analysis to Cassirer's more general description would give us an important tool for safeguarding the political world. Indeed, the goals of these authors coalesce in concluding that myth must be eliminated if we are to secure the conditions for the possibility of freedom. Suppressing the power of myth certainly does not guarantee the state of freedom, but not doing so dooms us to bondage.

SEMIOLOGICAL SYSTEMS AND SYMBOLIC FORMS

Barthes and Cassirer both inveigh against the dangerous power of myth, but merely sharing the belief that myth wreaks havoc in political life tells us little of the deeper convergences and divergences in the work of the authors. The metaphysical and ontological underpinnings of these theories of myth and political life are certainly at odds. Barthes is operating out of material dialectics and Cassirer out of critical idealism. Yet each author holds as his locus of investigation the work or activity of human being in shaping the world and the self in a meaningful fashion. Each understands Nature as a category opposed to what claims honorific status in his system—History for Barthes and consciousness or Spirit for Cassirer. Each holds that an adequate account of the truly human must embrace all types of meaning engendering productive activities, as well as investigate the internal mechanisms of development and the historical lineage of each area of meaning activity.

Barthes' use of the term 'speech' for myth connotes myth's status as an activity rather than as a substantial possession. This certainly accords with Cassirer's notion of symbolic activity. And as Cassirer makes room for many different sorts of material used as the medium of symbol formation,[34] Barthes uses a notion of language expansive enough to cover "any significant unit or synthesis, whether verbal or visual: a photograph will be a kind of speech for us in the same way as a newspaper article; even objects will become speech, if they mean something."[35] Cassirer uses 'symbolic formation' as the most general category of truly human activity, with myth, language, scientific knowledge, and so on, as particular kinds of symbol formation. Barthes has 'signification' or 'semiological system' as his most general category, with myth, spoken language, literary texts, and so forth, as particular kinds of sign systems.

Barthes and Cassirer describe their overall projects in similar ways. Barthes writes of the appropriateness of considering semiological analysis as the primary method of understanding human activity. He says that "we see culture more and more as a general system of symbols, governed by the same operations." He further justifies his global "semio-critical research" by claiming that there is a "unity of the human symbolic field: culture in all its aspects is a language." Barthes goes on to anticipate the possibility of a "unified science of culture" developing out of the wide variety of contemporary research, especially in the human and social sciences.[36] As we saw in chapter 2, such a unified science is precisely the goal of Cassirer's work, especially in the three volumes of *The Philosophy of Symbolic Forms* and in *An Essay on Man.*

The comprehensive categories used by these two thinkers to describe specifically human activity are in fact quite close. This is especially clear when we remember Cassirer's analysis of the emergence of the *animal symbolicum.* He takes the use of language as typical symbolic formation, especially when language attains the level of universal variability. The evolutionary development of human language systems and the achievement of certain linguistic skills in childhood serve to demarcate the bounds of the truly symbolic and the truly cultural.[37] But, for Cassirer, language is a particular type of symbolic formation, and the unities, identities, and so on, that are formed through this symbol system are quite different from those generated through other symbolic forms. Thus, language may be typical of symbol formation, but it is not the case that all other symbol systems can be reduced to the forms of the linguistic. When Barthes refers to a "translinguistics" as the future he envisions for semiology, he is trying to avoid equating his most general category with language in our "ordinary sense of the term."[38] As with Cassirer, for Barthes, language (spoken, for instance) is a particular semiological system, one among many. We ought not think of language as providing the general principles and norms under which all other semiological systems may be fit.

MYTH, NATURE, AND HISTORY

The transformation of History into Nature is the primary objective of mythical signification, according to Barthes. This transformation exhibits some of the same characteristics enumerated by Cassirer in his account of mythical consciousness. For Cassirer, mythical time is divided into the mundane or profane arena of ever-changing events and the sacred arena of unchangeable origins fixed forever in an untouchable past. This determines the alien character of certain explanatory schemes in myth. Events in sacred time demand no justification; they are immutable and support their own necessity.

Events in sacred time simply *are*, with no precedents determining or causing them to be as they are. "Specifically human existence—usages, customs, social norms, and ties—" in mundane time derives its justification through relation to events in sacred time. Insofar as traits of human existence can find their beginnings in primordial, sacred time, they are considered explained.[39]

On the face of it, Cassirer's description appears to be directly opposed to Barthes' contention that myth transforms history into nature. Cassirer is writing of the transformation of events in the everyday commerce of human beings with the world—production of tools, planting, hunting, thunderstorms, and so forth. The transformation is accomplished by establishing a necessary causal connection between these events and those occurring in a strictly demarcated temporal sphere of the "past." If mythical consciousness has the concept of history at all, it would be played out in this division. So we could read mythical consciousness, in Cassirer's understanding, as transforming nature into history, the reverse of Barthes' claim. But the formal characteristics of such transformations, either history into nature, or nature into history, are the same in both accounts. For each writer, events and traits of contingency are given mythical justification and explanation through a false connection between the contingencies and a wellspring of necessity. It is a false connection because the two ontological orders thus associated are actually irreconcilable. This lends a character of externally caused necessity to that which is actually under the rubric of human direction and production. Cassirer claims that the arena of ongoing human activity and experience, insofar as it is not yet fodder for fully symbolic formation, is part of nature. Relating this activity and experience to a realm impervious to human intervention (the sacred past) results in the deformations exhibited in the products of mythical consciousness. For Barthes as well, apprehending a causal connection between the ongoing, contingent events or traits of human life (what he calls History) and implacable events beyond the pale of human efficacy (his Nature) is a mythic deformation in understanding the real productive activity of human life. For both authors, myth also serves to obscure a certain measure of human responsibility for contingent events, by seeing them as necessary.

MYTH AND FREEDOM

The topography of these two systems of analyses may be quite similar, but the fact that Cassirer and Barthes have identified different signifying forms (the scientific-theoretical and the literary, respectively) as the exemplars and prophets of culture leads to a fundamental difference between the two theories. Cassirer maintains that we are able to chart the degree of development of a specific symbolic form by measuring the ability of consciousness to apprehend its representations within the form as purely of its own creation. Furthermore, as the symbolic form gains in sophistication, it loses its dependence on any reference to substance (either in the objective or the subjective features of existence) and the products of the form are apprehended as strictly functional, ideal unities. Given the gamut of cultural forms, each a coherent meaningful organization of self and world, an adequate account of culture must address each form and give it the respect it is due. Seen this way, no symbolic form is better or worse in terms of being the field or object of investigation for a critical philosophy of culture. Nonetheless, there is an implicit hierarchy found in Cassirer's systematic account of the varieties of symbolic formation. The mythical is at the bottom of this hierarchy, in large part because mythical consciousness lacks even the rudiments of a category of the ideal. Such a category is necessary for any representative functioning whatsoever. Therefore myth can never come to understand itself *as* a symbolic formative activity. At the pinnacle of this hierarchical arrangement is the sort of theoretical activity exemplified by the workings of quantum and relativity physics (and, of course, critical philosophy). This highly abstract symbolic activity knows itself as symbolic. It has also struggled diligently to strip its formative concepts of all taints of substance as some sort of entity that can be caught in a net of correspondence. The concepts in contemporary physics have become almost entirely functional—matter is not understood as self-subsisting substance, but as the functional equivalent of energy. This functionality clearly exhibits the formative and constructive processes enascent in any symbolic form. The history of scientific accomplishments can be read as the most successful and forceful attempt of consciousness to overcome its bondage to blind, mechanical nature by formulating and constructing the conditions of its own freedom.

As Cassirer understands scientific-theoretical symbolic organization as the avenue most suitable for attaining the goal of freedom implicit in every symbolic activity, it is no surprise that he has chosen critical philosophy (a branch of the scientific) as his method of analysis of culture. Cassirer's work can be seen as an investigation of the structure of that which he understands to be the pinnacle of symbolic formation in quest of freedom. He appropriates and makes explicit this structure, utilizing it as his means of investigation and his yardstick for measuring other cultural forms. Barthes understands certain literary forms as the pinnacle of nonalienated, free production of culture. So it is no surprise that he would model and extend his general analysis of semiological systems based on an explicit articulation of the structures of meaning formation found in such works. For Cassirer, the most efficacious method of analyzing culture is to use as a template the structure of the highest achievement of culture. This is true for Barthes as well.

All of Cassirer's work on the spectrum of symbolic forms posits freedom as the end toward which consciousness strives in developing and constituting the forms. As we saw in chapter 2, myth is the only symbolic form inimical to this movement of consciousness. Cassirer is more specific in denouncing myth when writing of political myths in our century. Freedom for consciousness is hard won; it "is not a natural inheritance of man[; i]n order to possess it we have to create it."[40] The tentative advances toward freedom made in the history of culture are erased when we allow myth to infect and surreptitiously control our lives.

Barthes claims that the work of the mythologist, in deciphering mythical signification, is radical political activity. The practice of the mythologist is founded on the liberation of language, postulating the freedom of revolutionary language to make the world and accepting full responsibility for such making. Barthes, of course, does not see consciousness as the driving force behind free productive activity. Barthes is a neo-Marxist and must understand consciousness as itself rooted in the forms of productive labor. Whatever differences Barthes' analysis may have with Cassirer's on the "force" that drives cultural production (and we will return to this important issue in chapter 6 and the conclusion), Barthes' description of freedom is remarkably similar to Cassirer's description. Language for Barthes, in its broadest sense, is the template through which the world and the self become organized and correlated. The only kind of language immune to mythical deformation and alienation is revolutionary language. Revolutionary language is the language of freedom in the sense that it "*harmonizes* with the world, not as it is, but as it wants to create itself."[41] We'll see that this is very similar to Cassirer's notion of the absolute freedom of consciousness to construe self and world; this is the *telos* of freedom that appears in each of the theories we're examining.

☙❧

If mythical symbolic formation or mythical signification is to be understood as the means by which the objective and subjective features of the world are constituted, as Barthes and Cassirer suggest, then we must look carefully at precisely how these regions are constituted. Both Cassirer and Mircea Eliade deal specifically with the spatiotemporal (the objective) features of the mythical world. This is the subject of chapter 4. Cassirer and James Hillman provide accounts of the constitution of the subjective sphere of existence in light of mythical and archetypal configurations. These accounts will be examined in chapter 5. The work of Eliade and Hillman is especially interesting in that these authors understand the mythical as an avenue toward greater freedom than offered by alternative modes of cultural organization.

4

Mythical Space, Mythical Time

Mircea Eliade's Account of the Sacred and the Profane

Working with much the same ethnological and anthropological data, Ernst Cassirer and Mircea Eliade portray important aspects of the mythical world in much the same fashion. For example, each concludes that the mythical is more than a set of particular stories or rituals; that it is a specific cultural formation in which and through which the entirety of human experience is shaped and determined in a systematic unity. This means, of course, a specifically mythic determination of the world in which experience occurs. Eliade notes that the mythical forms "express . . . a complex system of coherent affirmations about the ultimate reality of things, a system that can be regarded as constituting a metaphysics."[1] Similarly, Cassirer writes that the mythical spiritual function does not take its "departure from a world of given objects, divided according to fixed and finished 'attributes,' but . . . first produce[s] this organization of reality."[2] Cassirer and Eliade also agree that the basic ontological opposition giving shape to the mythical world is the division of the sacred from the profane, or mundane. The clear and absolute distinction between the sacred and the profane determines both the subjective and objective features of existence; that is, what belongs to the "self" and what belongs to the "world" as other than the self, including the powers that belong to each. The constitution of the subjective features of existence in the mythical world is discussed in greater detail in chapter 5. Insofar as the mythical world exhibits a metaphysical unity, an analysis of myth must include an examination of both temporality and spatiality, or objective existence, as peculiar to the mythical world. This is the primary task of the present chapter.

There is a second task to be accomplished in this chapter. Though there are many deep similarities in the accounts that Cassirer and Elide give us of the mythical world, there are important differences. The primary difference between Cassirer's estimation of myth and Eliade's is that Eliade accords myth *positive* value. Not only does he acknowledge myth as a legitimate concern for philosophic inquiry, he bestows an honorific status on the existential position of humanity in the mythicoreligiously structured cosmos.[3] Eliade's description of the mythical offers a means of balancing out or evening up the valuational score implicit in Cassirer's account. The denigration of the mythical in Cassirer's analysis and the valorization of the mythical in Eliade's are derived from remarkably similar descriptions. Juxtaposing the accounts should give us a clearer picture of the mythical, one that is not entirely dependent on the religious convictions of one author or the scientific faith of the other.

THE POSITIVE VALUE OF MYTH

By and large, Eliade's work on myth is a measured argument against dismissing the mythical as merely error or ignorance; and his words on this score echo the sentiments of Cassirer. Eliade writes of peculiar cultural practices we find in "pre"-Westernized, "traditional," or "primitive" groups, that:

> To understand them is to see them as human phenomena, the phenomena of culture, . . . not as pathological outbreaks of instinctual behavior, bestiality, or sheer childishness. There is no other alternative. Either we do our utmost to deny, minimize, or forget these excesses, taking them as isolated examples of "savagery" that will vanish completely as soon as the tribes have been "civilized," or we make the necessary effort to understand the mythical antecedents that explain and justify such excesses and give them a religious value. The latter is, we feel, the only one that deserves consideration.[4]

Eliade's demand that we take the mythicoreligious position seriously is more than a condemnation of ethnocentricity in philosophy of culture. It is also more than the claim that we must understand the full range of explanatory schemes and devices if we're to do an adequate philosophical anthropology. Eliade's work is, fundamentally, an indictment of the modern spirit of inquiry and explanation. In his view, the modern existential position is founded on the desacralization of the world and human activity in the world. The modern stance is a valorization of the profane. For Eliade, the sacred is prior to the profane—historically, logically, and ontologically. Thus, the modern, profane mode of human being can only be asserted in the denial of the sacred. The modern position can only exist by aggressively refusing to grant value and validity to the mythical.

Eliade's analysis of the mythical world is at the same time an examination of a "post"-mythical world. His recognition of the positive value of myth can be read simply as a device for overcoming the prejudices endemic in the modern period. But, at heart, Eliade is urging a return to, or at least a reintegration of, the mythicoreligious life, which would provide a greater degree of freedom than the freedom available in profane life. Real freedom, for Eliade, is the freedom to participate in the continual creation of the cosmos and of everything in the cosmos. This is possible only through myth, only through returning to the origin of creation in mythical narrative and ritual. The freedom afforded the modern, or "historical" person is merely the freedom to "make himself."[5] Eliade's conception of the freedom inherent in the mythical is in direct opposition to Cassirer's claim that the mythical symbolic form offers the least (if any) freedom of any of the symbolic forms.[6] We will return to the issue of the relation of myth and freedom.

Eliade claims there are sites or moments of "hierophany," places or times where or when the sacred manifests itself, breaking through the plane of the everyday. The sacred shows itself as wholly other in the context of the mundane; and the mundane can gain meaning only through being in relation to, or coming in contact with, the sacred. In manifesting itself, the sacred exhibits its power to create, and its power to transform, the world. Eliade finds the clearest and most consistent expression of the experience of the sacred in archaic or primitive cultures, though religious experience is certainly not confined to these. He contrasts the mythicoreligious or premodern culture with cultures founded on a profane ontology. Profane ontology is organized around a linear sequence of non-reversible mundane events. In a profane world, we understand human life (personally and *in toto*) as progressing toward a fulfill-

ment or completion along this future-oriented sequence of mundane events. We can also call this a historicized ontology. This way
of understanding the world seems to allow the hierophany, or the
sacred manifesting itself, only as private, individual religious
epiphany—another subjective experience to be absorbed in the ongoing historical progression of human accomplishment.

Archaic cultures are organized centripetally around moments
and places of hierophany. The manifestation of the sacred is the
point of origination around which the world acquires temporal, spatial, and meaningful structure. The mythical world and its inhabitants are determined by a sacred rather than a profane ontology.
Where the sacred appears, where the cosmos is born as an ordered
world, formed and meaningful, out of nonbeing, chaos, formlessness, and meaninglessness, is that toward which all human endeavor
is drawn in a "thirst for the real."[7] The mundane or the profane in
the ontology of the sacred is that which has not yet been aligned
with the center of the world, the hierophany. That which is profane
remains meaningless because it has not yet been brought under the
rubric of an ordered relation to the site of the origin of meaning.
That which is unformed, chaotic, and uninhabitable is so because it
is far from the center of efficacious, formative power; that is, it is
profane rather than sacred. Insofar as human activity is geared
toward the site or moment of hierophany, it participates in the
sacred and has obviated the meaninglessness of the profane. Returning to the originary moment via ritual enactment of the creation of
agriculture, for example, or locating and designing a ceremonial
house to mark and repeat the center of the cosmos, transforms the
mundane or profane into the meaningful and the sacred.

According to Eliade, it is the insistent drive to participate in
meaning and being that structures the life of the archaic person and
archaic culture. It is in this sense that we can speak of a mythical
world. Myths are accounts of, and ways of returning to, the origin of
Being. Insofar as human activity is directed toward this lodestar and
insofar as the cosmos has its center at the irruption of Being into
nonbeing, it is a mythical or sacred world. Human activity in a world
centered on the hierophany exhibits an "ontological obsession." Eliade argues against explanations of myth that derogate ritual return to
the originary moment, or building practices that depend on the site
of the hierophany, or other "alien" behaviors. Such derogatory views
of the mythical world ascribe to it a "paralysis" of primitive people
in the face of change. These interpretations of archaic patterns of
behavior see the mythical world as essentially conservative and

backward in refusing "to assume full responsibility for a genuine historical existence."[8] Rather, Eliade claims, the ontological obsession displayed in mythical life is the desire to participate in the emergence of Being. At the very least, it is the impulse to remain as close as possible to the source of Being and meaning.

MYTHICAL SPACE

Though there is an essential difference in the value that Cassirer and Eliade accord the mythical, they describe the formal characteristics of mythical space and mythical time (the objective features of the mythical world) in similar ways. Mythical space is neither homogeneous nor is it a contentless continuum. (As we will see, this is also true for mythical time.) Cassirer describes the "homogeneity which prevails in the conceptual space of geometry" as allowing for a distinction between "*position* and *content*." He contrasts this with the heterogeneity of mythical space, which "'is' only insofar as it is filled with definite, individual sensuous or intuitive content."[9] For Eliade as well, mythical space is discontinuous and heterogeneous. He writes, that for

> religious man, space is not homogeneous; he experiences interruptions, breaks in it; some parts of space are qualitatively different from others. . . . For religious man, this spatial non-homogeneity finds expression in the experience of an opposition between space that is sacred—the only *real* and *really* existing space—and all other space, the formless expanse surrounding it.[10]

According to Cassirer, mythical space proceeds outward from a center constituted through proximate, experienceable activity. This doesn't mean that there must be some sort of conscious apprehension or will, but rather that the structure of space radiates outward from the locus of active manipulation in the world. Space delimited through bodily experience and kinesthetic orientation is more like space in perceptual orientation than in, for example, space as geometrically structured. Perceptual space has a nexus of reality at the center of sensible experience, which appears to coalesce near the center of the body, with an ever decreasing degree of sensible reality at the far reaches of this nexus. Likewise, mythical space is organized around the concrete experience of the body. "Here and there," "above and below," "near and far," cannot be understood in myth as abstract relations, but are always apprehended in terms of particular bodily positions.

According to Cassirer, in the less primitively structured mythical world, the organization of space does not proceed directly from felt biological or kinesthetic states. But it is still organized around the body as a locus of reference for all other spatial distinctions. He writes, "wherever [myth] finds an organically articulated whole which it strives to understand by its method of thought, it tends to see the whole in the image and organization of the human body."[11] The most sophisticated spatial scheme in the mythical world is astrological space; in this as well, space is organized around the body. But in astrological space, the center of efficacy or action is manifested in many bodies rather than one, and the "body" is now celestial rather than personal. Astrological space accomplishes what we might call a Copernican Revolution in its move from a single, absolute center of space determined through bodily activity to multiple loci of structure. Astrological systems are quite well-developed mythical systems, and have begun to show the stresses that eventually destroy the bonds of mythical thought from within. The shift from singular to multiple structuring loci may indicate a movement out of mythical space; but insofar as it is the efficacy and substantial power of the heavenly *bodies* that determine the form of space, the scheme remains mythical.

Eliade's understanding of the structure of mythical space also includes the organization of the world around a center of efficacy and action. The world or cosmos radiates outward from the mythically apprehended center of the world, and the center is the point of orientation for much of human activity. The human world is spatially articulated according to the appropriate location for habitation or crop planting, the configuration of dwellings, the selection of a site for ceremonial buildings, and so on. Each of these has a proper place determined by relation to the center of the world. Furthermore, it is proximity to the center that determines what belongs to the cosmos; that is, what constitutes ordered reality. It is distance from the center that indicates chaos; that is, the uninhabitable, formless realm of nonbeing.

This center is not the human body and its activities and capabilities, as in Cassirer's description. Rather, Eliade writes, "where the sacred manifests itself in space, *the real unveils itself*, the world comes into existence."[12] The hierophany, as a breakthrough of the sacred into the profane, can always be marked by its location in space. The particular space then becomes sacred, becomes a gate or a threshold between the sacred and the profane. The places or objects at the site of the hierophany are sacralized, and, as such, are paradoxical in the strongest sense of the term. Eliade comments, "By manifesting the sacred, any object becomes *something else*, yet it continues to remain *itself* for it continues to participate in its surrounding cosmic milieu[; a] *sacred* stone remains a *stone*."[13] The sacred is an irruption in formlessness and meaninglessness. Being ingresses at the rupture and serves as the constituting center around which the world organizes centripetally. Space in the mythical world is certainly neither homogeneous nor continuous. Space is permeable and liable to being pushed apart or rent by the power of the sacred manifesting itself. But, in another sense, space cannot be rent, for there can be no space, indeed no cosmos, until there is a point of reference around which the world is organized spatially.

In the mythical cosmos, according to Eliade, the site of the irruption of the sacred is the site of the origin of the world. The force of creative power manifests itself at this point and flows outward. The efficacy of the sacred is concentrated at this center, and becomes dilute, so to speak, as it spreads toward a periphery. The archaic, mythically determined world is organized around its center, the place where the sacred has appeared. All spatial articulation has its locus at the site of the eclipse of the formless by the formative power of the holy.

MYTHICAL TIME

Of course, space is only one aspect of the objective world of myth. In fact, it appears that temporality is the predominant "architecture" of the mythical cosmos. This is especially true for Cassirer's understanding of the mythical. He writes,

> The mythical world achieves its true and specific articulation only when its dimension of depth, so to speak, opens up with the form of time. The true character of mythical being is first revealed when it appears as the being of origins. . . . It does not adhere immediately to the content of the given but to its coming into being, not to its qualities and properties but to its genesis in the past.[14]

Tracing origins back to a primordial, ontologically distinct realm results in a cutting-up of the world into particular temporal zones, each of which has its own "essence and efficacy," its own "intensive content."[15] Each of these sectors possesses its own time, which determines the rhythmic pulse, the ebb and flow, of all the transformations belonging to the zone. Eliade writes of the same sort of temporal organization and anchoring of the profane in the sacred. He writes that, "[b]efore a particular vegetable species was created [in sacred time], the time that now causes it to grow, bear fruit, did not exist."[16]

Time in the mythically structured world is never the non-reversible sequence of contentless, even-flowing instants we find in the scientific-theoretical mode of consciousness (according to Cassirer), or in historicized ontology (according to Eliade). Both thinkers understand time in the mythical world, as well as space, as radically heterogeneous. Eliade comments,

> For religious man time . . . is neither homogeneous nor continuous. On the one hand there are intervals of a sacred time, . . . on the other there is profane time, ordinary temporal duration, in which acts without religious meaning have their setting.[17]

Cassirer describes mythical time negatively, as lacking the principle of a generalized relational continuum of past-present-future under which particular events can be subsumed and ordered. Mythical time is never this strictly functional ordering principle. The distinct temporal zones in the mythical, each with its own content, "can be similar or dissimilar, corresponding or contrasting, friendly or hostile to one another."[18] This is the heterogeneity and discontinuity of time in the mythical world, according to Cassirer.

For Eliade, the hierophany is not only the center that structures mythical spatiality, it also determines mythical temporality. In the mythically constituted temporal features of the objective, we again have an organization that radiates outward from a core of efficacy—creation of the cosmos as ordered being—to a periphery that is the dissolution of this original power. Cyclical is perhaps not the best term to use in describing mythical temporality, though it is the term used most often by Eliade. In his description, mythical time seems more analogous to force fields. The integrity of anything in the system disintegrates as it moves away from its origin at/in the most concentrated moment of creative power. Then everything travels back to the center where it is not only renewed and rejuvenated, but recreated. So, for instance, the "new" year is never a commemoration of a year that is finished and a designation of a year that has yet to be. The celebration is a return to the origin of being and time after the cosmos has reached its nadir of decay, dissolution, and disorder. The sense in which the year is cyclical is that the temporal order has returned to its moment of inception and *re*born, and is thus the "same" year. But in a more fundamental sense, the year is not cyclical, because it is an absolutely new temporal progression each 'time' it originates in the moment of the creation of the cosmos. Mythical time does not, strictly speaking, repeat itself. In returning to the moment of creation, it returns to the absolute beginning of all being and all time. That which has not yet been cannot be repeated.

We can easily see the return to the moment of the hierophany in rituals and stories of the birth and death of particular temporal processes, such as the day, the year, or the fruition of crops. Eliade describes a number of other sorts of dissolution and decay that demand a return to the origin of being and time. He explains that the reenactment or recounting of the origin of medicinal plants, for example, is the deliberate return to the zenith of power and efficacy at the creation of the plant from the nadir of a diseased and enervated condition.[19] Or, we might imagine, returning to the moment of the creation of rain, which belongs to the moment of the creation of the cosmos and time, is the appropriate measure to take when rain has lost its power and being. The dissolution of the proper order of the world is seen in the desiccation of drought, a condition of nonbeing, meaningless, and chaos. Only a return to the power of the origin of the world will restore the world to its most fruitful condition.

In Cassirer's explication of the constitution of mythical time, we see the same formal characteristics as we see in Eliade's description, especially in the nonlinear, nonsequential, noncontentless structure of time. Cassirer understands mythical time as proceeding outward from a center of power, but the same difference that appeared in their discussions of mythical space appears in their discussions of mythical time. Where Eliade posits the manifestation of the sacred in the hierophantic moment as the center of mythical temporal organization, Cassirer locates the center in the body and its biological rhythms. He claims that mythical consciousness shows the "subtlest sensitivity" to felt biological and sensible rhythms and periodicities, especially to the differences between light and dark, day and night, and, presumably, waking and sleeping. These determine the first and most primitive temporal apprehension. This sense of time is like a kind of musicality, the varying tempos of felt organic existence defining particular configurations of "temporal gestalt."[20] Each of these configurations has its own intensive content, just as space is organized into particular zones of efficacy.

Certain transitions breaking the rhythm of the mundane course of life are accorded special significance, like a kind of musical coda. Rituals performed at births, deaths, comings-into-adulthood are means of intensifying the experience of the rhythm inherent in life. As we saw in chapter 2, Cassirer believes that myth does not distinguish between the animate and the inanimate, that it apprehends the world in its entirety as alive. This occurs because felt biological rhythms expand outward to encompass the cosmos as a whole; there is no differentiation between a personal, living self and an inanimate world. Cassirer writes that for mythical consciousness there is "a kind of biological time, a rhythmic ebb and flow of life, [which] precedes the intuition of a properly cosmic time." Myth determines the temporal manifestations of the world through "projecting" all change, all cycles it comes upon or experiences "into human existence, where it perceives them as in a mirror." This translation and transposition of all natural and cosmic phenomena into the "subjective form of life" organizes the temporal features of the world into a unity patterned on the body and its rhythmical changes of state.[21]

THE ORIGIN OF THE MYTHICAL WORLD

At this point we can examine more closely the formal similarities in Eliade's and Cassirer's descriptions of mythical temporality and spatiality. The authors agree that mythical space and time are not continuous, contentless, homogeneous ordering principles that allow for position of objects or events relative to each other according to some overarching, unchanging formal principle. Mythical space is never ordered or apprehended in the manner of Cartesian geometrics, for example, in which any point maintains its position relative to the field and relative to any other point within the field, regardless of which point on the grid is taken as the "origin." If we continue this analogy, and if Cassirer and Eliade are correct in their descriptions, mythical space is constituted and experienced as a kind of elastic spherical space in which locations are determined relative only to a constant center, never relative to each other. Space is divided in terms of what is closer to and what is further from this center. The spatial features of the world tend to converge at the center and to disperse at the periphery.

Events in mythical time are never ordered relative to each other in terms of an absolutely unidirectional flow of uniform constant instants. Time as well, if we can imagine it, is organized spherically around a center. Whatever is temporally "closest" to the center is most real; that is, is most efficacious and least subject to the vicissitudes of change and decay. Whatever is temporally "farthest" from the center is least real; that is, is least powerful and most subject to dissolution and destruction. Time in the mythical cosmos is periodic and rhythmic, apprehended as ebb and flow, an insistent pulse of the world of change and becoming. Nothing is determined as past or future in relation to a constantly moving present, in linear temporal progression. Events in mythical time can only be measured relative to a persistent center, never relative to other events.

For both Cassirer and Eliade, the center of mythical time is the same as the center of mythical space. Cassirer concludes that both mythical time and mythical space are founded in the most primitive biological and sensible experience. Eliade refers to the unity of mythical time and space in a different way. The center of the mythical world is the hierophany, the manifestation of the sacred. This is the origin of being and time and space. Though the center of the mythical world is different in the authors' descriptions, each draws a picture of a kind of unified spatiotemporality.[22]

It is essential to notice that although several of the formal characteristics of mythical spatiotemporality are remarkably similar in these descriptions, there is a fundamental asymmetry. For Eliade, the hierophany is both the determinant of the sacred sphere and the axis around which the mythical cosmos is organized spatially, temporally, and meaningfully. For Cassirer, the center of spatial and temporal organization is the determinant of the *profane* sphere, not the sacred sphere. In his account, the primary ontological division of the mythical world into the sacred and the profane depends on biological existence, concrete physical activity in the world, and the kinesthetic states and orientations of the body. There is a zone or nimbus of efficacy in human physical existence. That which is beyond the scope of human manipulative activity is outside the everyday commerce of human being and the world and thus properly belongs to the sacred. Cassirer writes that the "limits which the mythical consciousness posits and through which it arrives at its . . . articulations . . . are fixed on man's self-limitation in his immediate reality." Myth delineates "two *provinces* of being: a common, generally accessible province and another, sacred precinct which seems raised out of its surroundings."

Cassirer and Eliade agree that the mythical world is founded on a fundamental ontological distinction between the sacred and the profane. For Eliade, the sacred is the center of the cosmos and the profane gains meaning and being through the sacred. For Cassirer, the profane is the center of the cosmos and the sacred sphere is generated out of it. We can see the fundamental difference in perspective by examining how Cassirer and Eliade each use Rudolph Otto's ideas. Cassirer claims that Otto's work in *Das Heilege* (*The Idea of the Holy*)[23] expresses the essentially dual nature of the experience of the sacred. Cassirer hypothesizes that mythical consciousness, in apprehending and construing the sphere of the sacred, at the same time endows this sphere with the character of the "taboo."

> The consequence of the twofold character is that in differentiating itself from empirical, profane substance, the sacred does not simply *repel* it but progressively *permeates* it; in its opposition it still retains the ability to give form to its opposite.[24]

For Cassirer, the true power of mythical consciousness lies in its making progressively greater distinctions between the sacred and the profane, while sharpening the features of each through the lens of mythical symbolic activity. This eventuates in the crisis in which mythical consciousness apprehends its symbolically formulated world as its own creation, not as the expression of a "wholly other" force. Spirit and Nature are recognized as ontologically distinct, and consciousness identifies itself with the spiritual and disentangles itself from the material. But this crisis in mythical thought signals the demise of the mythical world.

Eliade congratulates Otto for describing the felt experience of the "living God" and the appearance of the "numinous" rather than "studying the *ideas* of God and religion" in analyzing the holy. Feelings of terror, fear, and fascination in coming upon the "wholly other," in its majesty and inexplicable power, are core features of all religious experience. The history of religion can be read as a chronicle of the revelation of the holy other. Eliade hopes to extend and deepen the insights gained by Otto, while avoiding Otto's claim of an essential opposition between the rational and the irrational in religious experience.[25] For Eliade, the moment of the manifestation of the sacred, the hierophany, is a fundamental moment in human life and ought not be discounted or explained in terms of anything but the recognition of Being.

Eliade begins with the disclosure of the sacred as an irreducible facet of human life, irreducible to psychological pathology, or perceptual misconstruals, or ignorance of the laws of the natural world. In all of these, he and Cassirer would agree. But Cassirer understands that the duality of the sacred and the profane, though specific to the mythical form, is the kind of distinction necessary for consciousness in any of its symbolic forms. The difference between mythical form and other forms is that myth cannot make its primary distinction, that between the sacred and the profane, co-valent with the *real* ontological division between the spiritual and the material. Eliade, on the other hand, finds the religious distinction between the sacred and the profane as a *direct* apprehension of a real ontological distinction. Eliade takes the sacred manifesting itself as the primary fact of the world and human experience. He offers us a broad phenomenological account of life in the mythicoreligiously structured world.

If Cassirer were to abide by his own admonition to examine a symbolic form as much as possible from "within" the form, his description of the constitution of the mythical world might well look more like Eliade's. For example, Cassirer tries to avoid claiming that the expressive features of the world are merely projections of the self not yet understood by the self as belonging to the self. The self, properly speaking, does not exist in mythical organization, according to Cassirer's analysis. He claims instead that the expressive features of the world are merely projections or objectifications of physiologically determined emotional states; that is, that myth identifies features of biological existence as the sacred. For Cassirer, this is proof of the inability of mythical consciousness to escape its immersion in nature, proof that myth must be conquered if consciousness is to find full freedom. Eliade avoids such a convoluted explanation. The sacred appears in human experience, but need not, should not, be accounted for in terms of *human* activity or experience.

THE SUBJECTIVE IN THE MYTHICAL WORLD

The central theme of the present chapter is, of course, the constitution of the objective features of the mythical world, at least as understood by Eliade and Cassirer. But a brief discussion of the constitution of the subjective, or the self, should make clearer the distinction being drawn between these two authors.

Though Eliade does not give an elaborate description of the constitution of the self in a sacred or mythically ordered cosmos, his more general description leads us to assume that a self would exist as meaningful and formed only insofar as it participates in the hierophantic moment. As all reality in the mythical cosmos is determined by proximity to the locus of formative, creative power, the reality of human existence must be so determined. Nowhere in his description of the mythical does Eliade allude to the individual human being, as body or consciousness or emotionality, as at the center of the cosmos. Human experience does not serve as the node around which the sacred cosmos is ordered spatially, temporally, meaningfully, or ontologically. The mythical constitution of the self is accomplished in the re-creation of certain archetypal or paradigmatic models of that which belongs to the sacred moment of creation.

The more that the profane, that is, the accidental, the meaningless, the nonexemplary, is shorn from human life, the more reality and meaning can accrue. In the repetition of the cosmogonic gestures of the origin of human being, the truly human emerges in pure and fully fashioned perfection. To return to the origin (via ritual and myth) is to abolish all but the originating and original form.[26] The *truly* human is individual only in the sense that there can be but one, the consecrated form of human being at the moment of creation. (Or, one supposes, at most two—the consecrated male and the consecrated female.) Eliade writes,

> This tendency may well appear paradoxical, in the sense that the man of a traditional culture sees himself as real only to the extent that he ceases to be himself (for a modern observer) and is satisfied with imitating and repeating the gestures of another[, the original human being]. In other words, he sees himself as real; i.e., as "truly himself," only and precisely, insofar as he ceases to be so.[27]

It is no coincidence that this description sounds vaguely Platonic. Eliade concurs with Cassirer's evaluation that Plato stands at the cusp of the mythically and nonmythically structured worlds. But there is a difference in how these authors view Plato. Cassirer understands Plato as transforming the notion of the *archē* from (mythical) origin to *archē* as universal ordering principle.[28] Eliade understands Plato as embracing the mythical insofar as the archetypes or Forms are taken as that which bestows meaning and Being, as that which determines whatever degree of reality there is in the realm of becoming. But Plato also rejects the mythical attempt to return to the moment of the creation of the original Forms and abolish profane time. Thus, for Eliade, Plato stands at the turn from sacred to historicized ontology. Cassirer would say that Plato stands at the crisis of mythical consciousness as it begins to give way to theoretical or scientific consciousness. But where Cassirer marks this as a point of great progress for culture, Eliade sees the downfall of sacred human existence.

THE FUNDAMENTAL ASYMMETRY

Cassirer attributes a sort of temporal and implicatory "flatness" to the mythical world, as we saw in chapter 2. This flatness is the result of the inability of mythical consciousness to construe idealities independent of immediate impression. Mythical consciousness lacks typicalities against which to measure the ongoing flux of experience; it has no representative function, and representation is essential for the constitution of the typicalities necessary for arresting the flow of experience. This means that there is no triangulation of what is present against what is nonpresent, and consequently, the mythical word lacks perceptual and conceptual depth.

In Cassirer's picture of the mythical world, mythical consciousness cannot constitute the relatively enduring in opposition to the relatively fleeting; therefore mythical experience has no thickness, there are no tendrils of meaning, significance, overlapping relations that give weight and density to sheer experience.[29] Such experience, if we could even call it experience, of the ever-changing world of absolutely fleeting impressions, cannot be woven into a thick tapestry of implication, relation, and possibility. These are patterns that can be achieved only through a sort of standing back or pushing away from the ongoing flux of untrammeled interaction of organism and environment and a filling in of the resultant opening with vectors of relationality and contrast.

If Eliade's description of the mythical world is accurate, then it would have this peculiar flatness *only* if it is viewed from the perspective of consciousness grounded in an individuated human agent. Cassirer understands the mythical cosmos, or rather, he attempts to reconstruct the features of the mythical world, through the lens of an incipient subject aligned with not-yet-self-reflective consciousness. It appears that Cassirer insists on describing the mythical world from the point of view of a unity he himself claims does not yet exist in the mythical cosmos. The self as personal and individuated principle of psychic or spiritual organization has not yet been determined or delineated, it is an *end* product of mythical symbolic formation. The physiological and biological states of an individual human organism might constitute a principle of internal organization for the human self, but Cassirer claims that these states deter-

mine a continuity with, rather than a division from, organic, material nature. In Cassirer's description of the mythical world, the rudiments of a self are immersed in the objective sphere of existence.
They remain within material existence and have not yet coalesced
with the spiritual. When Cassirer discovers the flatness of the mythical world, his discovery is based on positioning his surveying tools
within a unity that does not, according to his own account, belong to
mythical symbolic formation. The mythical world appears to have
no depth only when viewed from the point of view of a self constituted nonmythically.

Eliade's description of the mythical does not involve this flatness, there seems no possibility of viewing the mythical cosmos
from a personal locus or perspective. The mythical world does not
proceed outward from the human organism, it is generated around
the manifestation of the sacred. If this is the case, then looking at the
mythical world from the point of view of a human self would
account for the distortions that Cassirer attributes to the mythical
world itself. (We can use a perceptual analogy here. From the point of
view of the human observer, taken as the center of perceptual space,
the stars appear to be arrayed on a single, curved plane; there is
apparently no "depth" in the night sky. But the appearance of flatness disappears when we imagine the celestial bodies as radiating
outward from an altogether different center—the origin of the cosmos in the "Big Bang.") Eliade posits the hierophany as the means of
triangulation for the mythical cosmos. The depth of the mythical
world is determined by the lodestar of the appearance of the sacred,
not by consciousness accumulating typicalities in empirical perception, scientific-theoretical thought, and so on, as Cassirer describes.

Where Cassirer postulates an originary folding back of Life
upon itself, an interruption in the absolutely equivalent exchange of
organic existence in its environment (which results in the possibility
of Spirit constituting its own sphere of meaningfulness),[30] Eliade
describes the opening up of the world in the hierophany. This break
in the profane sphere is not a product of consciousness. The sacred
appears. And the appearance of the sacred fulfills all the require-
ments of ideality that Cassirer finds missing in the mythical, except
for Cassirer's faith that any ideality is the product of an act of consciousness. The appearance of the sacred also fulfills all the functions
that Cassirer ascribes to Spirit; but Cassirer's understanding of Spirit,
so closely aligned to the individuated human agent, cannot be taken
as equivalent to Eliade's notion of the sacred. This is the fundamental asymmetry in the two accounts. For Eliade, the appearance of

the sacred is not a product of consciousness, no matter how broadly we conceive of consciousness.

Cassirer does an injustice to the supposed integrity of the mythical world by recasting it in light of a particular sort of human experience, one that culminates in the achievements of theoretical activity. If Cassirer is correct in claiming the independence of development of the mythical and the scientific symbolic forms, then his claims about the flatness of the mythical must be denied. Cassirer does not seem to recognize the possibility that what appears as the flatness of mythical apprehension of the world is a flatness only to those for whom the relative thickness of experience is determined by the positing of internal, subjective states identified as the location of consciousness (as meaning constituting agency), a location around which change in an outer sphere is gauged.

According to Eliade's description of religious experience, we can say that Cassirer does not adequately recognize that what appears as an attenuated, out-of-focus field of experience and apprehension, marked by its flatness, is so only to our own nonreligiously or nonmythically determined sensibilities. Our sensibilities have been shaped by a particular understanding of the temporal as a nonrepeatable, historical progression of events. The flatness of the mythical world, as it is observed through the lenses of either theoretical or historically aligned modes of accomplishment, is a flatness not observable through the lens of myth itself.

Eliade's description of the mythical, taking seriously the appearance of the sacred as an irreducible fact of the mythical world, shows a world not characterized by its flatness, either temporal or implicatory, but a world in which depth is determined by means of triangulation according to the hierophany. The hierophany anchors the mythical world in time and space, performing the functions that Cassirer assigns to idealities or typicalities constituted by, and held in, consciousness.

MYTH AND FREEDOM

Eliade might well claim that Cassirer's account of the mythical is an account grounded in evaluations proper only to a profane or historicized ontology, not a description faithful to the forms of a mythical or sacred ontology. Cassirer has chosen the "risks" inherent in the project of gaining freedom in and through the profane arena. He does not seem to recognize an alternative freedom, the freedom possible, according to Eliade, in and through the sacred. Cassirer's description of the quest of consciousness for the unfettered freedom of self-creation or self-constitution fits precisely Eliade's description of the condition of "modern man." Eliade describes someone in this existential position as one who "can be creative only insofar as he is historical; in other words, all creation is forbidden him except that which has its source in his own freedom; and, consequently, everything is denied him except the freedom to make history by making himself."[31] History is the playing-out of time, from the moment of its inception. History belongs to the profane sphere. Only insofar as history can be obliterated through the "eternal return" of the cosmogonic moment, does it belongs to the sphere of the sacred.

History may also be absorbed into an eschatological, "metahistorical" scheme of divinely or cosmically ordered destiny. As history is either resorbed in the cosmogonic moment or absorbed in a metahistorical destiny, the "terror of history" can be held at bay, according to Eliade.[32] The terror of history is the terror in the face of meaningless, random suffering. The terror of history is the terror in the face of unredeemable, unsalvageable evil. The terror of history is the terror in the face of history understood as nothing other than itself, an arbitrary concatenation of events, having no meaning, merely unfurling in irrecuperable time. The terror of history is the terror in the face of a present and a future irrevocably determined by events and persons now beyond all culpability. Without recourse to a repetition of the cosmogonic moment there can be no erasure of the meaninglessness and violence of profane historical existence. There can be no recourse to an absolutely new beginning of being and meaning. There can be no return to the origin in which human actors participate in full creative power.

Eliade holds out only one other alternative for human existence. If the archaic, sacred world must be abandoned, and if the terror of history is to be averted and not merely ignored, then we must turn to faith and the acceptance of a "philosophy of freedom that does not exclude God." Eliade likens this alternative existential position to that recorded in Mark 11:22–24. Here Christian faith implies that, as for God everything is possible, so "everything is possible for man." Such faith guarantees the hope of an "absolute emancipation from any kind of natural 'law' and hence the highest freedom that man can imagine." This highest form of freedom is the freedom to "intervene even in the ontological constitution of the universe[;] a pre-eminently creative freedom."[33]

Cassirer exhibits this faith, I believe, though not a faith in God as Supreme Being. Cassirer has faith in the movement of Spirit toward its ultimate emancipation from the constraints of nature and substantiality. He understands the history of culture as the history of Spirit or consciousness as it imprints itself on the surface of Nature and then progressively frees itself from the foibles and fancies reflected there. Thus, the terror of history can be erased, can be subjugated to the not yet perfect or not yet free, but finally perfect and free domain of Spirit. In symbolic formation we find a "pre-eminent creative freedom." Cassirer writes that "man can do no more than to build up his own universe—a symbolic universe that enables him to understand and interpret, to articulate and organize, to synthesize and universalize his human experience."[34] The forms of culture exhibit a dynamic equilibrium of opposing forces (especially those of "subjectivity and objectivity, individuality and universality"). This delicate balance is brought about through the functional, not substantial, unity of human activity. This "organic" process "may be described as the process of man's progressive self-liberation." In the process and progress, "man discovers and proves a new power—the power to build up a world of his own, an 'ideal' world."[35]

For Cassirer, mythical consciousness is denied this route to freedom. Myth cannot construe an ideal world. But myth does articulate a line of demarcation between the sacred and the profane, and in so doing, paves the way for the heroic trek of consciousness in its quest for freedom. Cassirer chooses the faith of the modern, historicized ontology. But he denies a possibility offered by Eliade. Sacred, *mythical*, ontology allows a return to the site or the moment of origin or *archē* and allows participation in the creation of the cosmos. This is a real creative freedom, one denied by Cassirer. He demands we live the historical or profane ontology and accept the challenges and risks of creating and carrying forward the ideal principle or *archē* into uncharted and unsanctified territory.

THE SHIFTING ONTOLOGICAL PREMISES

The accounts of mythical spatiotemporality offered by Cassirer and Eliade show remarkable symmetry and many similarities. In an important sense, however, Eliade's description is the broader. We can place Cassirer's analysis within the framework of Eliade's, as an expression of the most favorable sort of outcome for historicized or profane ontology. Eliade's work also fulfills the promise implicit and explicit in Cassirer's work. This promise is of giving full and due respect to mythical symbolic formation. Cassirer subtly derogates the mythical, as incapable of apprehending itself as fully symbolic in determining the objective and subjective features of existence.

With a slight shift in ontological premises, Eliade is able to finish the task that Cassirer set for himself. Eliade locates the primary ontological distinction in the mythical world in the absolute difference of the sacred and the profane. All other distinctions flow from this originary division. The division itself is not the product of an act of consciousness. To posit the distinction between the profane and the sacred as the result of an activity of consciousness is to proclaim a second ontological division, that between consciousness and whatever does not belong to consciousness, and to predicate constitutive power to consciousness. Cassirer, of course, postulates this second ontological division and accords primacy to the acts of consciousness in determining the distinction between the sacred and the profane and in delineating the subjective and objective features of existence. If this is the case, then the experience of the primacy of the sacred as the constitutive power of the cosmos is mistaken. This is what leads Cassirer to maintain that mythical formation merely refashions the original material ties of Spirit to Nature into bonds that have only the appearance of true spiritual articulation.

Eliade's shift of the ontological premise allows for the mythical world to be understood as a completely legitimate, completely coherent organization of the objective and subjective features of existence. And perhaps *only* in this way—taking the sacred manifesting itself as a fundamental metaphysical fact of the mythical world, a fact that cannot be explained away or accounted for in any other terms—can myth be given a fair and adequate description. Cassirer cannot take this route, however, though it would fulfill his intention of analyzing myth as a legitimate symbolic form. Such a shift in ontological premise, from consciousness as the progenitor of spiritual form to the sacred as its own progenitor and progenitor of space, time, and the subject, would radically undercut Cassirer's work across the spectrum of cultural forms. His critical philosophy of culture depends on the unity of all cultural forms. His analysis cannot withstand a real ontological division that appears in only one of the forms. For Cassirer, the ultimate ontological distinction is between Spirit and Nature. Every symbolic form is evidence of consciousness articulating the world in such a way as to align itself with Spirit; every symbolic form except myth, that is. Myth delineates the spiritual, sacred aspects of the world, it is true. But myth finds Spirit in an extension of physical, natural existence. Thus myth impedes consciousness in its movement toward the absolute creative power to determine both the subjective and objective spheres of existence.

The difference between myth and the other symbolic forms, for Cassirer, is not that myth reveals a novel ontological configuration, but that mythical consciousness is never free but always bound to the biological, the physiological, the natural.

☙❦❧

In chapter 6 we will reconsider the notion of a *telos* of unmitigated creative freedom and analyze more fully the axiological commitments of these authors. But first we must examine, in closer detail, the constitution of the subjective features of the world as determined through myth.

5

Mythical Self, Mythical Soul

James Hillman's Depth Psychology

It is fitting to examine James Hillman's work *The Myth of Analysis*,[1] last in these analyses of theories about myth and myth-making. His work is not only rich and provocative in its own right, but it draws together and confronts many of the concerns already addressed here. Unlike Cassirer and Barthes, and like Eliade, Hillman judges myth as deserving of honor and respect. Accordingly, Hillman, with Eliade, sees myth as the gateway or threshold to true freedom, while Cassirer and Barthes conclude that myth is the greatest cultural impediment to human freedom.

Hillman admits that mythical speech can, and has, become mired in peculiarly conservative reifications (of similar function if not similar form), as described by Barthes. But Hillman allows for the possibility of mythical language transforming imaginative activity and propelling revolutionary change.[2] For Hillman, as opposed to Barthes, myth may be a *positive* power in the emancipation of human being from the forces that constrain it. Furthermore, we saw in Barthes' work a belief that scientific-theoretical discourse itself contributes to the covering-up of the historical conditions of the constitution of the self and the world. Barthes believes that radical semio-critical analysis must be applied to scientific semiological systems if we are to avoid a kind of tyranny fostered by hidden mythical tendencies of theoretical discourse. Hillman goes further than this in claiming that *all* scientific work is mythically determined. In particular, he castigates psychoanalytic and medical discourse as exemplifying pitfalls of "Apollonic" archetypal constructions. Whatever their own emphases on the relation of myth and scientific discourse, Hillman's and Barthes' work are each, in part, a criticism of the methodological position we find exemplified in Cassirer's critical philosophy of culture. In Hillman's work, especially, we'll see this appear as an indictment of any position that posits an absolute unity and hegemony of consciousness; in fact, we can understand this as an indictment of the basic ontological commitment held by Cassirer.

Hillman assumes a fundamentally dialectical structure in the relation of self and world, an assumption shared by Cassirer and Barthes. That is, these three authors understand self and world, subjective and objective, to be constituted in an obverse relation. Furthermore, each sees this constitutive relation as progressive, a moving forward in history to a state of greater perfection. The assumption shared by Cassirer, Barthes, and Hillman has different outcomes in each of the theories, however. The dialectical process eventuates in soul making itself, for Hillman; writing-itself, for Barthes; and consciousness construing itself, for Cassirer. As corollary propositions, Barthes and Hillman share the conviction that both consciousness and the boundaries of the ego are by-products of the dialectical process. Cassirer would agree that the boundaries of the ego are so constituted, but would deny that consciousness is a residue of the process rather than the driving force of the dialectical process.

Eliade, on the other hand, rejects the assumption of a dialectical relation between self and world, as this would be a denial of sacred ontology and an acceptance of profane, historicized ontology. As we've seen, he believes that the condition of perfect freedom for human being demands a return to the moment of the origin of the cosmos, or the hierophany. The notion of historical progress, no matter how the progress is construed, is antithetical to Eliade's basic contentions regarding the primacy of the sacred. But he does suggest, near the close of *The Myth of the Eternal Return*, that there is hope for "historical" human being achieving a correlative freedom to that achieved by mythically or religiously determined human being.[3] For this hope to be fulfilled, profane, historicized life must carry the sacred through the ravages and terrors of history, transforming the *archē* as temporal and spatial origin into the *archē* as a continuous principle of organization that transcends the natural lawful structure of the profane. Hillman alludes to something very much like this in his discussion of the archetypes as transcendental (in the sense of transpersonal and *a priori*) forms that are not themselves subject to the vicissitudes of history, biology, and so on. The archetypes stand in an imaginal realm; they provide a continuous fund of ideational constellations to which the soul appeals for order, for confirmation that the terrors of history or suffering are not blind, arbitrary, and meaningless. Regardless of where each locates the power of myth, in the movement of history, or in a nonhistorical absolute origin, Hillman and Eliade certainly agree that myth must be embraced if we are to fulfill the promise of our humanity. And in this they certainly disagree with Cassirer and Barthes on the relation of myth and freedom.

Most generally, we can say that all four authors understand the analysis of myth and mythmaking as essential to a coherent and satisfactory description of human being and the world. As well, each sees myth as implicated in the prevention or cure of a variety of cultural and/or personal ills. Of course the authors disagree as to whether myth is to be avoided or embraced to effect the cure. They also disagree as to whether myth is beneficial or detrimental in the quest for freedom. But for each author, freedom is the end or *telos* of human existence. In fact, the *telos* of human life is precisely the same freedom for these authors: each holds true freedom to be the unmitigated, absolutely creative power to constitute both the subjective and objective features of existence. And for each, myth must be understood (to be better evaded or embraced) if we are to be free.

The above comments foreshadow a more thorough piecing-together of these four theories of myth. Chapter 6 presents a complex, but unified, pattern of myth and mythmaking that can be exhibited by weaving together the various strands of analysis. The task at hand in the present chapter is articulating Hillman's account of the role of the mythical in the formation of the self or the soul. As in chapter 4, where we contrasted Eliade's account of mythical spatiotemporality with Cassirer's account, we will contrast Hillman's account of the mythical constitution of the soul with Cassirer's in order to explore more fully myth's role in this.

ANALYSIS AND THE *LOGOS* OF THE PSYCHE

In one sense, Hillman's work in *The Myth of Analysis* does not fit in the present investigation of the properties of mythical configurations and the effects of these configurations on the shape of the world, the self, or systems of signification. *The Myth of Analysis* is not the analysis of myth, except in a very restricted sense. Rather, according to Hillman, analysis itself is a mythical form. That is, analysis is mythically determined or guided in almost every one of its guises and methods.

The Myth of Analysis is really an examination of the role of psychoanalytic categories and practices, of psychiatric language concerning pathology and health, and of medical or biological models of reproduction and female anatomy. All of these are investigated for what they disclose of the now hidden possibilities for the soul in its free creative potential. As Hillman claims, his work is "applying psychology to psychology."[4] He traces and articulates conceptions about the psyche, or soul, as these conceptions have developed through history, *as if* the concepts themselves were dreams or parapraxes. And, as Hillman works in the Jungian or Neumannian tradition of depth psychology, he explores the ideational constellations exhibited in psychological explanation for their archetypal analogues. As psychology is the *logos* of the soul, Hillman expects to find the soul speaking through the symbolic formations of psychology. Though, as with any symbolic activity, we must be attuned to the distortions wrought on the "surface" of such activity as well as paying heed to the deeper archetypal dramas played out beneath the surface.

Hillman sees his work as an examination of mythical structures as they are exemplified in the processes of analysis. More specifically, he understands analysis, in the sense of "explanation," "definition," or "logic," to be the antithesis of the sort of work necessary to appreciate fully the scope of the soul's activities and its mythic or archetypal affinities. Hillman advocates "amplification," rather than analysis, as the only method sufficiently generous in its premises and focus to explicate the full range of the soul. He writes of "ritual dismemberment by psychological analysis," and claims that he himself intends "no definition, which limits and cuts, but rather, amplification, which extends and connects."[5]

Analysis, as used in therapeutic psychology, has led to a kind of desiccation of the soul. In part 2 of his work, Hillman traces the reduction of wide-ranging psychic processes to nominalistic categories. These reductions tend to erase the metaphorical nature of psychology, the *logos* of the psyche, or the "speech of the soul." The result of this analytic method has been the subsumption of rich and varied psychic phenomena to neatly labeled pathological "conditions" in the hopes that these conditions can then be cured or at least alleviated. But for Hillman, the soul *necessarily* suffers or falls ill in its quest for wholeness and freedom. If we eliminate the necessary suffering of the soul as it strives to identify itself and its powers with the archetypal or mythical forms, we obstruct its development. The soul needs to recover the language best able to fully express its suffering. Psychology is the speech of the soul in one of its dialects, and psychology must find its tongue, must wrest the speech of the soul from the professional practitioners of curing and healing. While analysis constrains the free development of the soul in its quest for wholeness, analysis *is* archetypally or mythically determined. The problem with psychoanalysis is not that it is mythically patterned; the problem is that the myth of analysis is no longer the right myth. The hope expressed in Hillman's work is that we will turn from outmoded mythic patterns to archetypes more amenable to the progress of the soul in its journey toward freedom.

In part 3 of his work, Hillman considers the "Apollonic" dimensions of our predominantly "masculine" psychological and medical models of analysis. He compares these to "Dionysian" models, which are predicated on the reincorporation of the "feminine," as it is fantasized as the "abysmal" nature of human being. The soul follows Apollo as depth-psychological lodestar in a phase necessary to the history of the soul; this allows the soul to pattern itself on a model of the fully individuated, heroic, masculine, rational, self-conscious ego. But the process of the individuation of the soul has reached its climax and the tales told on the psychoanalyst's couch tell of the suffering experienced by the soul as it attempts to move beyond the bounds of its Apollonic identification. The feminine principle, castigated throughout history and absent from the constellation of attributes coalescing in the Apollo archetype, must be re-envisioned, claims Hillman, if the soul is to apprehend itself as more than the rational, conscious ego. The end of misogyny would signal a radical shift in the archetypal form, or mythical configuration, that determines our understanding of consciousness, its functions, and its place within the vast landscape of the soul.

The continued development of the soul demands turning to the mythic exemplar of Dionysus, for Dionysus offers an archetypal form or drama that does not allow the exclusion of material, biological existence (the fantasied feminine) from the imaginal attributes constellated as the self or the soul. For Hillman, there is no avoiding a mythically determined self, but there is a possibility of aligning and identifying the self with an archetypal pattern that is much more conducive to the soul coming to fruition, a myth that encourages the inclusion of more and more attributes as belonging to the self.

SOUL-MAKING

Hillman understands the soul as evolving as it identifies itself with different archetypal patterns in a search for wholeness, an attempt to incorporate more and more of life into the sphere of the soul. The speech of the soul, through history, undergoes many transformations, as attested to by the changing dominant archetypal dramas to which the soul is subject. But Hillman also understands the mythical archetypes *themselves* as liable to historical transformations; and it is this that allows for the possibility of the free creative activity of the psyche or soul. *The Myth of Analysis* examines the transformations of the archetypes themselves and the evolution of the identification of the soul with particular mythic patterns, especially Eros, Psyche, Apollo, and Dionysus. The evolution of the archetypes is a process of stripping away the once necessary and now inadequate imaginal configuration of the mythemes, a movement away from the deadening reifications of the archetypal patterns. Hillman implies a progress and a development through history; that the soul comes to fruition as it engages more and more completely with the evolving archetypes guiding its development. However, Hillman is careful to avoid claiming that there is some sort of linear advance in the process of soul-making. The notion of continuous development is itself mythically determined, a mytheme of the rational, conscious ego as hero endeavoring to conquer the unconscious, or colonize the imaginal realm, a kind of "psychological imperialism."[6] This myth was once necessary to the soul making itself, but it has now become outmoded. The soul's shifts in archetypal identification are full of repetition and uruboric movement.

Hillman would never claim that our mythical bonds could or should be overcome or broken. He claims only that certain mythical patterns can (and have) become impediments in the evolution of the psyche in its inexorable drive to freedom and wholeness. In its journey, the soul frees itself from its historically determined archetypal identifications, as the snake sheds its skin. The skin is a product of the snake's necessary development, but is now outgrown and in need of renewal. As the soul is freed from its constraints, it is able to speak more and more directly of its triumphs and travails in its own distinctive language—that of myth and archetypal grammar. The once necessary and now outgrown mythical identifications must be overcome in the "transformation of psyche into life."[7] This progressive transformation frees psyche from the imposition of archetypal or mythical reifications (especially those of the analytic tradition and the science of psychopathology). For example, Hillman claims that a recognition of the archetypal fund from which the self is constituted as an integrity (that is, accepting the inevitability of mythic determination), and an embrace of the "feminine principle," will finally end the tyranny of the rational ego. The history of the evolving archetypal patterns is the history of the soul making itself, evolving "an archetypal psychology to meet its needs."[8]

Archetypal reification, such as equating the entirety of the soul with one of its manifestations—the rational ego, according to the archetype of Apollo—restricts the range of possible identifications for the soul, thus limiting the scope and richness of the soul's active life. Hillman's special concern is with the reifications that have been constructed by professional healers and academicians. If we recognize the archetypal necessities of psychological creativity (soul-making itself), the occurrence of transference relations in psychoanalytic practice can be understood as "soul-making as presented in the Eros-Psyche mythologem."[9] But the archetype is distorted and hidden in psychoanalytic practice. The archetypal drama plays itself out in transference as the scientific and therapeutic expression of the Eros-Psyche mytheme, opening up the soul to constitution through the other, through love and desire. This is a painful experience, transference causes the soul to suffer. But it is a necessary step in the soul's development toward wholeness. This suffering ought not be treated as an illness, but rather celebrated as the rite of passage that it is. We must let go of our insistence that the self or soul is equivalent to the rational, self-conscious, individual ego, we must move away from Apollo and toward Eros and Dionysus. If one partakes fully of the ritual and drama of the psychoanalytic process, one begins to partake of the mythic drama and ritual of the revelation of the soul in the act of loving and being loved.

The recognition of the archetypal necessities to which the soul appeals in its quest results in a revisioning of the soul, and a rehabilitation of a metaphor once rich and vivid, now professionalized and desiccated. Hillman writes,

> Psychological creativity as the union of eros and psyche was dreaming within us long before analysis became a historical necessity for its realization. . . . How necessary the ritual of analysis was and is for psychological creativity is evident; how much longer its hermetic vessel will be necessary we do not know.[10]

Breaking through the reifications causes pain and suffering for the soul, but it also allows the soul to seek better allies in the archetypal realm. The more expansive archetypes, Eros and Dionysus, for example, present the soul with a tremendously rich range of possibilities. As the soul strives for wholeness, for the amalgamation of more and more attributes, it recognizes these archetypal realities as its own possibilities. Then nothing in experience need be denied, all of human life will come to be understood as belonging to the symbolic or archetypal, and the soul will be able to incorporate more and more of life as its own.

The aim of soul-making itself—as it throws off the constrictions imposed by past necessities, suffers inevitable pain of loss, and lovingly embraces the entire constellation of archetypes—is to become wholly "transparent." This is the *telos* of the archetypally determined drama that is the history of human being. The transparent person is the one in whom the soul transcends the particularities of the mundane and reveals fully its archetypal determination. Hillman's suggestion is that the soul is truly free when all of life is experienced as a playing out of the archetypal dramas, with "life as a psychological adventure lived for the sake of the soul."[11]

The soul, in opening itself fully to the archetypal patterns that form the ground of possibility for the very constitution of the soul, not only revisions itself, but can focus more clearly on the end toward which it strives, that toward which it is impelled by its nature. Hillman writes,

> Now our image of the goal changes: not Enlightened Man, who sees, the seer, but Transparent Man, who is seen and seen through, foolish, who has nothing to hide, who has become transparent through self-acceptance; his soul is loved, wholly revealed, wholly existential; he is just what he is, freed from paranoid concealment, from the knowledge of his secrets and his secret knowledge; his transparency serves as a prism for the world and the not-world.[12]

The transformation of perspective or focus in the speech of the soul as it plays out the Eros-Psyche mytheme transforms and clarifies the *telos* of human life. Hillman writes that the goal, "Know Thyself," takes reflective consciousness as the telic force of the soul. Self-reflective knowledge is impossible, however, "only the last reflection of an obituary may tell the truth." The *telos* of the soul, fueled by Eros, and spoken of by the soul through the archetypes, is the command, "Reveal Thyself." As the soul speaks in its mother tongue, it regains the power of discerning its own proper desires.[13]

KANT, THE INTELLECTUAL FATHER
OF CASSIRER AND HILLMAN

Hillman's work is an attack on the reifications of the labile language of the soul's self-expressive speech. He offers us a revised conception of psychological pathology, one that asks us to understand pathology as a necessary feature of the soul's suffering in its journey to freedom. Hillman calls us to reexamine the history of professional fantasies concerning the soul and to find the archetypal patterns buried there. In these ways, Hillman's work certainly seems far from Cassirer's work on the mythical symbolic constitution of the I, the soul, or the subjective. Hillman's work is also a plea for reinvigorating the mythical elements and dramas through which the soul gains shape, meaning, and power. Cassirer, on the other hand, especially in his later writings, calls for stripping away any residual mythical elements in the constitution of the self and the objective features of existence. This is necessary, for Cassirer, if we are to foster the development of purely theoretical accomplishment, truly ethical life, and rationally organized political systems. Each of these is predicated on the freedom of consciousness from its original bondage to myth. For Cassirer, we may never be able to completely expunge myth from cultural endeavor, but we ought to restrict it, confining its power to foster certain imaginative activities—poetry, for example.[14]

Whatever the differences in their analyses, Hillman's work can be read with an eye for the positive connections to Cassirer's work as well. For both authors, the task is to investigate the history of cultural forms in order to discover otherwise hidden but important features of human existence. These concerns are, at least, the following: to find the driving or constitutive force behind mythical formations; to investigate the relation of myth's archetypal forms to the psychic representations of the constitution of individual human selves; to discover the possibility of free, creative activity for the individuated agent; and to delineate the role that mythical formations play in hindering or helping the movement toward freedom. One way of understanding the convergent interests of these two authors is to examine their common intellectual heritage; this will put their divergent conclusions in sharper relief.[15]

References to Cassirer's Kantian leanings are scattered through chapter 2 of the present work; we need only a brief reprise here. Cassirer undertakes a critical philosophy of culture and envisions his work as an expansion of what he considers the basically sound Kantian critique of reason and judgment. Cassirer tackles the spectrum of symbolic achievement as exhibited in the wide variety of cultural forms. He also thinks of his work as an advance on Kant's analysis of the conditions of knowledge, at least in his own description of consciousness. For Cassirer, consciousness is marked by a dynamic relation of subjectivity and objectivity in mutual definition and determination. As this relation is both dynamic and functional in its determination of the field available to experience and knowledge, Cassirer has added the possibility of an evolution of consciousness to the Kantian account. The evolution of consciousness is a progressive advance toward the *telos* of complete creative freedom for consciousness.[16] We can also see Cassirer's debt to Kant in the description of ethical action. Cassirer links the apprehension of the distinction between meaning and being to the distinction between "ought" and "is." In superseding the givenness of the substantial world, via meaning constitution, the *animal symbolicum* posits an ideal world to which it can aspire.[17] Further, Cassirer claims that true ethical freedom demands the renunciation of instincts and inclination, and a subservience to the dictates of (theoretical) reason.[18] Of course, this is Kant's description of actions having moral worth.

Hillman displays his Kantian colors as well, though in considerably more muted hues. But he does give direct acknowledgment to Kant when he describes *memoria* and its role in the development of the "imaginal ego." Hillman describes Frances A. Yates's work, *The Art of Memory*,[19] and notes that it "gives an account of the ways in which all the traits of the soul and the encyclopedic knowledge of the mind can be placed within an imaginal structure." Yates recounts quite elaborate mnemonic devices used by orators and scholars in antiquity. Hillman notes that the principles of organization used in these imaginal systems are "universals" in the sense that they bind disparate, particular elements into meaningful and memorable unities. These unities are neither *nomina* nor any sort of generalized concept, however. They are, most often, images of the "Gods and heroes and themes of classical mythology." All the particulars of experience may be classified through these imaginative organizing principles "because the archetypal configuration to which these details belong gives them inherent intelligibility . . . [an] inherent belonging within mythical meaning." Hillman goes on to claim that these "archetypal dominants" or "divine imaginal forms" correspond to "Kantian conceptual categories." Experience gains coherence only through this formal organization. According to Hillman, the archetypes themselves are "*a priori* structures of the immeasurable imagination." However, these supersede any of the Kantian categories, as even the "categories of logic and number, of science and theology, could themselves be reduced (i.e., led back) to more basic metaphors of myth."[20] The power of the archetypes in ordering experience lies in their visual attraction as well as in the wealth of associations available to the imagination via the mythical figures. These "personalized universals" serve to synthesize elements of experience, continually enriching the scope of the meaningful content represented in the figure.

Cassirer's understanding of the function of representation, at least insofar as the contents of perception are concerned, depends on a somewhat similar account of synthetic activity. As the perceptual world becomes organized through symbolic activity, the "particular contents that present themselves to consciousness are filled with increasingly richer and more diverse functions of meaning." Each element becomes "saturated" with progressively varied relations. As consciousness functions symbolically, it organizes the perceptual content of experience into "manifold meaning-groups which in turn are systematically related to one another and which by virtue of this relationship constitute the totality that we call the world of our experience." This is Cassirer's notion of "symbolic pregnance."[21]

For Hillman, the archetypes are transcendental in the sense that they are "transpersonal," or nonsubjectively determined, as well as *a priori*. Hillman writes,

> What transpires *in* our psyche is not *of* our psyche; both love and soul finally and from the beginning belong to the realm of archetypal reality. This psychological lesson gives an impersonal quality to the entire creative opus of soul-making within each individual's subjectivity. No matter how personally we feel them as our "own," eros and psyche are archetypal powers that find their final and original "home" when placed where they belong, as transpersonal events which paradoxically form the ground of personality.[22]

The archetypal patterns are determinations of "objective necessity" appearing in each and every instance of soul-making.[23] Furthermore, Hillman is claiming that the proper development of the soul depends on the submission of the subjective, personal, and contingent features of existence to universal law; as Kant describes the good will. Of course, Hillman does not claim that these necessary, objective principles are determinable through reason. Rather, the "imaginal ego" has access to archetypal reality. The transpersonal, archetypal realm is the source for all knowledge of that which must determine the activities and conceptions of the soul if the soul is to be truly free. The imaginal ego is able to apprehend the archetypes through the "art of memory," gaining entry into, in depth psychological terminology, the "collective unconscious." The archetypes are the objectively necessary, a priori principles to which the contingent, particular features of experience must submit. This submission entails "ritualizing all occurrences, turning events into mythemes, fixing the trivia [of life] into the precise details . . . of a legend."[24] The soul becomes "more," more real and more full of meaning, gains depth and scope, as it identifies itself with an ever wider range of the archetypal patterns and principles available through imagination.

THE INDIVIDUATION OF THE MYTHICAL SUBJECT

For Hillman, the archetypal is transcendental, transpersonal, and "psychoid"; in part it "stands completely outside the psyche."[25] The individuated soul is constituted out of and through its identification with the archetypal constellations, but the soul needn't confine itself to any particular archetypal patterns. By reinvigorating a notion of psychological creativity as soul making itself, we can see the soul as coming to understand itself as a function of the archetypes. In so doing, the scope of the soul is broadened to include its full capacity for creating itself according to the universal, imaginal principles found in the archetypal realm.

Cassirer finds that each symbolic form constitutes the I or self according to the form's own particular unifications. In each form, the I is correlatively and mutually determined with what is not-I, the world, with different features accruing to each as the unities are formed through the specific symbolic function. The mythical is, for Cassirer, the matrix out of which all other symbolic forms arise. So we expect that the constitution of the mythical I would be the most primitive of subjective formations. When he describes the first stirrings of spiritual activity out of its immersion in strictly biologically or organically determined existence, Cassirer claims that neither the soul nor the I nor the ego yet exists. These are *products* of symbolic activity. Furthermore, as we saw in chapter 2, mythical consciousness, even in its most articulate manifestations, cannot recognize itself as spiritual formative power. It remains embedded in natural existence, never achieving a true distinction between material being and spiritual meaning. Given all this, we can expect to find the machinery of the constitution of the I and its correlative world most crudely, and, therefore, most obviously, in operation in mythical symbolic formation.

Cassirer claims that the first wedge driven into the undifferentiated, boundaryless fluidity that characterizes human being prior to a demarcation of self and world is the "translation and transposition of the world of subjective emotions and drives into a sensuous, objective existence."[26] Mythical consciousness performs the act of differentiating the spiritual sphere from the material sphere in a manner foreign to all other symbolic forms. Emotional *reaction*, strong enough to arrest the ongoing flow of biological existence, allows for objectification of the emotional state. The objectification of emotional reaction marks a transformation from passive impression to the possibility of consciousness expressing and recognizing itself as the constitutive force behind the transformation. Furthermore, it is in the objectification of emotions that the first spiritual force is encountered, and this splits apart the original fluidity and undifferentiated flux of biological existence. In this split, the center of efficacy is not construed as belonging to a subject who "has" an intense emotional reaction. Rather, this "sheer immediacy," this being "overcome" or being "possessed," leads to an extreme compression of the experienced moment. Then "the subjective emotional excitement becomes objectified, and confronts the mind as a God or daemon."[27] The locus of spiritual efficacy moves into closer and closer proximity to the subjective sphere, though it is still apprehended as an objective, outside force. Spirit moves from its inception as a purely objective feature of the world, possessing the subject, impressing itself upon human being, through its incorporation as an internal, yet still nonsubjective principle of spiritual efficacy (as when the soul is experienced as a separate entity inhabiting in the body), and finally finds itself as a nonsubstantial, subjective attribute, as with the Socratic daemon.

This is the end of mythical consciousness, at least in terms of the constitution of the subjective features of existence. Consciousness accomplishes an ideal unity of spiritual efficacy located within the domain of personal, subjective experience. Consciousness has accomplished its telic task of sifting out the features of the *real* ontological difference and assigning the features to their proper place along the psychic/physical or spiritual/material line of demarcation. Mythical consciousness, through its dialectical activity of constituting a self, brings about its own demise. A "true 'self'" emerges, as an individuated, internally determined sphere predicated on the "intuition of free subjectivity." This formation belongs to religious consciousness, distinct from the mythical, in that there appears both the "idea of a unitary *subject* of creation" and the concept of a transcendent, universal ordering principle to which the contingent features of the world and the I must submit.[28] Again, as with all symbolic formation, Spirit first discovers such unities as objective before finding its own properties and operations reflected in the unities. So, as the bonds of mythical constitution are shattered, Spirit exhibits its power of self-definition more clearly, in opposition to material existence and in its self-reflective or self-conscious attributes. Furthermore, Spirit shows itself as the subject of its own creative endeavor and as accountable only to universal, *spiritual* ordering principles.

Much of what's just been said about Cassirer's description of Spirit at work in the mythical world could just as well be said of Hillman's account of the individuated soul and its relation to universal principles. Though using different terms, Cassirer and Hillman appear to agree that the subjective sphere, the I or the soul, is constituted via mythical configuration. They agree that the divinities that inhabit the mythical stand in a reflective relation with the subjective; that is, by examining the changing mythical configurations, we can read back to what the subjective must be. Cassirer and Hillman agree that the features of the mythical exhibit transformations that are directly correlated to transformations in the attributes or configuration of the subjective sphere. There is an essential difference to be noted, here, however. Cassirer claims that these mythical formations must finally come to be understood as the constructions of consciousness. Hence, the mythical formations will be swept away as the spiritualized subject comes to apprehend itself as the creative power behind any symbolic formation. Hillman claims that the archetypal cannot be evaded or destroyed. This is the case even as psychic creative power strives to align itself with archetypal determinants. Contrary to Cassirer's conclusion, this grants the subjective greater and greater scope.

For Hillman, the movement of the soul toward unification with the constitutive power of the archetypes is a unification that allows the freeing of the soul from categories once inevitable in its development and now reified and restraining. This can be seen as the obverse of the movement of Spirit as described by Cassirer, who traces, as we've seen, Spirit's symbolic activity as it diminishes its dependence on the substantial. This is dependence on the substantial in any of its manifestations—from actual organic embeddedness in natural existence to concepts in theoretical physics that have not yet been completely purged of the quasi-material imputation of force. Spirit frees itself in coming to apprehend the unities of knowledge and experience as purely formal, purely functional in determination. Spirit frees itself when it accepts and understands itself as symbolic activity articulating the world and the self in dialectical, functional opposition.

Cassirer's description of Spirit freeing itself is the obverse of Hillman's description of soul freeing itself in the following sense. Hillman outlines the process of the soul, as individuated principle of human being, in its coming to understand itself as, and align itself with, the archetypal, the transcendental, transpersonal ground of the possibility of the existence of the soul. Cassirer outlines the process of Spirit coming to understand itself as the ground of the possibility of the constitution of individuated human being. He describes the individuating process out of the transcendental ground, where Hillman describes the process of the individuated being released into the transpersonal. This obversion of perspective results in very different conclusions regarding human embodied existence. As we shall see, these conclusions are inextricably entwined with the very different values accorded myth by the authors.

THE EMBODIED MYTHICAL SELF

For each thinker, charting the transformations wrought in the mythical constellations shows us that the subjective moves toward encompassing more and more as its proper domain. For Cassirer, consciousness moves toward apprehending all of its milieu, including its own identification with a subjective self, as symbolically determined and that it itself is the formative power behind the symbolic. For Hillman, the soul moves toward recognizing all features in human life as moments of archetypal drama, and that it itself determines the form of life through identification of and with the archetypes. This is psychological creativity. So, for Cassirer, the mythical determinations of the subjective *must* be overcome if human being is to finally free itself from its natural constraints. For Hillman, the mythical determinations of the subjective *can never* be overcome, and ought to be fervently embraced if human being is to finally free itself from its contingent condition.

We can see a direct parallel of this difference in the authors' views on the nature of biological existence and the body's relation to the constitution of the subjective sphere. Cassirer and Hillman agree that the mythical is inextricably bound to material, physical existence. But while Cassirer claims that such embeddedness must be overcome, through the dissolution of the mythical and the apprehension of the strictly opposing spheres of nature and Spirit, Hillman claims such embeddedness can never be overcome. As a matter of fact, Hillman might say that Cassirer's contentions on this score merely show him to be living out an archetypal fantasy or drama closely aligned with the Apollonian mythical configuration. The Apollonian drama depends on the valorization of the conscious, rational ego and the denial of all other aspects of the psyche. The archetype directs the movement of the soul away from the body, away from materiality, away from the instincts, away from the unconscious. Hillman might very well read Cassirer's work as yet another account of an Odyssey of the Great Hero on the Quest, complete with the underlying themes of renouncing the Mother (fantasied biological origin of material dependence) and escaping the vicissitudes of the Maternal/Material through an identification with the Father (especially as exemplar of the rule of [universal] law).[29] For Hillman, this archetypal configuration was once an essential template for the soul; it allowed the soul to constitute its rational features and claim these for its own. But the exclusion of all other mythic patterns, for the sake of the Apollonic, impoverishes the life of the soul. The archetypal pattern of Apollo seduces the soul into entering on a heroic quest for freedom from all relations. It is a dedication to an absolutely *self*-determined and *self*-created ego that stands alone and free. There is no hidden darkness for Apollo, there are no secret constraints and impulses.

Hillman describes the Apollonic primarily in terms of the psychological and medical theories that have examined and pontificated on the female body, though Cassirer's analytic practices and commitments could surely be included in Hillman's indictment. The Apollonic must cast aside the "dark, material, and passionate part of itself."[30] The Apollonic has depended, through history, on relegating the "abysmal side" of itself to the feminine, and castigating the feminine as inferior and degraded. Thus, misogyny has been a dominant feature of the Apollonically determined soul. Even without direct denunciations of the female body as the representative of human material embeddedness, the Apollonic may show itself in any theory—if the theory depends on the exclusion of material, physical existence as the means of gaining freedom. For Hillman, this exclusion can never lead to a truly free condition for human being. Denial itself is a kind of bondage, and we can trace the deformations wrought in our understanding of human being in all theories dependent on exclusion, or denial, or castigation of biological existence. Hillman writes,

> It is very well to speak of new theories of matter, of the relativity of matter and spirit, of the end of materialism, of synchronicity and *unus mundus*, and of the possibility of a new, universal science, where matter and spirit lose their hostile polarity, but these are all projections of the intellect unless there is a corresponding change of attitude in regard to the material part of man himself, . . . a movement in consciousness in regard to bodily man, his own materiality and instinctual nature.[31]

To divorce the features of the living soul deemed too intimately connected with material existence from the features of the soul accorded purely spiritual functioning is really to deny the worth or perhaps the very possibility of the "human individual and the single soul."[32]

To strip away the particularizations imposed on the subjective by its embodied existence is precisely to define the soul or the self as an empty, purely functional determination. Hillman, as a psychologist, holds a primary commitment to the value of the *particular* soul in its creative endeavor to "become what it is." The individuation of the soul depends on biological existence and environmental conditions. For Hillman, Cassirer's description of the constitution of the individuated, subjective sphere of the I in contradistinction to the material conditions of particularized subject has little to do with psychology. Of course, Cassirer might well accede to this. His work more clearly fits what Hillman calls the "spiritual disciplines,"[33] which find their specific task in transcending the individual. But if this is the case, then we must wonder how much credence to give Cassirer's analysis of the constitution of the individuated self or I, in mythical symbolic formation.

Finally, we can see that Hillman's account of myth offers a way to incorporate the mythical in an understanding of contemporary life without recurring to the dire consequences that Cassirer foresees. As mentioned in chapter 2, Cassirer is forced to ignore several of his own discoveries concerning the mythical world in order to understand the political mayhem of the first half of the twentieth century as a resurgence of mythical consciousness. He leaves out of consideration such features as the fundamentally "sympathetic" nature of mythical consciousness, the apprehension of the world primarily as "thou" rather than "it," and so on, while referring to the ritualistic aspects of mythic activity and its penchant for word magic. If Hillman is correct in his assessment of the journey of soul-making, Cassirer serves as an exemplar of the kind of analytic thinker who attempts to divorce the erotic from psyche, a divorce that is doomed to failure. Cassirer has stripped his description of mythical consciousness in contemporary culture of precisely those aspects of myth that Hillman considers as belonging to Eros. These are the sympathetic identification with all living things, the inability to distinguish the spiritual from the material, and the reservoir of attractive power in the imaginal forms. According to Hillman, these are aspects that must be joined with Psyche if the soul is to continue on its journey to archetypal completion and its freedom. The travails of our century may be the symptoms of the necessary suffering the soul undergoes if Eros and Psyche are sundered.

CREATIVE FREEDOM

There is one last difference between Cassirer and Hillman that must be mentioned, and it too is predicated on the place of the body and physical, biological existence in the constitution of the subjective sphere. Cassirer and Hillman, as well as Barthes and Eliade, understand the freedom that is the *telos* of human being as a free, *creative* power of construal or constitution of the subjective and objective spheres of existence. We can trace the concept of creativity in the work of Cassirer and Hillman through their description of the relation of bodily existence to freedom.

Hillman predicts that analysis will finally discover its end when the "abysmal" or "feminine" or bodily aspects of human being are fully recognized as belonging to the soul, when it transforms the dominant archetype of Apollo and his exploits into the imaginal forms of Dionysus. The end of "misogyny," which Hillman equates with the refusal to deny the mythical representations of bodily existence entrance to the court of the soul, will open the self to a condition of greater and greater freedom. The self will no longer be identified strictly within the narrow bounds of the conscious ego, but will become diffuse, open to the calls of *memoria*, and free to experience its erotic nature through a "commingling of consciousness with the 'other' souls and their Gods, a consciousness that is always infiltrated with its complexes, flowing together with them."[34]

Cassirer regards the embeddedness of consciousness in material existence as the origin of the quest for freedom from these bonds and Hillman regards embodied existence as both the alpha and omega of the soul's striving. As alpha, embodiment is the motivating force behind the imaginal forms according to which the soul consti-tutes itself; as omega, archetypal images of the body are incorpo-rated as an essential feature of the constellated self. While both Cas-sirer and Hillman understand the mythical as indiscerptibly united with biological and physical existence, the former sees this as the entrapment of Spirit, while the latter sees it as creating the condi-tions for the freeing of the soul from illusion and deadly constriction.

For Cassirer, the body, or substantiality in general, is, more than anything else, a hindrance to the free, creative possibilities of Spirit.[35] This is so even though every symbolic formation depends on some sort of "matter" to which "form" is given. As we've seen, the more developed a symbolic form is, the less bound to substance is the material wrought through the form. For example, mathematical thought depends on number as its "matter" to be "formed," but number is already far removed from substantiality. Not only does mythical thought depend on nonsymbolically wrought substance, but it does not properly differentiate between the spiritual and the material, nor between the accomplishments of consciousness and the body and its physiological and emotional states. These condi-tions must be overcome if Spirit is to proceed on its path toward freedom. Symbolic forms other than myth are able to transcend this muddle of ontological nondifferentiation and clearly apprehend a distinction between the spiritual and the material; and consciousness in these nonmythical forms is able to identify itself with the spiritual and constellate these feature into a subjective realm of the I. The I as individuated agent is thus identified with the spiritual, constitutive acts of consciousness, at least in nonmythical forms. Only through properly distinguishing between the spiritual and the material, between meaning and being, is Spirit able to engage fully in free, creative symbolic production. Correlatively, the material trans-formed through symbolic activity is stripped of any suggestion of independent substance impressing itself upon the spiritual. The "matter" itself comes to be understood as the result of the creative power of consciousness. So, for example, theoretical physics uses the concept of force as an objective characteristic of its field of study *and* understands that force is a concept, the product of Spirit's own symbolic fashioning and not a substantial feature of the world. In this, consciousness has achieved a greater degree of creative freedom than when it has taken force as independent of symbolic formation. Obviously then, for Cassirer the creative freedom of human being lies in consciousness sharply distinguishing between substance and form, aligning itself ever more completely with the formative activity, and distancing itself more and more from bodily, physically determined substance.

We would still find this essential difference in the authors' concepts of creative freedom, even if we could equate archetypal reality with Cassirer's understanding of Spirit, purely in its nonparticularized but formal capacities. Hillman does not claim that the creative endeavor to individuate the subjective or the soul comes from the archetypal, as it originates in Spirit for Cassirer. For Hillman, the creative itself is absolutely dependent on physical, biological existence. Psychological creativity, the driving force in the constitution and individuation of the subject, finds its genesis in biologically determined instinct, according to Hillman. He would agree with Cassirer that the mythical is indissolubly linked to material existence. The two cannot be dissociated, for Hillman, because the archetypes, insofar as they provide a kind of evolving blueprint for the soul in its search for wholeness and completion, are given to us only as the psychic configurations constellated by the creative *instinct*.

One of the major tasks of exploring the *logos* of the soul is to discover the origin of the soul, or that which creates soul. This is the search for the "creative principle," which engenders soul in its wide array of configurations.[36] The principle of psychological creativity is the principle of determination of the soul. It is the "creating, engendering, awakening, enlightening, and individuating of the soul."[37]

Hillman's examination of the process of creativity is a reaffirmation and expansion of certain Jungian concepts. According to Jung, there are at least five "ectopsychic" forces that must be taken into account in understanding human being. These ectopsychic forces are instincts, or biologically determined patterns of activity. They are exhibited objectively as a compulsion or drive toward satisfaction of a particular kind. As ectopsychic, the instincts are "older than, prior to, and outside the psyche." Jung includes creativity as a separate, distinct, instinctual drive, adding it to a list of four others: "hunger, sexuality, the drive to activity . . . [and] reflection."[38] (These correspond roughly to the more traditional naming of the major instincts as feeding, reproduction, aggression, and flight.) The instincts may find representation in the psyche. The "psychization" of the instinct (or, as Freud would have it, the ideas or images cathected by instinctual drives) may modify or ameliorate the particular demands of the instinct. Only insofar as the instinct has been rendered psychically can it be known to the subject of the instinctual forces.

Hillman is quite willing to admit that Jung's characterization of the instincts, in general, has nothing extraordinary about it. In fact, it falls prey to the same sorts of criticism that most theories of an ill-defined instinctual force occasion. But, if Jung is correct in claiming a nonderivative status for a creative instinct (that it is not, for example, a sublimation of the reproductive drive), then, as any instinct must, the creative instinct must find satisfaction. Though, as any instinct is subject to modification via psychization, so too the creative may be channeled according to specific images or representations.

Jung's description of the instincts and their role in the psychic processes may not be particularly radical. However, his claim that the creative drive must be accorded the same status as flight or reproduction is quite unusual. It allows for certain important transformations in our understanding of the constitution of the soul and the soul's intimate relation to the body. The creative instinct, following Hillman's account of Jung's explanation, is the "urge to wholeness, the urge toward individuation or personality development, the spiritual drive, the symbol-making transcendent function, the natural religious function, or, in short, the drive of the self to be realized." Hillman writes that "we are driven to be ourselves." The creative instinct may indeed be thwarted or diverted or exaggerated in any particular person, but its drive to satisfaction cannot be denied as shaping subjective existence. Moreover, as ectopsychic, the creative instinct exerts "relentless pressure on the soul," and is often experienced as a "numinous power" before which one feels a "sense of helplessness." Hillman suggests that such experience in the face of overwhelming creative compulsion tends to align this instinct's cathexes with conceptions of the "immanent Gods in their creator roles [and as] 'beyond' the soul, neither in it nor of it."[39] The extreme power of the creative instinct, combined with the felt experience of its ectopsychic nature mean that the drive to create finds clearest expression and psychic representation in the guise of the gods and goddesses.

Hillman has a great deal more to say about psychological creativity, especially insofar as traditional theories of the soul tend to deny the destructive aspects of the creative process, and attempt to eliminate the truly erotic elements of the creative drive in favor of explanatory schemes that locate the creative solely in the reflective capabilities of human beings. But most important for the present work, Hillman demands that we understand the drive to individuate as inseparable from biological, material existence. This notion of creativity follows related claims that true freedom for the soul lies in the destruction of once necessary, but now outgrown and restrictive ideational, archetypal, or mythic patterns. There is an evolution of the archetypal patterns that can be traced and the evolution exhibits the erotic drive of the soul (mythically figured as Eros) toward its fulfillment in identification with the entire range of the imaginal field. As the drama of Eros and Psyche are played out, we discover the desire of the soul to incorporate incommensurable otherness. Hillman hopes this desire will express itself in the incorporation of the fantasied feminine, material, and abysmal aspects of human being. Finally, Hillman suggests that we may be on the brink of the death of analysis and misogyny. This is a shift from the Apollonic drama to the Dionysian. Dionysus is the figure of bisexuality and radical dispersion (rather than concentration) of power and activity. Living the Dionysian drama would mean "a world undivided into spirit and matter, imaginal and real, body and consciousness, mad and sane."[40]

☙❦❧

In chapter 4, we examined the work of Cassirer and Eliade and found striking similarities (amidst the differences) on the constitution of the objective features of the world through the lens of myth. In this chapter, we have again found striking similarities and disagreements, here between Cassirer and Hillman on the constitution of the subjective features of the mythical world. Hillman's description of the consequences of embracing the mythical in determination of the subjective sphere would be precisely what Cassirer would predict. But where Cassirer would recoil from such consequences, Hillman finds his own Dionysian joy. This skewing of the description of the mythical self arises from the particular value valence brought to bear by the authors. This difference, along with the confluence of the notions of freedom in all four of the authors we've been investigating, are major concerns of chapter 6.

6

The magic mirror
of myth . . .

The title of this chapter[1] is a quote from Cassirer. In *The Myth of the State*, he describes theories of myth that followed Schelling's:

> [T]he old spell was never completely broken. Every scholar still found in myth those objects with which he was most familiar. At bottom the different schools saw in the magic mirror of myth only their own faces. The linguist found in it a world of words and names—the philosopher found a "primitive philosophy"—the psychiatrist a highly complicated and interesting neurotic phenomenon.

This may indeed be true. But there is a correlative truth—at least concerning the theories of myth we're examining here. The reflection and the reflected are much more intimately related than Cassirer admits. If the subject of myth is a mirror reflecting our intellectual concerns, our intellectual concerns mirror myth as well.

The present chapter has two goals. The first is piecing together the investigative results of Cassirer, Barthes, Eliade, and Hillman into a coherent pattern of explanation and description. The second goal is more ambitious. We will examine this explanatory fabric for what it can show us of the function of the concept of myth in our theoretical endeavors. I will articulate the ways in which the theories of myth themselves exhibit the same characteristics as those the authors ascribe to myth. Though myth's guise has changed, its function remains the same: myth can be discovered at work in our

most sophisticated theoretical constructions about myth. Our theoretical accounts of myth serve the same purpose as the telling of
tales around an open fire.

A THEORETICAL QUILT

In chapters 2 through 5, we examined four theories of myth in a
rather straightforward way. I offered synopses of the intellectual
positions of the thinkers, outlined their views of myth, and pointed
out areas of agreement and disagreement among them. The analysis
I undertake in this chapter is more like making a quilt. We will take
bits and pieces of the four accounts of myth, rearrange them into a
harmonious pattern, and create something new without destroying
the texture, the color, or the fabric of the old.

The four authors we've been studying seem to have little in
common beyond the selection of myth as an important topic for
inquiry. Cassirer is a cultural critical idealist, investigating the
mythical for what it exhibits of the movement of consciousness
out of its embeddedness in organic, biologically determined existence and toward an ideal freedom, the fulfillment of the *telos* of
Spirit as it creates symbolic form. Barthes is a neo-Marxist structuralist semiologist inveighing against the furtive cover-up of contingent, historical processes; a cover-up performed by mythical signification, especially as bourgeois mythmaking attempts to stop
up free, revolutionary speech. Eliade offers an account of a sacred
ontology, an existential position of being human made possible and
available through reciting mythical narratives and participating in
ritual acts. Sacred ontology allows for the erasure of the terrors of
history and for full freedom for human being in participating in the
creation of the cosmos as a meaningful, ordered, spatiotemporal
unity. Hillman, a depth or archetypal psychologist, follows the path
of soul-making through mythical forms to the soul's destination of
freedom from analysis and misogyny, a movement toward a
"divine" psychology.

Given the great differences in perspective we find among these
theories, why have I chosen to compare them in my own work on
myth? First, I am doing a "second-order" analysis; I have not begun
at the beginning, so to speak, examining myriad examples of myth
and offering an original interpretation of them. That groundwork
has already been done by many other competent researchers, including Cassirer, Barthes, Eliade, and Hillman. I have taken for granted
that thinkers of such intellectual sophistication, despite their inerad-

icable differences, all have interesting and important contributions to make in our understanding of myth.

Furthermore, I believe that the deep differences among them have positive value. This book is an attempt to determine what myth is and how it affects human existence. What I have done is pose these questions to four thinkers with fundamental disagreements, given each a respectful hearing, and juxtaposed the answers to see if any consistent patterns emerge. I've assumed that, given the same object of research across the various theoretic endeavors, these disparate perspectives can be collated in order to provide a quadrascopic view of myth. This view will result in the richest understanding.

We need not take a position "above" these theoretical accounts in order to better judge which is the correct account, nor adopt one of the perspectives and reformulate or refute the others through that particular lens. I've sought a pattern, a description of myth, that is a complex but unified theoretical exhibition of the traits of the mythical. I have used Cassirer's analysis to set the broad outlines of our discussion because his work covers more territory than the others. This provides the basic organization, while the others' work provides counterpoint, highlight, balance of composition, and so on. This complex pattern need not do violence to the internal integrity of any of the theories, but rather may display the features of each within a larger context that adds to our understanding of the ways in which myth and theories about myth function. When we trust that each author has something important to tell us about myth, rather than trying to prove that one is correct and dismissing the others, interesting patterns do emerge.

One pattern has already become apparent, though it may be, in part, an artifact of using Cassirer's work to set the basic themes. However, the theories fit this scheme rather neatly. The emphases may differ, but the theories are remarkably consistent: myth is a culturally (or symbolically, or semiologically, or ritually) creative act through which human beings articulate and constitute the distinction between human being and the world for human being. Four authors of quite different political and intellectual commitments agree on this (while often disagreeing on the particulars of the process). We ought to give it credence. However, when we take this general picture of myth seriously and focus on *it* rather than on the particulars of the theories, we are able to see that the theories of myth themselves function in precisely the same way. That is, our accounts of myth are theoretically creative acts through which we articulate and constitute the distinction between human being and the world for human being.

We can also begin to elucidate more fully the means by which myth—and theories of myth—perform this task. We can identify these by piecing together our explanatory fabric in a different way. Rather than explicating the internal organization of a theory (for example, moving step-by-step through Eliade's account of the hierophany) and clarifying this through comparison with another theory, we can look for more subtle points of congruence across the four theories. We can find these congruences, and they exhibit a definite theoretical pattern. I will offer a schematic rendering of this pattern here; it will be examined in detail in what follows.

"Myth" is a functional construct with no definite and invariable content. The function that myth serves is to unite and separate two opposed ontological regions. Myth is irreducible to one or the other and at the same time is intimately related to each and to both. This is the paradoxical nature of the mythical; it is a kind of gateway, hinge, turnstile, or threshold. This undecidable quality of myth in service of distinguishing opposing ontological regions means that for myth to maintain its status as myth it must continue in its function as the boundary between incommensurables. The ontological regions delineated through the paradoxical function of myth are that which belongs to human being proper and that which is other. Myth also plays an important role in determining the ontological *priority* of the region that belongs to human being (however construed). The otherness of what belongs to the secondary region determined by the mythical makes it particularly intransigent for theoretical endeavor. However, certain features of what is mythically designated as other can be transformed and recuperated for the truly human region through a reduction of what is other to that of the same; myth works as a kind of permeable boundary.

This pattern of explanation is evident in each of the theories we've examined. But the same constellation of traits can be found in the way that each author uses the concept of myth. We will see how the *concept* of myth works as it alternately hides and betrays (sometimes) covert metaphysical, ontological, and valuational assumptions in the theories. The *concept* of myth serves as a gateway or threshold, the paradoxical site or the perfect alibi, demarcating antithetical ontological realms, one of which is honored and valorized, the other taboo. The *concept* of myth, like myth itself, serves to mark the limit of the truly human, however construed.

Myth is the means by which human being represents to itself the range, scope, and limits of being human. Whatever stories we tell, whatever rituals we engage in, whatever theories we develop: insofar as these cultural and social constructions function as means of telling ourselves or showing ourselves the *boundary* between human being and whatever is not, we have myth. Myths are human creations that create human being in the sense of being a unified integrity set over against its antithesis, or set within a larger context.

Each of the four authors we've studied offers us his own myth, each draws a picture of just where human being proper "ends" and where what does not belong to the truly human "begins." Though altogether different in terms of what is ascribed to human being proper, these mythical constructions of the scope of the truly human share two fundamental features. These theoretically constructed myths posit the *telos* of human existence as absolute freedom, an unbounded and unconditioned power to create. This, I believe, is a bankrupt myth, and we will examine it below. There is a mythical correlate to this understanding of human existence; and that is, that human being proper must transcend natural or inevitable determinations. This, I believe, is a dangerous myth; we will return to it in the conclusion.

MYTH AS PARADOX

The four authors, though using different terms, agree on the essential work of myth. This is true even though they disagree deeply on *what* is considered mythical. For example, we've seen that Barthes' notion of myth is any metalanguage that uses already constituted signs as its signifiers in a second-order semiological system. Eliade counts as myth those narratives and rituals that return us to the origin of the meaningful, ordered cosmos at the irruption of the sacred into the profane. The concept of what counts as myth could hardly be more different. Yet each author describes how myth *works* (whatever myth *is*) in very much the same way. For Barthes, mythical speech functions as a kind of "turnstile"; for Eliade, myth functions as a "paradox" or a "gateway." But it is not only that each author ascribes this paradoxical work to whatever is considered mythical. On a deeper level, we can see that the concept of myth performs the same service in the theory itself.

Generally speaking, we find that myth, for each of the four authors, stands as a dividing line between antithetical regions. It does not belong to either "side," but rather to both and to neither at once. This is especially clear in Eliade's description of the site of the hierophany, the appearance of the sacred. He writes of the site of the sacred irrupting through the mundane,

> It is impossible to overemphasize the paradox represented by every hierophany, even the most elementary. By manifesting the sacred, any object becomes *something else*, yet it continues to remain *itself*, for it continues to participate in its surrounding cosmic milieu.[2]

Mythical narratives perform the same sort of work as the sacred object. The narrative and its attendant rituals are the means by which the human actors can return to the scene of the origin of the cosmos. As a means of access, the mythical is both sacred and profane, and at the same time, neither sacred nor profane. The myth and the sacred object mark the division between two antithetical realms, two ontologically distinct arenas: sanctified existence and profane existence. The marks themselves are truly paradoxical; they both unite and separate the sacred and the profane. The mythical is irreducible to one or the other ontological region. If it loses its function as undecidable, it is absorbed into either the sacred or the profane, losing its paradoxical property and its status as mythical.

   Barthes as well writes of the paradoxical quality of mythical signification, calling it the perfect "alibi." In the oscillation of meaning and form, the basis of mythical second-order signification, there is no way to pin down the mythical sign as (contingent, historically determined) sign. The visual image that Barthes uses is a neat one. He writes,

> [in myth] there is never any contradiction, conflict or split between meaning and form: they are never at the same place. In the same way, if I am in a car and I look at the scenery through the window, I can at will focus on the scenery or on the window pane. At one moment I grasp the presence of the glass and the distance of the landscape; at another, on the contrary, the transparence of the glass and the depth of the landscape; but the result of this alternation is constant: the glass is at once present and empty to me, and the landscape unreal and full.[3]

Barthes locates the mythical between the antithetical realms of History and Nature. Mythical signification presents itself as signifying both and neither of these regions; insofar as the signification can be identified as a product of one or the other region (that is, it no longer has its perfect "alibi"), it has become decidable and no longer functions mythically. The mythologist, by practicing the art of restoring the object of language and the second-order signification to their proper spheres, disturbs the oscillation of meaning and form, moves deliberately between the two, and destroys mythical speech.

Eliade posits the mythical as the "threshold" between the sacred and the profane, and Barthes understands myth as the "turnstile" between Nature and History. In each case, we see the mythical as uniting and separating two distinct and opposed ontological regions, opposed regions that, together, exhaust the metaphysical field. In other words, for Eliade, whatever is belongs *either* to the sacred or the profane—there is no third category. For Barthes, whatever is belongs *either* to History or Nature. Myth, for both of these authors, serves as the paradoxical boundary between the metaphysically exhaustive opposed regions.

Hillman's understanding of the mythical as irreducible paradox can be seen in two of his lines of analysis. The first is that of the transcendental, imaginal *a priori* archetypes. These must maintain their transpersonal status while at the same time become particularized in the individual through the cathexes of the creative instinct in the biologically driven human organism.[4] The soul suffers in this transubstantiation, but the suffering of the soul is a symptom of ultimate well-being. Illness and neuroses are the signs of the vitality of the soul in its creative endeavor toward wholeness and life. The second domain of the paradoxical in Hillman's work is that of the *coniunctio* achieved through the archetype of imaginal Dionysus. This is a means of "leading consciousness into bisexuality." Bisexuality is neither unisexuality, nor a leveling out of the (primarily fantasized) differences between the masculine and feminine, nor is it a domestication of one by the other, nor a transmutation of one into the other. It is rather the incorporation in the soul of both the material and the spiritual according to an archetypal pattern that cannot be distinguished as either material or spiritual. Hillman remarks that,

> bisexual consciousness here means also the experience of psyche in all matter, the fantasy in everything literal, and the literal too, as fantasy; it means a world undivided into spirit and matter, imaginal and real, body and consciousness, mad and sane . . . when we take Eve back into Adam's body, when we are no longer decided about what is masculine and what feminine; what inferior, what superior, what exterior, what interior.[5]

The function of the Dionysian archetype is, at one and the same time, to maintain an abysmal, material, inferior femininity and to weld the feminine to masculine clarity, spirituality, and ego-consciousness. The mythical archetype both separates and unites the masculine/feminine, the spiritual/material, consciousness/unconscious. The mythically determined *coniunctio* is the undecidable, irreducible paradox. These oppositions are all representations of the fundamental opposition that exhausts the metaphysical field. For Hillman, there is embodied existence and existence as imaginal or spiritual, and myth stands as the gateway between these.

In Cassirer's work on cultural form, this paradoxical quality can be seen in any symbol. As we've seen, his notion of the symbol entails the conjunction of material and formal attributes, though as the symbolic form becomes progressively more sophisticated, the material aspect of the symbol loses all connotations of the substantial. The material transformed in the spiritual activity can itself be a product of symbolic work. The material incorporated in the symbolic activity of contemporary physics, for instance, is most often mathematical material, itself the product of symbolic formation. The primary difference between mythical symbolic formation and other types of symbols is the inability of mythical consciousness to apprehend the products of its own work as divisible into material and formal properties. Such acknowledgment depends on the ability of consciousness to recognize its own acts of transformation in the world as its own accomplishment. The inability of mythical consciousness first to recognize as its own and then to claim that which is spiritual for itself means that the mythical symbolic form is an indiscerptible union of antithetical properties: the substantial and the spiritual. As the matter or substance and the form begin to peel apart (as when religious symbolic formations emerge and consciousness locates the seat of spiritual efficacy not in substance but in a universal principle), the mythical symbol disintegrates. Again we see that as the paradoxical and undecidable nature of the mythical symbol is resolved, it loses its status as myth.

However, it is not only the specific formations of mythical consciousness as described by Cassirer that can be characterized as paradoxical; the mythical world in its entirety is paradoxical. Nature, as material, substantial ontological reality, is both united to and separated from consciousness or Spirit as Nature's ontological nemesis. For Cassirer, mythical symbolic formation, the constitutive force of the mythical cosmos, is incapable of correctly distinguishing the contributions of Spirit as Spirit, instead attributing spiritual efficacy

to Nature. Again, the mythical marks that which cannot be dissociated and yet is ontologically distinct. The mythical is irreducible to
either Nature or Spirit and at the same time belongs to each and
differentiates the antithetical regions.

Each of these four authors identifies as mythical that which
serves the function of threshold or gateway. And by examining the
way each author describes myth, we can see the underlying
dichotomy he assumes as fundamental to existence as such. The
concept of myth works in precisely the same fashion as the authors
insist that instances of myth do. The concept of myth stands as the
paradoxical boundary between antithetical ontological regions; and
whatever the fundamental opposition posited through the concept of
myth, each author assumes it provides the primordial distinction
giving structure to the world.

ONTOLOGICAL ANTITHESES

The antitheses at the heart of the ontological assumptions of Cassirer, Barthes, Eliade, and Hillman are easy to discern. These are
noted in the preceding description of regions united and separated by
the mythical, and outlined more completely in the chapters devoted
to the individual authors. Here we need only a brief recapitulation.
Cassirer holds a real ontological opposition between Nature and
Spirit, a position that becomes apparent only in a close examination of his analysis of the difference between mythical symbolic formation and the other symbolic forms. Implicit in Cassirer's work on
myth is the characterization of the mythical form as not quite fully
symbolic. This lower status is accorded to myth primarily because
the fundamental, symbolically articulated antithesis determining
the structure of the mythical world—the sacred and the profane—is
not constituted according to the "real" ontological distinction
between blind, mechanical, natural forces and the transformative
power of Spirit. Mythical consciousness improperly imputes the
products of its own activity to the power and efficacy of substantial
nature, and in doing so, is incapable of determining an accurate unity
of spiritual attributes that can be aligned with and reappropriated by
the subjective sphere of existence.

Barthes posits a real ontological distinction between Nature
and History. The blurring of this distinction makes possible the
inequities and oppression associated with particular political, economic, and social orders. For Barthes, myth functions as a system of
signification that substitutes Nature for History, that presents what

is really historically determined as naturally occurring or as inevitable. Insofar as a human being experiences his or her position in the world as naturally rather than (really) historically determined, that person is manipulated or oppressed. Barthes identifies as mythical any semiological activity or product that presents itself as both and neither History and Nature.

Eliade's ontological opposition is also quite clear. There is sacred ontology and there is profane ontology. Sacred ontology is structured according to the hierophany and, by means of myth and ritual, allows a return to the creation of the cosmos. This is a return to the moment or site of the inception of the world as a meaningful, ordered whole and an escape from the ravages of the profane—the disintegration that the world and everything in it suffers as it moves away from its origin. Profane ontology is historicized ontology that does not recognize the possibility of expiation or renewal at the source of meaning and being. The opposed ontologies are the basis of the opposed existential positions Eliade ascribes to human being: sacred being or historical being.

Lastly, Hillman predicates his analysis of soul-making on an ontological opposition between the transpersonal, transcendental archetypes and embodied existence. The archetypes must maintain transcendental status if the soul is to have access to anything beyond its particular bodily life. The creative instinct, cathecting representations that belong to the transpersonal, unites the individual biological organism with the transcendental sphere. But the organism cannot be absorbed into this sphere, it must maintain its integrity as bodily existence. Here the mythical is the means by which the opposed ontological realms can forge a kind of uneasy alliance of the spiritual and the material. The other distinctions utilized by Hillman (masculine/feminine, conscious/unconscious, etc.) are imaginal or ideational substitutes for the basic ontological distinction.

ONTOLOGICAL REDUCTION

As we see, what counts as a myth is quite different for these authors, but the notion of how myth functions or works is identical. Whatever myth is, it serves as a kind of permeable border, separating and uniting opposed ontological regions. Where each author locates myth makes clear his own assumptions regarding fundamental ontological distinctions. But each author's concept of myth (what he counts as a myth in articulating the theory or critique) also serves to indicate which of the opposed ontological spheres he considers primordial. That is, the mythical line is drawn, and drawn in such a way as to give ontological priority to one of the regions demarcated. Two opposed and ontologically distinct regions, distinguished through myth, collapse into a primary region and a secondary region whose reality is merely borrowed from the first. We can call this "ontological reduction," and by tracing out the reductions in the analyses of the four authors, we'll see quite clearly the unargued metaphysical assumptions at play.[6]

Ontological reduction serves to erase the peculiarities of some orders or categories in favor of a more highly valued order. The criteria for bestowing higher value on one rather than another of the orders is seldom made explicit or argued for. Furthermore, the analyst makes an (almost always implicit) assumption that what s/he finds more *valuable* is in fact also more *real*. Whatever traits are irrelevant to this more highly valued category are then taken not merely as irrelevant, but as ontologically negligible. When describing what is other than relevant to the dominant order, the elements that determine its internal integrity or coherence *as* other are discarded as less than real, and only those elements or characteristics that can be subsumed under the more highly regarded category are considered relevant or meaningful.

Ontological reduction must always convert as much as possible of what is other to what is more of the same. For example, if the order of religious belief is most highly valued, it is not enough (in the thrust of ontological reduction) to claim that only God's work is real and that whatever is not God's work is unimportant or inessential. The true believer must be able to transform what appears to be absolutely other than belonging to the dominant order into more of the same. The debate on the nature of evil is a case in point. If God is good, then how can evil exist? The true believer's answer often is that God's goodness demands evil as a kind of teaching or testing tool: evil is not other than good; evil is not even real, it is merely a misapprehension of a deeper or more profound good. In fact, the true believer may be able to subsume every facet of existence to God's handiwork, from the starving millions in Somalia to the outcome of a political race to the loss of a job. The reductive process transforms and then absorbs as much as possible of the plurality of existence into a single, highly valued category or order.

Ontological reduction is quite apparent in Cassirer's description of mythical consciousness. He assumes as fundamental the distinction between Spirit and Nature; whatever is, belongs to one of these spheres. But on closer scrutiny, we see that Spirit is granted greater weight. Nature is essential, or real, only insofar as it becomes symbolically articulated and available for reappropriation by consciousness as its own achievement. That is, what is in fact distinct about Nature (at the very least, that it is not Spirit) is effaced. Nature loses its ontological integrity and becomes merely what has not yet been converted from "other-than" Spirit to "more-of" Spirit.

For example, Cassirer attributes the existence of gods and goddesses in the mythical world to expressions of extreme emotional or physiological states. These are first experienced as objective. They appear to belong not to the subjective sphere, but as manifestations of nature, apprehended as divine *and* material. These divine powers are gradually incorporated into, and understood as, features of a subjective constitutive power aligned with the formative activity of Spirit. The process advances, step by step, until the "really" spiritually determined products become disengaged from the material conditions of natural existence. The products of spiritual transformation of the material are finally located where they "belong," in an ideal, unitary, universal ordering principle absolutely independent of material efficacy or substantial content.

This new apprehension of the spiritual accomplishment of a symbolically articulate world by the actual agent of accomplishment, Spirit or consciousness, spells the doom of mythical consciousness and the birth of a different symbolic form.[7] As each symbolic form progresses from its more primitive manifestations to its most complete, or as myth is overcome in the birth of any other symbolic form, consciousness or Spirit raids the world, and returns from these forays with its own products, its own possessions. What originally appeared as other, as a feature of the objective world, gradually comes to be seen as spiritually wrought. The locus of such work may be apprehended as either divine or human, depending on the religious or nonreligious nature of the symbolic form—but in either case, Spirit is the agency. The formal properties of the symbolic remain, attributed to the activity of Spirit or consciousness, while the substantial properties drop out as inessential.

Barthes opposes History to Nature, giving much more ontological weight to the former. Existence, according to Barthes, really *is* historical and contingent. Though, to be sure, "History . . . unveils, while making itself, unimaginable solutions, unforeseeable syntheses."[8] Nature is a distortion of History; Nature is what History looks like when our vision is obscured by the reifications of myth. Myth distorts and alienates reality, because myth is "read as a factual system, whereas it is but a semiological system," juggling differential values.[9] Mythical speech substitutes a bogus naturalized essentiality for the really historically contingent character of all signification production. Myth thereby stymies the movement of History by substituting a quickly congealing "false Nature." The mythologist, in making apparent the second-order or mythicized system of signification, clears a path away from the immobilization of the world in the ahistorical, reified, false, and alienated mode and toward revolutionary, radically productive speech.

For Eliade, there is the sacred and there is the profane. But the profane is really a corruption of the sacred. The profane is the ever-weakening of meaning, order, and being that occurs as we move outward from the origin of the cosmos at the site or moment of the hierophany. Sacred ontology is driven by the elimination of the profane. The decay or disintegration of reality and meaning, time and space, that occurs the further the cosmos strays from its origin can only be offset by the radical reversal of the profane. Perfect and complete reality occurs at the irruption of the sacred. This cosmogonic moment or site must be repeated or returned to, for any temporal or spatial distance from the hierophany results in the progressive corruption and final fall into chaos of all that has its space, time, meaning, and being played out in the profane. Only the determination to repeat the cosmogonic moment, to return to the site of the creation of all meaning and being, can halt this progressive movement toward absolute chaos. What does not partake of the sacred has no meaning, no being, no order or significance. The profane is more than irrelevant in terms of the sacred, its only reality is its reunion with the sacred, a union that obliterates the otherness of the profane by absorbing it and destroying it in the fire of the sacred.

For Hillman, there is an imaginal realm of archetypes and there is embodied existence. The latter is real and meaningful only insofar as it is aligned with archetypal reality, everything else is meaningless. Hillman understands the process of soul-making as reintegrating, in revised form, the historically proscribed symptoms of mental illness as the valuable and inescapable modes of suffering experienced by the soul in casting off its outgrown symbolic achievements. According to Hillman, the progression of dominant archetypes marks the successive phases of psychological creativity (governed by Eros) in its insistent desire for the incommensurable other to remain as other and yet unite in a new conjunction of opposites, constituting an increased field of "wholeness" for the soul.[10] But these claims made by Hillman must be tempered with the acknowledgment that the incommensurable other—the body, the abysmal, the feminine—can be incorporated *only* as archetypally represented. What is other must be shorn of its otherness, transformed into more of the same. The body is not united with the soul, archetypal representations of the body are united with those archetypal representations providing greater scope for the soul's identifications.

We can see ontological reduction at work in each of these theories. It skews the outcome of the analyses; it is a sleight-of-hand that attaches legitimacy or value or priority to one ontological category while denying it to all others. What is plural is first reduced to a dualism, and then even this plurality is effaced by subsuming and erasing what may be in fact ontologically irreducible. The concept of myth not only marks the distinction between fundamental and opposed ontological regions, as we saw in the preceding section. Recalling Barthes' image of the pane of glass: by focusing our attention on instances of myth, the theorist obscures from view the surreptitious work of the concept of myth.

MYTH INDICATES OTHERNESS

As we saw in chapter 1, myth, in its technical and its more casual uses, is a very peculiar notion. There is no broad consensus as to what belongs to the category of myth nor what role myth plays in human life. There seems no stable *content* to the concept of myth. I am arguing that this is not merely the result of incomplete or inadequate analyses of myth; but rather that the meaning of "myth" can only be determined by the work it performs. "Myth" is not a concept in the sense of including definite particulars under its general and abstract rubric; rather, it is a means of functional determination. "Myth" performs the function of indicating what does not belong, what is not our own, what is other. In doing so, it at the same time indicates what does belong, what is our own. This is true of each of the variety ways that "myth" is used. "Myth" is used to identify or indicate that which cannot be considered as belonging to the existential, social, intellectual or historical context of the one identifying what is mythical. We can also say that what is other and what is same is an entirely relative determination depending on the perspective of the analyst. Whatever value is assigned to the mythical, theoreticians of myth and casual users of the term employ 'myth' to designate what is other, what is alien. To say that 'myth' indicates what is other and therefore what belongs, is not the most illuminating claim that can be made, but it is certainly an essential component of understanding myth. When we put this together with the other functions of myth we've discovered, a much more complex, coherent, and adequate account of myth emerges.

Above, we examined the ontological antitheses delineated by the four authors as these became apparent in their discussions of myth. Because the opposed ontological regions are united and separated through the concept of myth, we expect to find that one or the other member of the opposing pair is assumed to be "our own," while the remaining region is assumed to be "other." Whether myth is accorded positive or negative value, each theorist assumes that his own position is nonmythical.

Cassirer claims that his critical philosophy of culture belongs to scientific-theoretical activity, the antithesis of mythical consciousness. Barthes sees himself as the practicing mythologist, one who interrupts the inherent oscillation of mythical signification, restoring proper order to the object-language and the second-order system. As mythologist, Barthes recognizes the historical determination of signification systems, including those at play in his own work. He understands his own writing as political and revolutionary (or at least radicalized), not the depoliticized and conservative speech of myth. Eliade understands our existential position as being historical and profane; and he includes himself in this. We no longer live in a sacred cosmos, no longer live according to myth. That era has passed away, though we may be able to understand and appreciate it. Eliade's description of the mythical is a lament for a lost world and a call to remember it with respect rather than dismiss it as inconsequential. Hillman's work is also a call, but to the future rather than to the past. The suffering of the soul at our moment in history attests to the fact that the archetypal identifications we cling to, the Apollonic and the myth of analysis in particular, have lost their mythic power to transform and have become dead weight for the soul in its journey to completion. Hillman attempts to convince the reader and the practitioners of psychoanalysis that it is a mistake to remain in the realm of the desiccated and defunct images left to us by a passing era which professionalized and secularized the archetypal. We are trapped in the shrouds of moribund archetypes and deadening language; vibrant, living myth lies ahead of us and we must aspire to it.

There is another, and more important, sense in which the concept of myth designates what is same and what is other. And here we must note an essential isomorphism between the function of the concept of myth and the function of those cultural manifestations we call myths. The concept "myth" is used to indicate or identify what is other than the position of the one providing the identification. If we look closely at the examples of what is named as myth, we find that many of these share the same trait. The tales and legends from ancient cultures, the stories told by "primitive" peoples today, many of which would be considered examples of myth, also serve to indicate what is other than the existential position of the one telling the tale or performing the ritual. Stories of the origin of the tribe, totem figures, legends of heroic deeds, explanations of the inception of language or particular subsistence practices: all these serve to identify what belongs to the truly human sphere and what does not, what is other.

The story with which we began this study is a case in point. The Pelasgians told the tale of Eurynome and the inception of the world as an ordered place fit for human habitation out of Chaos. The story tells of the construction of the human abode of sun, moon, earth, and so on, and of the birth of Pelasgus, forebear of the people. This "myth" provided its participants a framework for identifying the human and the other than human. Cosmic order maintained by the various titans and titanesses is the mark of the world for human beings; Chaos is other. Descendants of Pelasgus are full members of the human family; those with another lineage are alien. The story of Eurynome divides existence into opposing spheres (Chaos and Order, the Pelasgians and others, etc.) and identifies which of the opposed spheres belongs to human being proper and which does not.

When we examine theories of myth, we find that it is not only that the concept of myth serves to delineate, through negation, whatever particular *theoretical* position is claimed by each author as his own. The territory indicated as belonging, as opposed to what is alien, is much broader than this. For each of these thinkers, myth distinguishes what is *truly human* and what is other than human. Cassirer may claim that he is doing philosophy of culture; Barthes, semiological analysis; Eliade, philosophy of religion; and Hillman, depth psychology. Whatever each calls his own work, they are all involved in describing human ontology. The core, though most often unarticulated, question in all the works we've examined is: What does it mean to be a human being? And for each thinker, the concept of myth is used to demarcate what is essentially human from what is not. The ontological antitheses mapped by the concept of myth are more than descriptions of the fundamental categories of existence assumed by the authors. Through ontological reduction, each author grants greater existential priority to one region over another, claims this region as the truly human, and eliminates from serious consideration that which cannot be absorbed into the region or order given ontological priority.

The placement of the mythical in each of these theoretical accounts as a gateway between two antithetical ontological regions, along with the use of the reductive method of transforming what is other into more of the same, shows us the means by which the value commitments of each author become translated into the descriptive accounts. Though ostensibly explications of myth and myth-making, these are theories that elaborate or bolster the author's assumptions of the "correct" ontological distinction between what belongs to human being and what does not. The *concept* of myth functions in each case as a boundary between the ontological territory claimed for the truly human and what must remain outside as foreign. When we recognize the ontological and valuational weight accorded to the territory claimed for human being, we can reread these theories of myth as thinly disguised metaphysical positions shot through-and-through with anthropocentric biases: what's most real is what is most human.

There is a value-determined ontological valence apparent in each theory. That is, greater weight is given to certain features of existence; these are considered to have greater reality than other features, are precisely those features that are claimed for the human sphere, and are taken as most valuable. Cassirer claims that his work is to be an examination of culture, an exegesis of symbolic forms for what they can tell us about the constitution of the subjective and objective features of experience. But his analysis of myth makes it quite clear that consciousness holds preeminence and that it is consciousness or Spirit that truly belongs to human being. Material, organic existence cannot be incorporated or allowed equal ontological status in the arena of human being, except insofar as it is symbolically wrought. Cassirer marks as mythical those cultural productions that do not make clear this ontological division and yet are determinative of the division.

"Momentary" gods, for example, are prototypical mythic formations. The momentary god is an indivisible mix of the material and the spiritual. The god is apprehended as a feature of natural processes, that is, of the objective world beyond the ken of human control, and yet the god is spiritual in that it is the product of human creation. At the same time, the momentary god does divide the world into the spiritual and the material by making the distinction between the sacred and the profane.[11] Myth makes the distinction between the spiritual and the material, but it errs in two ways: it does not *know* that it itself creates the distinction and it cuts up the world incorrectly; it does not align the spiritual with the sacred but aligns the material with the sacred. By naming this kind of "mistaken" cultural production as mythical, Cassirer stakes out the territory that must be recuperated and reunited as the true contribution of consciousness and what must be discarded as the trap of substantial determination. The former belongs to human accomplishment and has a greater degree of reality, while the latter is error, a misapprehension, and a means of bondage. Cassirer thus transforms a descriptive distinction between differently constituted ontological regions into a system exhibiting the ontological priority of one region over another, and claims this region of priority as the true habitat of human being. He uses the concept of myth and the method of reductive analysis to determine, delimit, or demarcate what human being is and what belongs to human being as its essential property.

We can see the same process in Barthes' analysis of mythical signification. Myth exhibits itself as the undecidable "alibi" between Nature and History, disguising itself as one or the other in an oscillating manner that blurs the true difference between ontologically distinct regions, thereby allowing the unwary reader of myth to see inevitable conjunctions of signifier and signified where the conjunction is arbitrary and contingent. This fascinating power of mythical signification, especially in the hands of bourgeois ideology, obscures the reality of the historically contingent character of human being. The truly human—unalienated productive labor in its changing forms through history—can be marked in its ontological boundaries by the machinations of myth. Mythical signification, the irreducible mixture of History and Nature, sets the limit between these ontological regions and sets up the possibility for appropriation of one of the regions as that which truly belongs to human being while draining of any value what myth marks as other.

This characteristic function of myth is perhaps most clearly drawn in those theories that castigate myth. But it appears in Eliade's and Hillman's work as well, though in these what is truly valuable for human being cannot be equated with the human condition as it is now. Eliade's analysis is a lament for the condition of human being in the profane or historicized existential position. Again, myth marks the boundary between two antithetical ontological realms, and what belongs to human being is separated from what does not by this paradoxical line of demarcation. What belongs to the human condition is the suffering that attends the terrors of history, the inability to appeal to the cosmogonic moment for relief and surcease. Hence, there is the necessity for creating, within the unfurling of the historical, profane process, a transcendental accompaniment that will ensure that our suffering is neither arbitrary nor meaningless. Eliade's analysis of the mythical is a means of articulating what *was* provided in the sacred ontology through the return to the cosmogonic moment and a means of suggesting how a profane ontology could constitute itself in ways that would allow access to expiation, renewal, and creative freedom. Historical humanity does not have recourse to the sacred ontology, that is determined as on the "other side" of the line of demarcation determined through the irreducible, paradoxical region of myth. Rather, historical human being in its profane or mundane mode of existence must accept the existential risk of the path it has chosen and must find new means of creating self, world, meaning, and order. Here, myth indicates what is assumed to be the truly human sphere: free participation in the cosmogonic moment.

Hillman as well valorizes what lies beyond the line of demarcation posited by the irreducible function of myth. For Hillman the truly human is the transcendental region of *a priori* archetypal configurations. These must remain as other in order for particularized human existence, the present character of human being, to have access to the imaginal, to the fund of representations in the halls of our collective *memoria.* The most valuable aspect of the nature of being human is the necessity for the creative instinct to push toward unification with the incommensurable other. Hillman describes the love involved in transference, the erotic, and the archetype of Dionysus as the means by which the soul defines itself in opposition to the other. But it is also the case that for Hillman what is truly human, the soul as it creates itself, belongs to the realm of the archetypes as opposed to the body. The soul constitutes itself through incorporating archetypal representations. The field of the soul increases as it manages to allow itself full expression of Eros, finally taking into its own sphere the *representations* of bodily, material existence. The otherness of organic, particularized existence cannot be digested by the soul (though the archetype of Dionysus includes this as a feature of its imaginal attributes). Only the imaginal analogues of this ontological region can be so incorporated.

Cassirer claims that mythical symbolic formation, as any other sort of symbolic formation, determines the distinction between the subjective and objective features of existence. Even without his elaborate explanatory machine, we can see that the stories most of us would consider mythical do, at least, distinguish what is considered the truly human from the rest of existence. And we can add to this claim: theories *about* myth and mythmaking serve the same function.

In each of these four accounts, myth serves to demarcate what belongs to human being and what does not. The ontological territory claimed for human being is ringed about with the mythical, a boundary that serves as both means of exclusion and means of inclusion. Myth defines and determines the human in opposition to what cannot be corralled within the mythical border. Precisely *where* mythical demarcation occurs, that is, between which two ontological regions, is determined by the value commitments of those investigating. The value determined ontological valence exhibited in theories of myth not only determines what belongs to human being, but determines which ontological sphere holds the position of preeminence, and which sphere is derivative of the other.

MYTH AND FREEDOM

One more pattern in this theoretical quilt must be traced. It is the most important one, I believe, and concerns the nature of freedom. It is in this that we see most clearly the abiding strength of myth. The four authors offer us a powerful version of the *telos* of human existence as unfettered freedom.

Evident in the work of Cassirer, Barthes, Eliade, and Hillman is the concern with discovering the possibility of complete freedom for human being and the steps necessary to attain and secure such a condition. For each author, myth separates and unites two distinct ontological regions, one of which is valorized as the realm of true freedom and one of which is castigated as continued bondage. But also for each author, freedom itself is marked as other, and, consequently, the concept of freedom exhibited in these theories is bound by myth.

Thus, for each of these authors, freedom for human being, freedom in the strongest and most coveted sense, does not belong to the human condition as it stands. Freedom rings throughout the work of these writers; freedom is the *telos* toward which we strive, and the works are chronicles of the journey toward unmitigated freedom. Each author is arguing for a means of overcoming the confines of human existence. Freedom itself is not considered to be mythical, yet freedom is to be garnered for human life by means of properly identifying the mythical and capturing for human existence a power or attribute guarded by myth. Whether the mythical conceals or reveals true freedom, whether myth is to be embraced or eschewed, it is the threshold that must be crossed in order to obtain complete and unconditioned freedom for the human ontological condition.

Each author claims that understanding myth is a necessary step on the road to freedom, and each author understands freedom as the unlimited creative power on the part of the truly human to constitute itself—as locus of ideal spiritual unity, as historically contingent agent transforming self and world through productive labor, as participating in the creation of human being at the cosmogonic moment, or as soul making itself archetypally. The unlimited power of human being to determine its own constitution implies the correlative freedom of determining the opposed sphere, the world.

An important difference in the theories is whether the author suggests abjuring or embracing myth in order to attain this state of full creative freedom. For Cassirer and Barthes, the mythical must be tamed, or kept outside the range of the truly human, if it cannot be altogether eradicated. The domestication of the mythical proceeds from making quite clear the distinction between what lies within the realm of human being proper and what lies without. This distinction must be bolstered, strengthened, and clearly marked to avoid the continuing bondage to myth's seductive powers. For Eliade and Hillman, the mythical must be mined for the possibilities it holds out for freedom. The divine or sacred character of that which is marked by myth offers hope of our overcoming, through transcendence, the limits of historical, particularized human existence.

Cassirer envisions a world in which the last vestiges of the mythical will have been erased. The result will be the full flowering of scientific-theoretical consciousness in symbolically constituting the reciprocal spheres of the subjective and objective as obverse ideal entities stripped of all dependence on substance (materially or conceptually determined). He also has a political commitment to destroying the vestiges of myth that undercut the rational organization of public life aimed at the good. Cassirer fears that myth will again erupt in political life, as it did earlier in this century in the machinations of the fascist state.[12] Myth is a shadow that continually threatens to blot out the tenuous gains we have made in civilizing our social and political relations. Though the symbolic activity of scientific-theoretical consciousness may finally eliminate myth in its own internal abstractive development, rationality shows itself as quite fragile when faced with the vagaries of economic and social realities. Only by stripping myth of its seductive power can we begin to eliminate it as a destructive force rending our achievements in rationally organizing political life for the good and freedom of all.

Both intellectual freedom and political freedom (the latter is, for Cassirer, a special case of moral or ethical life) are obstructed by the mythical. These correlative commitments reflect Cassirer's deeper value commitment to the absolute freedom of Spirit or consciousness from material constraint and the absolute freedom to create self and world, subjective and objective, through the agency of symbolic activity. Only when there is no recourse to substantial determination will the free creative power of the symbolic activity of consciousness hold sway.

Barthes inveighs against the stultifying effects of bourgeois ideology, which are immensely bolstered by the mythical significations produced in the bourgeois/capitalist economic order.[13] The alliance of the mythical and the bourgeois has absorbed so much into its domain, implies Barthes, that the revolution has all but withered away. If the bourgeois order can succeed in delaying History (by transforming the historical order into an inevitability of Nature), then History cannot move to its next stage, or step any closer toward the free transformation of the world through productive labor unclouded by false consciousness. Mythical signification displaces the contingent, historical origin of events; this is a powerful tool in the hands of the bourgeois/capitalist. On its own, the attempt of bourgeois practices to reify and present the capitalist system as an inevitable outcome of natural rather than historical processes would fail under the pressure of real historical necessity. However, the usurpation of the contemporary modes of dispersion of myth (mass media and instruments of popular and folk culture) by bourgeois ideology threatens the historical progression from capitalism to socialism, threatens the possibility of free productive labor and its attendant social and political forms.

Barthes conceives of freedom as the state of being human in which there is no disguising or erasure of productive labor. Direct human transformation of the world, through labor, must be recognized as the foundation of human reality. Any speech (parole) that distorts this state of affairs is mythical and sets the stage for a usurpation of labor and the subsequent inability to understand one's actions and one's life as political. Barthes obviously desires the complete elimination of depoliticized speech, the prototypical example of which is mythical signification, especially in its contemporary manifestation as the loyal servant of bourgeois ideology.

Myth must be overcome if we are to escape our immersion in a congealed history, a state in which inherent contradictions have been made smooth or erased, as bourgeois mythmaking transforms all in its path into false nature. Myth must be overcome if we are to reinstate the transitive relation of labor or action in/with the world and allow this relation to wend its historical way. Only when the falsely natural has been tamed and lost its persuasive power will the direct transformation of the world through free productive labor so determine our knowledge and consciousness as to eliminate oppression and free human being to take full charge and responsibility of historical progression.

Eliade laments the condition of contemporary humanity, living a profane existence, unable to avert the terrors of historicized, non-sacralized life; unable to expiate the errors and dissolution of existence, as mythical human being does, through a return to the purity of the cosmogonic origin.[14] Modern human being has forfeited the birthright of an absolutely free creativity. Free participation in the cosmogonic moment is denied to "historical," "modern" human being, for we are unable to return to the origin of the constitution of the world and human being. We are constrained to be the endlessly determined products of an endlessly unfurling historical process beyond our knowledge and control. "Sacred" or "archaic" human being had recourse to a return to the creation of the cosmos (including the creation of human being) through myth and ritual. Such a return offered the most complete condition of freedom for humanity: to participate in the creation of the entirety of existence. For Eliade, mythical life provides the pinnacle of the possibility of freedom, while our profane existence is one of bondage.

Eliade's notion of freedom and its relationship to myth is the most impassioned plea we find in these four theories. The historically determined human being cannot be free, for such a being is always subject to the vicissitudes of the arbitrary compulsion of linear, profane temporality.[15] There is no way to undo the past, for the present is the necessary consequence of irrecuperable past events. The best we can hope for is that the actions of the present will determine a future as a less troubling and troubled era. But as the present is always already determined by the past, there seems no way out of the inexorable terrors of history. Eliade's description of sacred existence is of the power to participate in the creation of the cosmos in each of its respects. This is a description of an absolute creative freedom, a freedom unconditioned in any way. When the particular human actor returns to the cosmogonic scene, through myth and ritual, s/he is stripped of all history, all mundane determinations and begins anew as the original human being.

The result of the embrace of the mythical is not a condemnation to the eternal repetition of the playing-out and winding-down of the profane. The result of embracing myth is the ever renewable chance to begin—unconditioned, indeterminable freedom to create. Historical human being is precluded from the most fundamental mode of creative freedom. Where archaic human being could return again and again to the moment of the creation of the cosmos, participating in the absolutely unconditioned creation of all meaningfulness, all order, all space and time, and actively participate in the creation of human being itself, historical human being can only hang on to the slim chance of influencing the process of history in some small way—as a twig may divert the course of a river. This is our only access to creative freedom. Since our ontology is profane rather than sacred, we do not have the means of achieving the unconditional freedom of being human at the creation of the cosmos.

Hillman describes a soul chafed and deformed, shrunken almost out of existence, desiccated, sterile, cut off from its true source of nourishment by a medical and psychoanalytic establishment that cannot abide the identification of its own mythically determined nature. Contemporary translators of the "speech of the soul" seem bent on achieving a minimal health of an adumbrated psyche at the expense of the soul's free and untrammeled expression. Psychology and psychoanalysis attempt to ignore or erase the pain and suffering experienced by the soul as it hurls itself against the bars of its analytic and Apollonic cage. The soul is held captive by the residue of its own activity. The soul's journey toward complete freedom is a chronicle of the articulation, incorporation, and acknowledgment of the mythical determinations of the soul. Myth is the means by which the soul recognizes and appropriates its own constitutive possibilities and therefore myth opens the path to a complete freedom for the soul in its self-creative power.

Like Eliade, Hillman understands the possibility of true creative freedom as the outcome of the embrace of myth. The soul's creation of itself demands the shattering of analytic models and language that constrict the imagination and thwart Eros in its drive to unite with Psyche. Hillman's description of the "Transparent Man"[16] is a description of humanity when it has lost all compulsion to lie, to deny, to conceal, to obstruct its own transcendental nature. Being Transparent, the goal of all soul-making, is a state of freedom from all mundane determinations and conditions. The soul discovers and accepts itself as divinely creative—of itself and as a "prism for the world and the not-world." Participating in the archetypal drama of Eros and Psyche finally means freedom from the particularities of the human condition and the strictures of outmoded *logos*, and the freedom to participate in divine creative acts. Hillman writes:

> Precisely this insight—that neither psyche nor eros can be identified with our souls and our loving—is the upshot of the long discussion. . . . Love starts in the personal and means me; then it means my soul and my whole being. Then it moves me, my soul, and my being into archetypal being, into a sense of interiority; an interior process contained within me, and myself contained within the interiority of a chaotic universe transformed by love into a cosmos.

Here again we have a notion of the *telos* of human existence, a state much valued but not yet achieved. This state is the unconditioned freedom of the soul to create itself, through its own fund of archetypal forms, and in so doing create the world.

☙❦❧

These four conceptions of true freedom are remarkably similar—freedom is the unbounded, indeterminable creative power of human being to constitute itself and, conversely, the world. And they are remarkably similar in locating the conditions for such freedom in breaching the mythical. The fact that the mythical demarcates the truly human ontological sphere means that it also serves as the boundary that must be crossed if the limits of the human condition are to be transformed. Insofar as the mythical presents the boundary of the human condition as the region of ontological priority, it also presents the obstacle or challenge that must be overcome if there is to be some trait of human existence (such as creative freedom) that is limitless. Once again the mythical exhibits its paradoxical nature—now as the limit that discloses the possibility of the limitless, the boundary that separates human being from the boundless, the gateway, hinge, turnstile, or threshold that must be crossed in order to reach the absolutely other, complete freedom rather than our own existential bondage. Myth, whether valorized or denigrated, is the condition of the unconditioned freedom so coveted.

What is it that impels us to secure a condition of complete freedom? What is the "driving force" behind the constructions of culture in general, and myth in particular? Cassirer claims that it is Spirit in its drive to free itself of the constraints of Life that accomplishes symbolic formation of any sort. Barthes' analyses imply that the creative force impelling the constitution of mythical signification is the machinations of a particular historical political-economic interest. Eliade describes the driving force behind mythical organization of the self and world as an ontological desire, a thirst for the real. It is the hierophany, as a kind of Prime Mover, that draws human beings again and again to the site or the moment of the origin of the cosmos. Hillman offers us Eros as the imaginal archetype of the compulsion of the soul to constellate itself as the field of all imaginal activity.

These attributions of the driving force behind the constitution of the mythical seem utterly incompatible. Which is correct? Is it possible to adjudicate among these competing contentions regarding the origin of mythical processes and products? Spirit, History, the hierophany, Eros . . . which of these determine mythical formation, and, by extension, cultural formation in its vast scope? Which is the driving force behind the postulation and determination of the limits of human being, and, conversely, the nonhuman? I think we must finally conclude that the question of which "driving force" directs mythmaking is a dead-end.

The assumption of a driving force behind the constitution of the features of existence in a mythical manner is merely the necessary obverse of the assumption of a *telos* of absolute creative freedom for truly human existence. Each of the four authors takes as the aim of human productive activity the acquisition of the state of unfettered and unconditioned creative power—the power to determine both the subjective and objective features of existence (whatever is believed as belonging to each sphere). If true creative freedom is conceived as the overcoming of the "natural" (however construed) determinations of human being, then it becomes necessary to import an "extra"-natural force that will enable us to hurdle our limits. So, consciousness has the possibility of surmounting our natural embeddedness in organic existence; so, contingent (and therefore malleable) History is the antithesis of the inevitable processes of Nature; so, the return to the hierophany is the means of escaping the terrors and decay of nature's cycles; so, Eros and Dionysus are the imaginal ways to overcome the particularizations of embodied existence.

Each of these methods of explanation is a method for obviating the *natural* conditions of human being. Such obviation demands an extranatural or supernatural impulsion. Only reformulating human existence in terms of some transcendent accomplishment or impulsion can lift human being, as it were, from the conditions that seem to irrevocably determine our existence within a context of natural imperatives, debts, and possibilities.

Each author posits unconditioned creative freedom as of extreme value, as the proper and fulfilling aim of human life, and yet does not find it in human existence as it stands, but only as a possibility jealously guarded by myth. Absolute freedom for human being, an elimination of all forms of determination and an unbounded power of creation is located in the same irreducible, undecidable region as myth. This notion of freedom belongs to the mythical, and as such plays a role in demarcating that which human being claims for itself. But freedom, as the possibility of somehow going beyond the limits determining the human position, undercuts the foundational assumption that human being is self-creative in determining the limits between subjective and objective, self and world, the I and the not-I.

The constitution of the limits of human being through the agency of human processes of creative endeavor is at one and the same time an expression of our *freedom* to create and of our *bondage* to such creation. Insofar as human being determines and delimits its own ontological realm, it forecloses the possibility of unbounded, unlimited extent. If human being is in some respect self-creative, we cannot be mythless and we cannot determine our boundary as boundless, our limits as limitless, our creative construals of human existence as unconditioned.

Human being is, at least in some respects (which we'll examine at greater length in the conclusion), self-creating. As cultural creatures, our creative and productive activities shape our world, and in turn shape ourselves. One important trait of human being in the world is human representation of the boundary between these, and our construal of such limits is mythical. In this sense, mythical determination is inescapable. But it is a poor myth, I believe, that posits the creative process of being human as not subject to conditions, determinations, and demands of the world. I would like to offer an alternative myth, one more consonant with our experience and one offering greater hope for the future.

Conclusion:
The Nature of Culture

Members of the Snohomish Tribe of what is now called the Olympic Peninsula of Washington State, tell the following story:

The Creator and Changer first made the world in the East. Then he slowly came westward, creating as he came. With him he brought many languages, and he gave a different one to each group of people he made.

When he reached Puget Sound, he liked it so well that he decided to go no further. But he had many languages left, so he scattered them all around Puget Sound and to the north. That's why there are so many different Indian languages spoken there.

These people could not talk together, but it happened that none of them were pleased with the way the Creator had made the world. The sky was so low that the tall people bumped their heads against it. Sometimes people would do what was forbidden by climbing up high in the trees and, learning their own words, enter the Sky World.

Finally the wise men of all the different tribes had a meeting to see what they could do about lifting the sky. They agreed that the people should get together and try to push it up higher.

"We can do it," a wise man of the council said, "if we all push at the same time. We will need all the people and all the animals and all the birds when we push."

"How will we know when to push?" asked another of the wise men. "Some of us live in this part of the world, some in another. We don't all speak the same language. How can we get everyone to push at the same time?"

That puzzled the men of the council, but at last one of them suggested that they use a signal. "When the time comes for us to push, when we have everything ready, let someone shout 'Ya-hoh.' That means 'Lift together!' in all our languages."

So the wise men of the council sent the message to all the people and animals and birds and told them on what day they were to lift the sky. Everyone made poles from the giant fir trees to use in pushing against the sky.

The day for the sky lifting came. All the people raised their poles and touched the sky with them. Then the wise men shouted, "Ya-hoh!" Everybody pushed, and the sky moved up a little.

"Ya-hoh," the wise men shouted a second time, and everybody pushed with all his strength. The sky moved a few inches more. "Ya-hoh," all shouted, and pushed as hard as they could push.

They kept on shouting "Ya-hoh" and pushing until the sky was in the place where it is now. Since then, no one has bumped his head against it, and no one has been able to climb into the Sky World.

Now, three hunters had been chasing four elks during all the meetings and did not know about the plan. Just as the people and animals and birds were ready to push the sky up, the three hunters and the four elks came to the place where the earth nearly meets the sky. The elks jumped up into the Sky World, and the hunters ran after them. When the sky was lifted, elks and hunters were lifted too.

In the Sky World they were changed into stars, and at night even now you see them. The three hunters form the handle of the Big Dipper. The middle hunter has his dog with him—now a tiny star. The four elks make up the bowl of the Big Dipper.

Some other people were caught up in the sky in two canoes, three men in each one of them. And a little fish also was on its way up into the Sky World when the people pushed. So all of them had to stay there ever since. The hunters and the little dog, the elk, the little fish, and the men in the two canoes are now stars, even though they once lived on earth.

We still shout "Ya-hoh!" when doing hard work together or lifting something heavy like a canoe. When we say "Hoh!"

all of us use all the strength we have. Our voices have a higher pitch on that part of the word, and we make the o very long— "Ya-hoooooh!"[1]

☙❦☙

We have made ourselves a home; we have made the world a place fit (and fitting) for human habitation. We have carved out a niche where we can live "without bumping our heads." We work, in concert and in resistance, with other natural products and processes, to shape what we find in nature into a human abode. But the sky is now closed to us; this is the price we pay. In creating a space for human being, we not only secure what is within our enclosure, we create a boundary, we draw a line between what is ours and what must remain outside our domain. This boundary may shift—our communal work ("Ya-hooh!") enlarge our range—but a boundary there must be.

Some creatures secrete substances from their bodies, others move into the abandoned abodes of different species. The human organism builds slowly and communally, in the manner of the coral—an accretion of the work of the organism, deposited amidst the currents of the ocean, offering a firm hold against the tide on which we yet depend. We humans create culture—our own environment. What a wondrous work.

I believe Cassirer is writing of this fundamental trait of being human when he claims that in order to know human being we must look to human work, human fashioning, human creation. We must look to, and appreciate, what we have wrought of and in the world. I think that Cassirer is right in this assessment; and I think that he is right in believing that human being is inseparable from cultural activity. What needs radical reappraisal in Cassirer's work is, so to speak, the *nature* of culture.

NATURALISM

As stated in the introduction to this work, my own philosophical home is naturalism. It's time to give a bit of flesh to that position. After outlining this perspective, I will sketch a picture of how culture and myth fit, and also how mythmaking and the theories of myth that we've been examining can be more clearly understood from this perspective.

Naturalism traces its roots to Aristotle, though perhaps only in his non-Christianized form.[2] Spinoza also belongs in the lineage, as do Charles Pierce, George Herbert Mead, and John Herman Randall, Jr., as do John Dewey and William James, in many respects. There is a related, but quite different strain of philosophic inquiry called "naturalism" following W. V. O. Quine's work. Naturalism is not a unified philosophical theory. Its proponents are often at odds with one another, and there is much disagreement as to any positive claims that could be made in its name. There are a few generalizations we can make about the naturalist position, however.

First, and foremost, naturalists refuse to found their metaphysical speculation on any pair of opposing categories. In describing the generic characteristics of whatever is, in whatever way that it is, most philosophers begin with an opposition: Being and becoming; Being and non-Being; appearance and reality; matter and spirit; *res cogitans* and *res extensa*. These metaphysicians often go on either to ignore one of the members of the opposed pair as inaccessible to human inquiry, or to eliminate the opposition by reducing one member to the other as a kind of epiphenomenal excrescence. For example, in one version of the mind/matter dichotomy, we can "prove" that as all sensation occurs within us, we can never prove that there is something without causing that sensation. Instead, we avoid such "illegitimate" assumptions and proclaim that matter itself is an idea (and nothing but).

The philosophical naturalist does not begin in this way. Whatever is, in whatever way that it is,[3] whatever we discover, belongs to "nature." In this way, "nature" is not a category, it is not a term used to distinguish one region of the metaphysical field from another. Randall writes that naturalism:

> can be defined negatively as the refusal to take "nature" or "the natural" as a term of distinction. . . . [Naturalism] is opposed to all dualisms between Nature and another realm of being—to the Greek opposition between Nature and Art, to the medieval contrast of the Natural and the Supernatural, to the empiricist antithesis of Nature and Experience, to the Idealist distinction between Natural and Transcendental, to the fundamental dualism pervading modern thought between Nature and Man.[4]

"Nature" is a locution meant to convey the contention that nothing need be excluded from inquiry, nothing need be closed to scrutiny because it is metaphysically irrelevant, nothing need be ignored because it is nonreal, or irreal, or unreal, or quasi-real.

There is no term to oppose to nature used in this way; it does not function the way most other metaphysical terms function. It does not work to divide whatever is, providing a contrast that can then be used in granting ontological priority to one of the divisions. We neither assert nor predicate anything when "nature" is utilized in this manner. Nor do we accord any honorific status to what is "natural" (as in opposing it to the "artificial"). What we claim is that there is nothing "outside" of nature, nothing excluded from nature, nothing distinct from nature.

This brief gloss on "nature" is not enough to distinguish naturalism as a philosophic position from other positions. One could hold that everything belongs to nature, and then proceed to explain nature in terms of matter in motion, or as physicochemical processes. As a matter of fact, one of the reasons naturalism fell into some disrepute is that it became identified with reductive materialism. With the latter, one could refuse to exclude the products of mentation from the rest of nature, for instance, by claiming that ideas may be understood *as* the firing of neurons. This reduction of nature to one of nature's aspects is anathema to the philosophic naturalist. Neurological activity and ideation are closely linked, of course. But one cannot be reduced to the other: neither is more or less real than the other, both arise in nature, each has its own specific traits, and each has an identifiable integrity. For example, thought seems to be a quite public sort of activity; it is symbolic and communicative. Even "internal" conversation *is* conversation, and is essentially social in character.[5] On the other hand, neurons firing are so private that I have no access whatsoever to my own, and with any luck, nor will any one else. Mentation and neurological function are quite distinct; whatever affinities they may have, they are not identical. That ideation in some respects "depends" on neurological states may be the case (unless we are able to develop thinking machines), but that does not mean that ideation can be *reduced* to brain activity. The human species emerged out of another species, could not exist as it does without this dependence, but we do not say that human being is "nothing but" that of our species' ancestor. Nor would we be content to say that the symphony performed is "nothing but" the score.

All monistic metaphysical systems assert the undivided character of the metaphysical field. Naturalism as well makes a similar claim. In this sense, naturalism could be mistakenly conflated with certain forms of idealism as well as with eliminative materialism; though again, only if we allow the *reduction* of whatever is, in its ontological diversity, to one trait of nature. The idealist claims that the metaphysical field is unified, that there is nothing "outside" of Spirit, or Mind, or consciousness. But idealism, materialism, and all other monisms take the further step in according privilege to certain aspects of the metaphysical field as "more like" the pure expression of the fundamental character of what is. Then whatever is "less like" is accorded the status of epiphenomenon, or accorded a status of somehow "less real." Naturalism refuses to eliminate plurality, it refuses to reduce all of what is to any one region or feature of what is.

In this context, we can say a bit more about "dualistic" metaphysics. Dualisms are, if rigorously maintained, a species of pluralism. But dualisms generally are "mirror-image" monisms. That is, a division of the metaphysical field is postulated, and then we see that, in fact, one of the divisions is considered "more real" than the other, and, most often, the progenitor of the less favored division. For example, Plato, in his *Republic*, has Socrates describe whatever is, in whatever way that it is, as belonging *either* to the visible realm or to the intelligible realm, to the arena of becoming or the arena of Being. Of course, it turns out that the reality of the realm of becoming and everything in that realm owes its existence to the Forms in the intelligible realm. Whatever degree of reality anything has, it has by virtue of its participation in the Forms. On the other hand, a dualism that refuses to employ this maneuver remains a type of pluralism, but it must relegate many traits of the world to an extremely problematic position. For example, a staunch nontheological Cartesian, maintaining the absolute metaphysical distinction between mind and matter, recognizes a plurality of existence. However, the ontological status of *knowledge* of matter, the relation between the two metaphysical realms, then becomes enormously difficult to decipher. (It seems to me that dualist systems present the most impoverished of metaphysical descriptions. The dualist refuses to see both the fundamental unity of existence and the fundamental diversity of existence.)

These two negative characteristics of naturalism, that it is not founded on a metaphysical dualism and that it is not a monism of either the idealist or the materialist stripe, leaves the option that existence is *indefinitely* plural. (We could postulate a definite number of divisions within the metaphysical field—four basic elements, for example. But such systems, I would argue, have the same shortcomings as monistic and dualistic schemes.) That is, within this broadest conception of the metaphysical field, there are many kinds, and many ways of existing.[6] Atoms, ideas, minds, hallucinations, ignorance, chairs, and computers: all are equally natural, and each is available for philosophic consideration. The task of the naturalist philosopher is not to decide which of these has greater reality, or which is "really" real. As naturalists we must admit to ontological parity and eschew granting *ontological* priority of any one over another.[7] We may certainly accord *valuational* priority of one over another, but, I would argue, evil is no more nor no less real than God,[8] whichever we may find of greater interest or value. The task for the naturalist is to investigate the ways in which things exist. This entails, at least, describing the traits coalescing in a unique integrity as well as what relations this integrity has with other unique integrities or nexuses of traits.

This brings us to a third tenet of naturalism, one not as unambiguously shared by proponents of the perspective. Most naturalists believe that as whatever is belongs to nature, there is *a* method of investigating whatever is. This is often identified as the "scientific" method, though the usually narrower conception of this is insufficient for the naturalist. Naturalists see the enormous strides made by scientific inquiry in its more restricted sense. Biology, chemistry, physics, and medicine, for example, have made tremendous strides in furthering human knowledge and improving human lives. As with many other late-nineteenth- and twentieth-century philosophic explanations and schools of thought, naturalism hoped to profit, intellectually, by emulating the kind of inquiry that proved so fruitful in the "natural" sciences. This kind of inquiry can perhaps best be described as controlled manipulation of features of nature, with observation of outcome and application of the results to further contexts of inquiry. This is classic experimental method.

One further condition of scientific inquiry has been very much taken to heart by many naturalists, and here we see the close connection between certain types of naturalism and pragmatism. For the working scientist, "truth" is a functional concept. Something is true if it fosters continued experimentation and inquiry. And it is true only until proven otherwise. I would add, in agreement with Pierce and Mead, and in distinction from James and Dewey, that truth is a function of what Mead calls the "objectivity of perspectives." Truth is contextually bound, but the contexts may be fleeting and transitory, or stable and long-lived. Furthermore, perspectives are social in being created through relations between and among all the constituent members of the perspective, some sentient and some not. This means that truth is also social, or based on some consensus between co-participants in the perspective.[9]

With the rapid advance of scientific knowledge in the past 150 years, we are all quite aware that scientific truths are essentially and irrevocably hypothetical. Science in a stagnant state may lull us into believing that "it has always been thus," but this myopia is impossible with controversies and challenges across the board of scientific canons. This does not mean that we cannot have great confidence in a good deal of what science has discovered. For example, the amount of counter evidence that would have to be amassed to overturn the theory of evolution is almost unimaginable. But it is a hypothesis, one that's tested with every new experiment in embryology and molecular biology. On this view, we may have to admit that the "truth" of a hypothesis is potential or conditional truth, at least until all the results of all possible experiments have been performed.

Scientific method has most often been understood as appropriate only for investigating certain kinds of things, most often spatiotemporally located objects and their attendant processes. Even this may be too broad a description of the scope of science as it is usually understood. A work of art is spatiotemporally located, yet aesthetic experience of such an object appears excluded from the domain of scientific inquiry except perhaps insofar as aesthetic experience is seen as a physiological response and measured as such. But the scientific method of investigating nature is limited in range of applicability only as much as our concept of nature is limited.

William Dennes writes of the methodological principle at the heart of naturalist philosophy:

> There is for naturalism no knowledge except that of the type ordinarily called "scientific." But such knowledge cannot be said to be restricted by its method to any limited field of subject matter—to the exclusion, let us say, of the process called "history" and the "fine arts." For whether a question is about forces "within the atom," or about the distribution of galaxies, or about the qualities and pattern of sound called Beethoven's Second Rasumowski Quartette and the joy some men have found in them—in any case there is no serious way to approach controlled hypotheses as to what the answers should be except by inspection of the relevant evidence and by inductive inference from it.[10]

There have been many ways of naming the naturalistic method: Dewey uses "experimental naturalism," Buchler, "query," James, "radical empiricism," and so on. By and large, however named, the method of naturalism is indefinitely wide in its range. This must be so if the method is applicable to the vast variety of traits of nature. Works of art belong to nature, as do religious dogmas, as do paramecia, as do quarks, as do fear of the unknown, hope for the future and extinct animal species.

How is it that *one* method of human investigation is somehow muscular enough to approach such diversity? Only, I believe, when we come to understand that the "scientific" method, as social and as controlled manipulation, observation, and application to further contexts, is *the* method of human investigation. In other words, it is not that we ought to think of a narrowly conceived method of scientific inquiry as the only legitimate avenue to knowledge of the world. Physicists, chemists, and others, employ the only kind of knowledge seeking process that human beings engage in, but they apply this to a quite narrow range of objects. Professionalized scientific endeavor is a species of human inquiry, sharing in the generic properties of human inquiry, but applied to a specific range of nature's features. It is incorrect, I believe, to identify the narrowly scientific with the range of "true" human knowledge seeking, while discarding other means of controlled inquiry as irrelevant and something other than the means to knowledge of nature. Writing a play, trying out a new recipe, traveling to a foreign country, contemplating the heavens, falling in love, all are, in some respect, social and all seem to include, in some way or another, manipulation, observation, and application. All seem, in some respect, to provide hypotheses then tested or testable.

I do not intend to offer a full-fledged epistemological theory here. What I would like to suggest is that much of human activity is creative in the sense of shaping features of nature, acquiescing in how these respond to our work, and then using what we have discovered to shape again. We may squeeze clay, bring together ideas, dissect frogs, glance at a stranger—in any case, we are manipulating features of nature. The clay may resist, the ideas harmonize, the nervous system be exposed, the glance returned. Then the clay is pulled, a sentence written, the musculature exposed, a quick smile given. I would hesitate to say (following Dewey) that these are all situations of problem solving or of overcoming obstacles; I may just enjoy the silky feel of moist clay or a subtle flirtation.[11] But I would suggest that all of the situations described are instances of natural investigation.

If we use this broad conception of the "naturalistic method" then we can see that any philosophic method itself belongs to nature;

that the naturalist cannot pretend to a method of investigation that is not itself an integral part of the field of investigation. The naturalistic method cannot be thought of as "objective" in the sense of transcending the particulars of the contexts of inquiry. The naturalistic method must admit that, as itself a strand or trait of nature, it is inevitably constitutive of the things investigated. This does *not* mean that the objects of human inquiry are "subjective" in the sense of not given by nature, but provided by mind. But it does mean that the act of investigation is as real and as creative of the context constitutive of any object, as any other relations the object of inquiry may have.

Furthermore, this recognition of philosophic method as a constituent trait of what is investigated does not mean that we can never have knowledge of nature because we are always viewing it through the veil of human experience. As Sterling Lamprecht writes, nature "may of course be, and probably always is, much more than it is empirically found to be. But the point of the argument is that everything is at least what it is given as in experience."[12] For example, however I investigate a painting, whether I analyze the chemical properties of pigment to determine the age of the work or contemplate the play of light and dark on its surface, I can admit that at least one of the paintings salient features is its interest to an observer. And this, in turn, allows us to acknowledge that aesthetic appreciation, as a kind of investigation, is a real feature of nature—not something imposed by human consciousness on an unaesthetic world. And, aesthetic appreciation of the work is as much a real feature of the painting and its context of relations as is the painting's provenance and its physical properties. None of these may be excluded from the reality of the work.

Naturalism is a metaphysical *hypothesis.* According to its own ground rules, its truth is conditional and provisional. Its assumptions must be tested in many contexts, and only its efficacy in furthering inquiry justifies our holding it as a hypothesis. I would like to suggest that naturalism offers us interesting and important insights on culture and mythmaking.

ↀ

Before we move on to culture and mythmaking as seen from the perspective of the naturalist's metaphysical hypothesis, we can draw in the work of Cassirer, Barthes, Eliade, and Hillman, to see where their contentions on the nature of myth might fit in the territory claimed by naturalism. Some accommodation is possible between these theories and the naturalist perspective, and we can only gain from seeing how we might do this.

The work of Cassirer, Barthes, Eliade, and Hillman exhibit a widespread tendency in philosophic inquiry—to predicate and ground metaphysical assumptions and perspectives from the vantage point of human being. This in itself is not entirely problematic. Randall offers a persuasive (and radicalized and naturalized Kantian) argument that insofar as it is human beings who investigate the metaphysical properties of existence, we have the responsibility to include the process of inquiry and articulation as co-gredient with the other properties and characteristics investigated.[13] But Randall's understanding of the necessity for including the contribution of the inquirers in the general picture developed as a metaphysical stance— and this does not mean that metaphysics is irredeemably "relative" or "subjective"—does not demand giving priority (ontological, logical, constitutive, or valuational) to the inquirer. The four authors under consideration bring to bear inarticulate axiological commitments as the determinants of the entire metaphysical scheme. Human beings certainly see and understand the world in human ways, but this does not immediately translate into a claim that therefore human being is the most important feature of the world, or in extreme instances, the only *real* feature of the world.

Cassirer, Barthes, Eliade, and Hillman also bring undefended notions of the truly human into the metaphysical scheme and grant these ontological priority. So, there is a twofold surreptitious importation of specific values into the articulation of the metaphysical scheme: the superior value of human being (over every other kind of being), and an idiosyncratically determined most valuable feature of human being as synonymous with the entirety of the truly human. To complete the picture, the authors posit a *telos* of greatest separation between the truly human region and the "rest" of what is. This is given the honorific title of "freedom," and we may be seduced by our own commitments to freedom.

The problem with coming to understand and identify human being in this manner is *not* that values are drawn into the metaphysical investigations or the metaphysical schemes. Values are, and are in important ways, in nature and in human endeavor and accomplishment; and therefore values must claim a significant place in an adequate metaphysics. The inextricable relation of value and metaphysical field is much too intricate to elaborate here. However, we can at least hope that the values held as essential by an author are made overt. For example, Cassirer takes as the most general description of existence its division into two antithetical and indefatigably opposed ontological regions—Spirit and Nature. From this originary metaphysical condition flow all other traits of existence. But the originary difference proposed by Cassirer (in subtle and often hidden ways) is a metaphysical distinction and description driven by his commitment to human being as Spirit. The process and project of culture is then traced from this originary distinction through all the means by which consciousness (the individual appropriation of Spirit) makes more and more distinct the "real" metaphysical difference between itself and Nature. In this way, Cassirer masks his commitment to understanding human being as purely spiritual functioning by devising a metaphysical scheme that will allow for the outcome he desires. And we can certainly trace the same sort of pattern in the reconstructions of the most general features of existence as these provide the results desired by Barthes, Eliade, and Hillman.

The most interesting feature of this kind of metaphysical reconstruction is that if the value commitments of the author were made overt and taken seriously into account, the author would have to admit that value does not belong strictly to the human realm but that value is a feature of existence as such. However, once this is admitted, the ontological priority of human being (as the progenitor of value) is undercut and the absolute distinction between human being and whatever is considered to lie outside of, or in metaphysical opposition to, this being, can no longer be held. Human being then returns to its location, its continuities and contrasts with other features of the metaphysical field. The ontological duality that was postulated and devised as a screen for ontological priority dissolves, and metaphysical plurality reasserts itself. Thus we may return to our metaphysical hypothesis of pluralistic naturalism.

NATURE AND CULTURE

What does the naturalist perspective give us in terms of our examination of culture? How is the naturalist perspective conducive to understanding more fully the role of myth in human life? What I hope to convey is, first, a sense of human being squarely within the larger expanse of nature, and of human activity as discovery and creation within nature. Human nature is not opposed to Nature, it nests within nature.[14] Understanding human being is a matter of recognizing the continuities human life may have with other natural processes, as well as the discontinuities we may find. Both continuities and discontinuities are many and varied—nature is indefinitely plural. Second, naturalism disallows a metaphysical distinction between culture (with mythmaking as a species of cultural activity) and nature. Culture, as a natural product of a natural activity of a natural creature, itself rests within nature. Third, not only is culture not irrevocably divorced from nature, but because the naturalist perspective admits the essential plurality of nature, we cannot reduce culture to some other aspect of nature. That means, for example, that however intimately related our complex nervous system may be to the products and processes of culture, we cannot reduce culture to biology or neurophysical life. Fourth, the "realist" naturalist insists on the resistance of nature to much of human endeavor; there are "brute" aspects of nature to which we must acquiesce. This is not to suggest a necessarily passive position of human being vis-à-vis nature; but if clay did not resist our attempts to shape it, we could never fashion a pot, we would always end up with a puddle of viscous fluid. What this implies is that human interaction with other natural processes and products is social—there are both transitory and stable resistances with which we interact. Lastly, human existence, in many respects, is social existence "intra"-species, as well. We are born into a social group, and our identity is in large part shaped by the relations holding between and among the members.[15]

In investigating the nature of culture, and its specification in mythmaking, we can follow two main avenues. One is recognizing that human being as cultural being emerges out of biological existence. Needless to say, this does not mean that culture can be reduced to biology. But in terms of the emergence of traits of nature, culture seems "closer," or more intimately and obviously connected to our biological traits than to our traits as physical objects, for example, or as conglomerations of chemical processes. In fact, I will argue that humans as social creatures arise out of biological existence, and that culture is the product of human beings insofar as we are social organisms. Our second avenue of investigation is in resuscitating the idea of human nature as, in part, self-creative nature. We will reexamine the notion of the *telos* of human existence as unbounded creative freedom to constitute both the subjective and objective features of the world. There is an important insight in this contention, I believe, but only if we relocate human creativity within the context of nature.

Nature, as at least, but not exclusively, an indefinitely complex arena for the activity of organisms, provides an incredible variety of opportunity. Jacob von Uexküll, as noted by Cassirer,[16] claims that for every kind of creature there is a corresponding "world." There is a "fly-world," a "horse-world," an "amoeba world." He seems partly correct in this. The world, or to use a less contentious and less ambiguous word, the environment, of each kind of organism is determined in mutual relations of constitution. It is not only the case that sunlight (or something much like it) is necessary for the appearance of chlorophyllic plant life. That there are chlorophyllic organisms determines sunlight as a source of direct food production. This property of sunlight (and therefore of the environment) does not emerge until an organism with a compatible and reciprocal trait emerges. Plant life selects and coaxes into the environment features and traits that are peculiar to the ongoing process of the plant and its environment. The plant-environment also includes such creatures as use plants for food. The plant is selected as an essential feature of its predator's environment insofar as the seeds of the plant are not destroyed by the digestive processes of the animal and insofar as it can use the predator's dung as germinating material. The implication of von Uexküll's description is that there are mutually exclusive worlds. I would suggest that the various environments, determined by the variety of organisms, overlap in essential ways. The environments of the fly, the horse, and the oat grass all include dung as an important feature of the individual environments. However, it does seem the case that the adaptability (or the spread and scope) of most organisms is fairly circumscribed while the variety of overlapping environments appears indefinitely complex.

The indefinite complexity of environment is nowhere more apparent than in the environment of human being. As far as we can tell, the human creature is the only creature for whom the environment is so generally porous or plastic. This trait of the human natural context is a result of the mutually determinative processes of the organism and the environment, as must be the case for the relationship that holds for any creature. Every organism shapes its environment in specific ways and the human organism etches its environment through its activity. What seems peculiar to the human process is that human beings produce as well as reproduce. The production of tools, images, judgments, rituals, and so on, are no less intrinsic to human activity than is reproduction of the species. Moreover, human beings are extremely prolific creatures. The environment for human beings, always a "human-world" in the same way there is a "fly-world" for that organism, has become more and more a human environment, nature is increasingly transformed by human endeavor. Our landscapes, our atmosphere, the objects around us, the animals and plants we encounter, the objects of our intellectual curiosity are more and more the products of human invention and fashioning in concert with nature. This production augments or diminishes certain features of nature, which in turn, in interaction, varies the shape and limits of the human process. This is merely a recognition of the mutual constitution of organism and environment.

We may call the specific environment of human being "culture." As the environment of human being, culture is the product of the mutual adaptation of the organism and the wider natural sphere. It is only within the environmental context of culture that we can speak of a human process at all, just as no other organism can be completely dissociated from its environment. Culture is the medium of human existence—the medium in two senses of the term. Culture is the supporting context of human existence, and culture is the means by which and through which we create in specifically human ways. We've been examining a naturalistic notion of culture in the first of these senses, we now turn to a notion of culture as medium, or means. For this, we can expand George Herbert Mead's insights on the relation of a self to the social organism.

CULTURE AS THE INTERPRETIVE GESTURES
OF THE SOCIAL ORGANISM

Sociality, according to Mead, is an attribute of all adjustment to changing conditions. Emergence of novelty of any sort, any occasion of transition from an old system or state to a new one is a social process.[17] Sociality is a fundamental trait of all emergent existence and this trait is expressed in *human* existence in the evolution of the self, mind, community, perception, and consciousness out of conditions void of these traits. As in any evolution, what evolves is dependent on, but not reducible to, that out of which it emerges.

According to Mead, any individual organism adjusts to changes in its environment. These acts are social in that adjustment is always mutual adjustment of the organism and its context. Out of this biotic context, social organisms evolve out of individual existence as further adjustment to an increasingly varied environment. The individual organism is now first and foremost "part" of a social organism and its behavior can only be accounted for in the context of the behavior of the social organism. The development of highly sensitive central nervous systems allows for finer modulation of the behavior of the social organism as it interacts with its environment. The actions of members of the social organism become features of the burgeoning environment (i.e., become stimuli calling out for response). This is the emergence of gesture or communication. There is coordination of the behavior of the social organism in the accomplishment of its social acts through the response of one "part" of the social organism to the behavior of other "parts." The gesture may be vocal or may be specific movements of the limbs or facial configurations. In any of these the primary function of the gesture is the unification of the organism as it performs a complex task. The societal organism "speaks" to itself in the taking up of the communal gestures by the members of the community.

Mead describes the gesture, at the level of its *significant* functioning in human communication, as the calling out in the gesturer the same response as that called out in others; the gestures that a part of the social organism takes up and uses to indicate the role to be played *by* the one using the gesture, *to* the one using the gesture.[18] A significant gesture is one that is not only a response to another but a stimulus to the gesturing organism. It appears that only the human central nervous system is so sensitive to its environment that the organism's own indicative gestures are features of the environment as stimuli to which the organism responds.

Mead assumes that the basic unit for inquiry in philosophical anthropology is a social rather than an individual unit. The picture that this affords of the complex organism (organization) of the social unit is the coordination of the various parts or roles that must be accomplished if the organism is to survive. We can broaden Mead's account of the small social unit (tribe or clan, perhaps) to that of the human process as such. The "as such" means the human process, through its entire temporal span. We can also broaden his notion of the gesture to that of culture as such, again the "as such" meaning the entire span of the process of human being organizing itself and its constitutive/constituting members into a coherent activity of mutual adaptation to/with its environment. The image to be drawn is one of the human process itself as an organic whole interacting with its environment and in this interaction and mutual determination shaping both the organism and the "providingness" we call nature.[19] The human process, at least in one of its respects, is the unbroken chain of organic existence stretching from its inception or evolutionary specification through its wide but still unified organization up to and including its present manifestations. If the human process is considered in its integrity in this light, as a vast organism (in temporal, spatial, and varietal terms), in which individuated human agents take a role that is both active and passive, then we can begin to understand the notion of a naturalistic philosophy of culture as the investigation of the gestures used by the human social organism in determining itself, and interpreting and shaping its environment.[20]

Culture is the agglomeration of products, results of the interaction of the human social organism with its environment, and the means by which this organism discovers, defines, and determines itself and its world. The cultural process is a process of interpretation, which must be understood with the emphasis on "inter-," with its necessary connotations of "between," "mutual," "reciprocal." Interpretation always entails more than the imposition of either the interpreter or the interpreted on the other. Interpretation is a process that prevails between the human social organism and the products of natural (including human) processes found, discovered, and constructed. Interpretation is a means of both separating and uniting the human organism and its wider natural environment.

Dewey calls this process one of "experience," with the caveat that experience must be understood as "'double-barreled' in that it recognizes in its primary integrity no division between act and material, subject and object, but contains them both in an unanalyzable totality."[21] Experience is the region of undecidability out of which the human organism determines itself and its world. Later in his career, Dewey was to drop the use of the term 'experience' in describing this irreducible region, thinking that 'experience' carries too much privatized freight to ever be understood except as having its location somehow within an already constituted subjective sphere. The British psychoanalyst, D. W. Winnicott, however, does use 'experience' in precisely the way that Dewey originally imagined it. As a matter of fact, Winnicott uses the term interchangeably with the one chosen as a substitute by Dewey—'culture'.[22]

Interpretation, experience, culture all refer to that which cannot be reduced to either the subjective or the objective, which refers to both and neither of these, and which allows for the possibility of either arising. Culture is the region of undecidability that both separates and unites the human organism and its natural environment. Winnicott writes of this as "potential space," as the arena of experience, and as the region of the creative.[23] Culture is the potential space in which paradoxical "objects" emerge, objects of which we cannot decide, as observers or participants, their status as discovered or created. Winnicott claims that for *human* life to occur, the paradox must remain unresolved. Culture is the space in which features of existence appear that are neither subjective nor objective, but irreducibly both and neither, irreducibly both discovered and created. If the paradox is resolved into one or the other of these positions, the cultural space or the space of experience disappears, the field of creativity dries up, leaving either things-in-themselves absolutely beyond the range of human ken or "subjective objects" entirely determined by instinctual desires or ego projections. When the space of culture, creativity, or experience disappears through the resolution of the paradoxical character of what is discovered/created, either the world is reduced to hallucinations and dream projections or the self is reduced to compliance to the demands of an external reality.[24]

⊛⊛

Cassirer is correct in claiming that an investigation of the nature of human being must find its locus in an investigation of culture; but he is incorrect in importing a transcendent notion of Spirit or consciousness as a necessary progenitor of culture. To make a tool for planting seeds is certainly a cultural activity. It is the fashioning of the found world; it is a creation and discovery of an aspect or feature of nature that exhibits meaning and value. Finding or locating value in the world and intensifying this value by removing extraneous elements (cutting the twigs off a branch in order to bring forth its value as a digging tool); adding to its value (giving it a name that can be used when the tool is on the other side of the field); augmenting its value (through repeated use and finally handing the tool down to a daughter for her ease in planting); destroying its value (burning the digging tool when the planting season has ended)—all these are cultural activities, all depend on the discovery and creation of meaning and value. Through such activities the world and human being gain shape, in mutual determination. None of these activities demands the incorporation of an extraneous, transcendent element; nor do we see any evidence of Spirit or consciousness creating its own means of distancing itself from its own material, organic, biological matrix.

As a matter of fact, it appears that cultural activity of most sorts ties us firmly to the earth, to the processes and products of nature. To gaze at the Parthenon is to open oneself to meanings that human being has wrought, with the earth, through centuries of lives. To discover the value that long-ago human being had unearthed is to remind ourselves that the human process is a living process, subject to all the vicissitudes of life, and death. The human process is a living process within the changing features and fortunes of the wider natural processes that in concert with human finding and making have constituted our home on earth. Agriculture, architecture, painting, music, science, language: all of these are found, all of these are created. All are aspects of culture, all are transformations of the providingness of nature: soil and seed, stone, pigment and canvas, sounds and rhythms, the regularities of existence, our vocal cords and social groupings. The paradox must remain unresolved if we are to have truly human, truly cultural existence.

THE SOCIAL ORGANISM AND THE SELF

The gesture is the way the human social organism talks to itself, telling itself about the salient features of its environment, and providing the roles to be played by the parts of the larger organism. For Mead, the self, as an individuated agent—what we generally conceive of as the individual human being—is constituted through the use of significant gestures.

Though Mead defines significant gestures as those to which the gesturing organism itself responds, the response (or meaning) is not necessarily the same as those of the other participants. Similar response within a social act constitutes "universality" of meaning; and this may be accomplished between two individuals or among many. This occurs when the gesturer takes up the attitude (tendency to respond in a particular way) of the other as the gesturer's response to his/her own gesture.

Social activity of the most finely calibrated kind occurs when the members of the social organism are able to adopt an "objective" or "impersonal" attitude toward their own behavior. That is, a participant in the social act can respond to (i.e., modify, elaborate, or eliminate) her/his own behavior from the point of view of the social organism and its aim. This is the emergence of self-consciousness. Consciousness of being a self arises out of universality of significant communicative activity. The individual anticipates the responses of others to his/her own gestures, and in this anticipation takes on the attitudes of the other participants in the social act. Self-consciousness is a highly sensitive response of the organism to its environment. Not only are its own indicative gestures parts of its environment as stimuli, but the gesturing organism itself, as a unified locus of behavior, becomes part of the welter of stimuli to which the organism responds.

The import of Mead's explanation is that the individual human agent, insofar as that agent is a self, is a product of the society of which s/he is a part, while at the same time, and in mutual constitution, determines its social matrix in essential ways. The society is prior for Mead, both logically and temporally. The individual is constituted through the taking up of gestures formulated by the society as a means of managing the various positions the organism (the society) must take in ensuring its survival.

Again, we can expand Mead's hypotheses. Human beings, as strictly individuated agents, do not create culture. If we *can* speak of causal determination in this regard, culture creates human beings. Culture provides the conditions for individuated agents, whatever we take the boundaries and scope of the individuated to be. There is no individual prior to enculturation. Culture provides the means by which the individual becomes articulate. This is articulation in both senses of the term: in the sense of individuated and in the sense of capable of discerning, discriminating, and reporting individuation—whether of the self or of the world. All the features of what we call the subjective are predicated on the efficacy of culture. The subjective sphere is a product of the social organism in that culture provides the personal pronoun around which certain features of experience are constellated. Culture provides the means in which and by which publicly accessible and shareable features of existence are discovered and constructed; the exhibition of such features are used as a gauge to what does not belong to the public, and therefore located in the private sphere.

One essential strand of cultural activity is the discovery and creation of the boundary of human being as such, whatever the range and scope of this being may be. It is this function of culture that I am identifying as myth-making.

RE-ENVISIONING MYTH AND FREEDOM

The paradoxical character of all cultural activity is the generic feature of which we found the specific in our investigation of mythical production. Mythmaking is an essential strand of the cultural process, a pervasive trait of the process of the human organism in determining itself and its environment. Mythmaking is a type of interpretation, a finding and creating of meaning and value. But this is an interpretation of a specific feature of the human process—the scope and limit of being human. Myth stakes out, as it were, the region of human being, not necessarily only in opposition to the nonhuman, but also in concert.

Mythmaking is a gestural activity, as is all cultural production. Myths are the gestures by which the human organism depicts its own range and its own limits. In this sense, myth is the prototypical cultural product, serving as the backbone or spine of significant cultural formation. The limits of the truly human may be discovered or created as so "spacious" as to include in its scope the entirety of the social organism from the moment of its evolutionary specification. The limits may be discovered or created in as narrow a fashion as to include only the internal, necessarily private experience of self-consciousness acknowledging its own reflective capacity. The freedom inherent in being human is exhibited through the many ways and the variety of spread and scope accorded the designation of the truly human. It is this creative freedom that we investigate when we examine myth and mythmaking.

I have argued that Cassirer, Barthes, Eliade, and Hillman themselves engage in the process of mythmaking. The accounts contribute, mythically, to our understanding of what it is to be human. The myth exhibited in the work of these authors is manyfold. One of the features of their common myth is the conception of contemporary humanity, at least in its more "sophisticated," intellectual form, as mythless. Another aspect of this theoretical myth is that human being, or what is *truly* human, must be divorced—entirely—from all other ontological regions; that, in fact, the integrity and identity of human being can be determined only through discontinuity with the natural and the mundane. We can add to this the authors' commitments to the ontological priority granted to the human sphere. Only by standing alone can human being be truly human. The corollary to this is that human being can escape the responsibilities inherent in the self-creative power of being human. This is the implicit promise of predicating the truly human on the achievement of an absolute creative freedom that is unconditioned, unconstrained, undetermined, and illimitable.

But the freedom of creation exhibited by mythical and other cultural activity cannot be understood as unbounded and unconditioned. Human being is constrained by biological, chemical, and physical imperatives. We cannot be reduced to these, but the claims of these imperatives must be heeded. We are also constrained by valuational imperatives, which are no less real, no less objective, no less demanding than any other imperative discovered and created. However we construe human being, such creation must occur within a context of constraint and providingness. In this, human creation is no different from any other sort of creation. The painter, no matter what level of genius, must work with materials found in the world, must make a work available to visual perception, must take into account the varying values of color, tone, texture, contrast, rhythm, and intensity. A reorganization of these features of nature (including the painter's own eye for detail and shape, interest in narrative, etc.) is a work of creation. The freedom of the painter does not lie in refusing to paint, refusing to give new shape to what s/he finds in the world. To refuse to give definition, set limits, provide and accept boundaries and specifications for painterly provisions is to refuse the act of creation.

The alliance of human self-creative power, a power exhibited and manifested through mythical and cultural processes and products, with a notion of unbounded creative freedom reveals a contradiction that is impossible to overcome. The very notion of creativity (of whatever sort) entails the process of determining, discovering, discerning, and constructing boundaries and limits. The attempt to create human being as the sort of being with *no* limits or boundaries makes as much sense as attempting to create a sculpture that has no shape. The project of construing human being as the sort of being that can create itself in such a way as to ultimately overcome the determinations that it itself provides is a project that ultimately is bankrupt.

The refusal to accept and create the constraints of human being, the refusal to accept the act of self-creation as always the act of limitation is a refusal of the responsibility of the creative process of human determination. To embrace an ideal of complete freedom from all constraints and imperatives is to refuse to create human being.

The study of myth provides wonderful evidence for the claim that human being is self-creative being. Human being, in concert with the world, creates and discovers its own possibilities and actualities, its own range, scope, and limits. But as artistic creation necessarily entails what is found in the world as well as what is transformed of the world and the creator, with the products of the creative act remaining in the world as repositories and commemoration of created and discovered material, meaning, and value, so self-creation of human being need not appeal to extranatural or extracultural functions that are divorced from all other processes and features of nature. In order to rehabilitate the notion of self-creative freedom for human being, maintain an understanding of the necessity of myth in the constitution of human being, and avoid the bankrupt schemes we've examined, we must place the entire discussion of mythical (*self*-creative) constitution within the ongoing processes of culture and within the ongoing processes of nature.

⊚Ϯ⊚

Analyses of mythmaking participate in the constitution of the fluctuating determinations of the human process, as do myth and mythmaking, as do analyses of theories of mythmaking. Insofar as my own inquiry attaches itself to and ramifies the original cultural formations we call mythic, it is adding to the exhibitive power of myth in construing the bounds of determinateness of the human process. The exercise of focusing on the horizon of human existence, the boundary conditions of what it means to be human, is an exercise at one and the same time in discovering and constructing these boundary conditions. If the human creature is the sort of creature that has great leeway in determining its spread and scope in the larger natural processes, and if it is through the products of mythical and cultural processes that the determinateness becomes the determination of human being, then philosophical inquiry into these processes is a further act of mythmaking.

There is an insight found early in our Western history, at least as early as Plato's *Republic*: We cannot escape the necessity of mythical determination, but justice and wisdom demand that we choose or construct our myths carefully. This is both the freedom and the responsibility of being human.

Notes

INTRODUCTION

1. "The Pelasgian Creation Myth," collected in *The Greek Myths: 1*, ed. Robert Graves (Baltimore: Penguin, 1955), 27.

2. Plato's *The Republic*, trans. B. Jowett (New York: Vintage), book IX, lines 614–21.

3. W. V. O. Quine, "Ontological Relativity," in *Ontological Relativity and Other Essays* (New York: Columbia University Press, 1969), 27.

4. Margaret Atwood, *You are Happy* (New York: Harper & Row, 1974), 45–70.

5. See especially, Estella Lauter, *Women as Mythmakers: Poetry and Visual Art by Twentieth-Century Women* (Bloomington: Indiana University Press, 1984), chapter 3.

6. Catherine Keller, *From a Broken Web: Separation, Sexism, and Self* (Boston: Beacon Press, 1986), 5–6.

7. The variety of forms cannot be understood as constituting some sort of linear progression of cultural achievement—art, religion, language, science do not give way to one another; each remains a coherent and legitimate avenue toward freedom.

8. For a concise description of this method of understanding the constitution of the "self," see A. T. Nuyen's essay, "The Fragility of the Self: From Bundle Theory to Deconstruction," *The Journal of Speculative Philosophy* 6.2 (1992): 111–22. Of course, Lacan and Derrida would sharply disagree with Cassirer's ascription of formative power to consciousness or Spirit. However, the "poststructuralist" analysis of language shows many other formal agreements with Cassirer's analysis of the nature of language.

9. J.H. Randall, Jr., *Nature and Historical Experience: Essays in Naturalism and in the Theory of History* (New York: Columbia University Press, 1958), 12.

1. WHAT IS MYTH?

1. James M. McPherson, "The Art of Abraham Lincoln," *New York Review of Books* 39.13 (16 July 1992).

2. Collected in *American Indian Myths and Legends*, ed. Richard Erdoes and Alfonso Ortiz (New York: Pantheon, 1984), 14–15.

3. Northrup Frye, *Anatomy of Criticism* (Princeton: Princeton University Press, 1957).

4. Edith Hamilton, *Mythology* (New York: Mentor, 1953), 14.

5. Sir James Frazer, *The Golden Bough* (abridged), ed. Theodor Gaster (New York: Mentor, 1964), author's introduction.

6. Ibid., 738.

7. G. S. Kirk, "On Defining Myths," *Phronesis: A Journal for Ancient Philosophy*, suppl. vol. 1 (1973): 61–69.

8. Lauri Honko, "The Problem of Defining Myth," in *The Myth of the State*, ed. Haralds Biezais (Stockholm: Scripta Instituti Donneriani Aboensis, 1972), 7–19.

9. William Bascom, "The Forms of Folklore: Prose Narratives," *Journal of American Folklore* 78 (1965): 3–20.

10. The three-way argument among Peter Winch, E. E. Evans-Pritchard, and Alasdair MacIntyre is an interesting example of this sort of debate. See Peter Winch, "Understanding a Primitive Society," in *Understanding and Social Inquiry*, ed. Fred R. Dallmayr and Thomas A. McCarthy (Notre Dame: University of Notre Dame Press, 1977), 159–88.

11. Joseph Campbell, "Mythical Themes in Creative Literature and Art," in *Myths, Dreams, and Religion*, ed. Joseph Campbell (New York: E. P. Dutton, 1970), 138–75.

12. Ibid.

13. Bronislaw Malinowski, *Magic, Science, and Religion and Other Essays* (Garden City, NY: Doubleday Anchor, 1954), 83.

14. Ibid., 101.

15. Claude Lévi-Strauss, *The Raw and the Cooked: Introduction to a Science of Mythology*, trans. John and Doreen Weightman (New York: Harper, 1969), 1–34.

16. Ibid., 6–9.

17. Claude Lévi-Strauss, *The Elementary Structures of Kinship*, trans. James Harle Bell and Richard von Sturmer, ed. Rodney Needham (Boston: Beacon Press, 1969); and *Tristes Tropiques*, trans. John and Doreen Weightman (New York: Atheneum, 1975).

18. Claude Lévi-Strauss, "The Structural Study of Myth," in *Structural Anthropology*, trans. Claire Jacobson and Brooke Grundfest Schoepf (New York: Basic Books, 1963), 206–31.

19. Ibid., 209.

20. Hans Blumenberg, *Work on Myth*, trans. Robert M. Wallace (Cambridge, MA: MIT Press, 1985).

21. Ibid., 5.

22. Ibid.

23. Ibid., 12.

24. Ibid., 21.

25. Ibid., part 5.

26. Ibid., 34.

27. Estella Lauter, *Women as Mythmakers: Poetry and Visual Art by Twentieth-Century Women* (Bloomington: Indiana University Press, 1984).

28. Paul Ricouer, *The Symbolism of Evil*, trans. Emerson Buchanan (Boston: Beacon Press, 1969), 10–11.

29. Ibid., esp. 161–64.

30. The examples I cite here are all taken from a normal daily reading of the *New York Times* over a period of several months in 1988.

31. Walter Gropius, *Bauhaus: 1919–1928*, trans. P. Morton Shand (New York: The Museum of Modern Art, 1937). Reprinted in *Paths to the Present*, ed. Eugen Weber (New York: Dodd, Mead and Co., 1960), 321–30.

2. ERNST CASSIRER'S THEORY OF MYTHICAL SYMBOLS

1. Ernst Cassirer, *Mythical Thought*, vol. 2 of *The Philosophy of Symbolic Forms*, trans. Ralph Manheim (New Haven: Yale University Press, 1955; rpt. 1971), xiii.

2. Ibid., xiv.

3. Ibid., xv.

4. Ibid., xvi.

5. Ibid., xvii.

6. Ibid.

7. Ernst Cassirer, *The Myth of the State* (New Haven: Yale University Press, 1946; rpt. 1970), chapter 18.

8. Ibid., 297.

9. Ibid., 296.

10. Ernst Cassirer, esp. "Critical Idealism as a Philosophy of Culture" (1936), in *Symbol, Myth, and Culture*, ed. Donald Phillip Verene (New Haven: Yale University Press, 1979), 64–91.

11. Cassirer claims for his own the task of articulating the "purely functional unity" of knowledge, to gather into a systematic whole the various branches of scientific inquiry and the concomitant variety of methodologies. According to his description of the development of theoretical activity, knowledge progresses through the dialectical movement of discovering unity first in the object of inquiry, then in the conceptual framework uncovered in the investigation of the object, which in turn exposes a "new" unity of the object, and so on. Through history, this dialectical movement has led to the penultimate positing of the strictly unitary "thing-in-itself," unavailable to direct apprehension. Cassirer's self-proclaimed position in this movement is as outlining the necessary unity of thought to which this unknown "X," the absolute unity of Being presupposed, is correlated. The absolute unity of being, culminating in the assumption of the thing-in-itself, is divorced from the realm of multiplicity and refractive phenomena. The latter are then taken up by the various specialized sciences, which make no claim to having a unified object of investigation and which freely admit to objects of inquiry shaped by the particular perspectives of the specific sciences. The outcome of this epistemological fragmentation need not be understood as the final denunciation of the unity of Being, but rather as the turning point of the dialectical movement back to the work of reformulating the unity of thought. For Cassirer, unity is the end toward which thought must aspire, whether it seeks unity in the object or in the form of consciousness giving rise to objects in general.

12. Ernst Cassirer, *Language*, vol. 1 of *The Philosophy of Symbolic Forms*, trans. Ralph Manheim (New Haven: Yale University Press, 1955; rpt. 1971), 77.

13. Ibid., 81.

14. Ernst Cassirer, *An Essay on Man: An Introduction to a Philosophy of Culture* (New Haven: Yale University Press, 1944; rpt. 1970), 68.

15. Ernst Cassirer, "'Spirit' and 'Life' in Contemporary Philosophy," in *The Philosophy of Ernst Cassirer*, ed. Paul Schillp (New York: Tudor, 1958).

16. This is a theme that runs through much of Cassirer's work. For a succinct account, see *Language*, 93–105.

17. See especially *Language*, pp. 80–81, and *Mythical Thought*, 14.

18. For a fascinating analysis of the development of nonmimetic concepts of art, see Irwin Panofsky, *Idea: A Concept in Art Theory*, trans. Joseph J. S. Peake (New York: Harper & Row, 1968; originally published in Leipzig, in 1924). For a discussion of similar developments in literature, see Erich Auerbach, *Mimesis: The Representation of Reality in Western Literature*, trans. Willard Trask (Princeton: Princeton University Press, 1953; first published in Switzerland, in 1946).

19. Cassirer, *An Essay on Man*, 23.

20. Ibid., 24.

21. Ibid., 29.

22. Ibid., 32.

23. Ibid., 34–35.

24. Ibid., 37.

25. Ibid., 36.

26. Ibid., 38.

27. Ibid., 25.

28. Ibid., 41.

29. Cassirer, *Mythical Thought*, 33.

30. Ernst Cassirer, *The Logic of the Humanities*, trans. Clarence Smith Howe (New Haven: Yale University Press, 1960; rpt. 1974), 94–96.

31. Cassirer, *Symbol, Myth, and Culture*, 246.

32. Ernst Cassirer, *The Phenomenology of Knowledge*, vol. 3 of *The Philosophy of Symbolic Forms*, trans. Ralph Manheim (New Haven: Yale University Press, 1957; rpt. 1973), 229–32.

33. Cassirer, *An Essay on Man*, 37.

34. Ibid., 77.

35. Cassirer, *The Myth of the State*, 14–15.

36. Cassirer, *Mythical Thought*, 13.

37. Cassirer, "'Spirit' and 'Life' in Contemporary Philosophy," 868–70.

38. Cassirer, *Mythical Thought*, 156.

39. Ibid., 166.

40. Ibid., 30–35.

41. Ibid., 35–36.

42. Cassirer, *The Phenomenology of Knowledge*, 61–62.

43. Cassirer, *Mythical Thought*, 44–46.

44. Ibid., 46.

45. Cassirer, *An Essay on Man*, 81.

46. Ibid., 82.

47. Ibid., 82–83.

48. Ibid., chapter 7.

49. Cassirer, *The Phenomenology of Knowledge*, 74.

50. Ibid., 62–67.

51. Ibid.

52. Cassirer, *The Myth of the State*, 47.

53. Cassirer, *An Essay on Man*, 37.

54. Cassirer, *The Myth of the State*, 43.

55. In this, Cassirer follows William James, understanding emotion not in (pre-Freudian) psychical or "mentalistic" terms, but in physical terms. See ibid., 26–27.

56. Ibid.

57. Cassirer, *The Logic of the Humanities*, 110.

58. Cassirer, *The Myth of the State*, 43.

59. Ibid., 28.

60. Ibid., 38. Of course, mythical consciousness, having no recourse to the representative function, could not use the concepts of 'substitution', 'role', or 'part'. As a matter of fact, the 'individual agent' is a concept we export to the mythical world.

61. Ibid., 37.

62. Ibid., 45–46.

63. Cassirer, *An Essay on Man*, 42–43.

64. Cassirer, *Mythical Thought*, 83–84.

65. Ibid., 108–11.

66. Cassirer, *An Essay on Man*, 50–55.

67. Cassirer, *Mythical Thought*, 111–18.

68. Ibid., 85–88.

69. Ibid., 75.

70. Ibid., 81.

71. Ibid., 94–95.

72. Cassirer, The *Phenomenology of Knowledge*, 150.

73. Ibid., 151. See also *Mythical Thought*, 101–2 and 107.

74. Cassirer, *Mythical Thought* 105–6.

75. Ibid., 109.

76. Ibid., 111–12.

77. Ibid., 157–58.

78. Ibid., 157.

79. Ibid., 73–77; see also *Language and Myth*, 63–67.

80. Cassirer, *Language and Myth*, 35–37.

81. Cassirer, *Mythical Thought*, 168–72.

82. Ibid., 62

83. Cassirer himself did not often address the form of art, but Suzanne Langer incorporates many of his insights in her work. See especially *Problems of Art* (New York: Scribners, 1957).

84. Cassirer, *The Myth of the State*, 37; and *An Essay on Man*, chapter 9.

85. Cassirer, *Mythical Thought*, 24.

86. Cassirer, *An Essay on Man*, 228.

87. Ibid., 225.

88. This notion of the ethical has many variations. Ethical freedom may be the freedom to unswervingly obey the laws of reason; it may be the freedom to enhance, through rational inquiry, one's chances of augmenting the benefit and avoiding the misery inherent in biological existence, etc.

89. Cassirer, *An Essay on Man*, 57–61.

90. Cassirer, The *Myth of the State*, chapter 18.

91. Cassirer, *Mythical Thought*, 26.

92. A succinct account of the theory of evolution in terms of random occurrence and successful repetition of such occurrences can be found in Jacques Monod, *Chance and Necessity: An Essay on the Natural Philosophy of Modern Biology*, trans. Austryn Wainhouse (New York: Vintage, 1972). I am also indebted to my father, Dr. Harold Baeten, for our discussions of embryology, biology, the theory of evolution, and related topics.

93. An interesting exposition of the theory of evolution sans overarching principles was presented by Professor Abner Shimony in the Boston University Colloquium for the Philosophy of Science, Spring 1988.

94. See especially Cassirer's references to Heinz Werner's theory of psychological development, in *An Essay on Man*, 45, and in *Language and Myth*, 87.

95. Cassirer, *An Essay on Man*, 31.

96. The inherent responsibility entailed in freedom has been addressed in an interesting and fruitful manner by Robert Cummings Neville. See especially *The Cosmology of Freedom* (New Haven: Yale University Press, 1974) and *The Puritan Smile* (Albany: SUNY Press, 1988).

3. MYTHICAL SYMBOL, MYTHICAL SIGN

1. Roland Barthes, *Mythologies*, trans. Annette Lavers (New York: Hill and Wang, 1972; rpt. 1986).

2. Ibid., 11.

3. Ibid., 109.

4. Ibid., 111.

5. Ferdinand de Saussure, *Course in General Linguistics*, trans. Wade Baskin, ed. Charles Bally and Albert Sechehaye (New York: McGraw-Hill, 1966), 16–17. A few years after the publication of *Mythologies*,

Barthes reexamined the relationship of semiology and linguistics and was prepared to invert the Saussurian formula of language as a province of semiological systems. He maintained that "linguistics is not a part of the general science of signs, even a privileged part, it is semiology which is a part of linguistics." Barthes was willing to take this position because of the demands of unifying the discoveries made in a wide range of research based on analyses of signification mechanisms. All such findings in anthropology, psychology, sociology, literature, etc., are formulated linguistically. Furthermore, all "nonsuperficial" semiological systems appear to incorporate spoken or written language "as a model, . . . component, relay, or signified." However, this is not the position that Barthes held some seven years earlier while working on his theory of myth, though a glimmer of this inversion shows through the fabric of his arguments. At the earlier time, his conceptual scheme was closer to Cassirer's. See Roland Barthes, *Elements of Semiology*, trans. Annette Lavers and Colin Smith (New York: Hill and Wang, 1968; rpt. 1978).

6. De Saussure, *Course in General Linguistics*, 79.

7. Barthes, *Mythologies*, 112–13.

8. Ibid., 113.

9. De Saussure, *Course in General Linguistics*, 67.

10. Barthes, *Mythologies*, 114. Barthes' emphasis.

11. Ibid., 115–19.

12. Ibid., 117–18.

13. Ibid., 129.

14. Ibid., 122–23.

15. Ibid., 142.

16. Ibid., 140.

17. Ibid., 155.

18. Ibid., 145–48. See also p. 132 on the concept of "zero degree signification."

19. Ibid., 145–46.

20. Barthes, *Elements of Semiology*, 23–30.

21. Roland Barthes, "Science versus Literature," in *Introduction to Structuralism*, ed. Michael Lane (New York: Basic Books, 1970), 414. This article is reprinted from the *London Times Literary Supplement*, 28 September 1967.

22. Ibid., 411.

23. Roland Barthes, "To Write: An Intransitive Verb?" in *The Structuralist Controversy: The Language of Criticism and the Science of Man*, ed. Richard Macksey and Eugenio Donato (Baltimore: Johns Hopkins Press, 1970; rpt. 1979), 143.

24. Ibid., esp. 141–43.

25. Barthes, "Science versus Literature," 412–13.

26. Ibid., 14.

27. Of course, it is no surprise that there would be similarities in the work of Barthes and Lacan. Lacan has radicalized the insights of de Saussure and applied them in the area of psychoanalysis. Lacan's essay, "The function and field of speech and language in psychoanalysis," deals specifically with the constitution of the subject of/by discourse, in part reinventing de Saussure's notion of the signifier through Freud's understanding of the function of the symbol. Lacan's work is rich and fertile, with much to add in a discussion of the function of the mythical. See especially Jacques Lacan, *Écrits*, trans. Alan Sheridan (New York: W. W. Norton, 1977); and Lacan, *The Four Fundamental Concepts of Psycho-Analysis*, ed. Jacques-Alain Miller, trans. Alan Sheridan (New York: W. W. Norton, 1981).

28. Barthes, "To Write," 144.

29. Barthes, "Science versus Literature," 415.

30. Ernst Cassirer, *An Essay on Man: An Introduction to a Philosophy of Culture* (New Haven: Yale University Press, 1944; rpt. 1970), 224.

31. Ernst Cassirer, *The Myth of the State* (New Haven: Yale University Press, 1946; rpt. 1971), 282.

32. Ernst Cassirer, *Symbol, Myth, and Culture*, ed. Donald Phillip Verene (New Haven: Yale University Press, 1979), 236.

33. Barthes, *Mythologies*, 9.

34. Cassirer, *An Essay on Man*, chapter 3.

35. Barthes, *Mythologies*, 111.

36. Barthes, "To Write," 144.

37. Cassirer, *An Essay on Man*, chapter 3.

38. Barthes, *Elements of Semiology*, 10–11.

39. Ernst Cassirer, *Mythical Thought*, vol. 2 of *The Philosophy of Symbolic Forms*, trans. Ralph Manheim (New Haven: Yale University Press, 1955; rpt. 1971), 105.

40. Cassirer, *The Myth of the State*, 228.

41. Barthes, *Mythologies*, 156.

4. MYTHICAL SPACE, MYTHICAL TIME

1. Mircea Eliade, *The Myth of the Eternal Return, Or, Cosmos and History*, trans. Willard Trask (Princeton: Princeton University Press, 1954; rpt. 1974), 3.

2. Ernst Cassirer, *Language and Myth*, trans. Susanne Langer (New York: Dover, 1953), 66–67.

3. Eliade certainly distinguishes between various mythical and religious traditions; however, there is no distinction to be made in the mythical *as opposed to* the religious. Eliade uses these two terms interchangeably, along with 'archaic', 'primitive', etc. The defining opposition is, rather, between the "religious" person and the "historical" or "modern" person. This distinction is founded on the opposition between sacred and profane ontologies.

4. Mircea Eliade, *Myth and Reality*, trans. Willard Trask, ed. Ruth Nanda Ashen (New York: Harper & Row, 1963), 3–4.

5. Mircea Eliade, *The Sacred and the Profane: The Nature of Religion*, trans. Willard Trask (New York: Harper & Row, 1961), 203.

6. I will return to these contrary evaluations of the relative merits of the mythical within the variety of cultural achievements. Such considerations belong to an analysis of the function of the *concept* of myth within a broader metaphysical scheme. This is especially true when the concept serves to carry the extrasystematic ethical and/or political freight of the author. These considerations are not altogether necessary in explicating the writers' understanding of the function of the mythical itself in cultural activity or organization.

7. Eliade, *Eternal Return*, 92.

8. Eliade, *The Sacred and the Profane*, 93–94.

9. Ernst Cassirer, *Mythical Thought*, vol. 1 of *The Philosophy of Symbolic Forms*, trans. Ralph Manheim (New Haven: Yale University Press, 1955; rpt. 1971), 84.

10. Eliade, *The Sacred and the Profane*, 20.

11. Cassirer, *Mythical Thought*, 90.

12. Eliade, *The Sacred and the Profane*, 63.

13. Ibid., 12.

14. Cassirer, *Mythical Thought*, 105.

15. Ibid., 108.

16. Eliade, *The Sacred and the Profane*, 76.

17. Ibid., 68.

18. Cassirer, *Mythical Thought*, 108.

19. Eliade, *Myth and Reality*, 29–31. See also *Eternal Return*, 83–85.

20. Cassirer, *Mythical Thought*, 108.

21. Ibid., 109.

22. Strangely, mythical space-time seems closer in some ways to that of contemporary physics than to the Newtonian explanation, in which the temporal features of the world are "detachable" from the spatial. This convergence of contemporary physics and mythical cosmology is too complex an issue to be dealt with fairly here. But we should remember that space and time in the mythical world are nondifferentiated in certain crucial respects.

23. Rudolph Otto, *The Idea of the Holy*, trans. John W. Harvey (New York: Oxford University Press, 1923; rpt. 1958).

24. Cassirer, *Mythical Thought*, 78.

25. Eliade, *The Sacred and the Profane*, 8–10.

26. Ibid., esp. 65 and 95–96.

27. Eliade, *Eternal Return*, 34.

28. Parenthetically, we can see that according to Eliade's description of the mythical, Cassirer is incorrect in claiming that true philosophic inquiry is born out of its mythical matrix when the concept of the 'archē' is transformed from a concept of actual, historical origin to a concept of a universal ordering principle. It would be more correct to claim that philosophic inquiry distinguishes between these two senses of the *archē*, and attempts to eradicate the former. In Eliade's version of the mythical cosmos there can be no clear distinction between *archē* as origin in time and space and *archē* as the formal ordering principle of reality. The *archē* of the mythical world is both the origin of the world and that which gives order to the world. See Ernst Cassirer, *The Myth of the State* (New Haven: Yale University Press, 1946; rpt. 1971), chapter 5.

29. Cassirer, *Language and Myth*, 85–92.

30. Ernst Cassirer, "'Spirit' and 'Life' in Contemporary Philosophy," in *The Philosophy of Ernst Cassirer*, ed. Paul Schillp (New York: Tudor, 1958).

31. Eliade, Eternal *Return*, p. 156.

32. Ibid., chapter 4.

33. Ibid., 160–61.

34. Ernst Cassirer, *An Essay on Man: An Introduction to a Philosophy of Culture* (New Haven: Yale University Press, 1944; rpt. 1970), 221.

35. Ibid., chapter 11.

5. MYTHICAL SELF, MYTHICAL SOUL

1. James Hillman, *The Myth of Analysis: Three Essays in Archetypal Psychology* (Evanston, IL: Northwestern University Press, 1972; rpt. New York: Harper & Row, 1978).

2. Ibid., 120–23.

3. Mircea Eliade, *The Myth of the Eternal Return, Or, Cosmos and History*, trans. Willard Trask (Princeton: Princeton University Press, 1954; rpt. 1974), 162.

4. Hillman, *Myth of Analysis*, 40.

5. Ibid., 30–31.

6. Ibid., 184.

7. Ibid., 3.

8. Ibid., 298.

9. Ibid., 108.

10. Ibid., 112–13.

11. Ibid., 5.

12. Ibid., 92.

13. Ibid., 88–92.

14. Ernst Cassirer, *Symbol, Myth, and Culture*, ed. Donald Phillip Verene (New Haven: Yale University Press, 1979), 245–46.

15. Whether Hillman is *correct* in his appeal to Kant as forebear is a separate issue. The demonstrable links of Cassirer's work to Kant's are also an

issue. However important these questions may be, they are not entirely germane to the present discussion. What's more helpful is comparing what each *believes* to be his Kantian inheritance.

16. Ibid., 83–88.

17. Ernst Cassirer, *An Essay on Man: An Introduction to a Philosophy of Culture* (New Haven: Yale University Press, 1944; rpt. 1970), chapter 5.

18. Ernst Cassirer, *The Myth of the State* (New Haven: Yale University Press, 1946; rpt. 1971), chapter 18.

19. Frances A. Yates, *The Art of Memory* (Chicago: University of Chicago Press, 1966). Yates' impressive work offers a history of methods for prodigious feats of recall, methods for developing what appears to be something like a complete photographic memory. Such achievement, explains Yates, depends on a "spatialized" organization of elaborate images offering metaphorical clues to what is "stored" in various memorial rooms, hallways, etc. Yates also details "memory theatres," zodiacal configurations and other devices, all methods for organizing an enormous body of material through what seem to be very peculiar categories. These categories, or "rooms" in memory, relate a wide array of material largely through imaginative, metaphorical connections. Yates' work is certainly intriguing, but its primary interest here is the use that Hillman makes of her painstaking documentation, and the fact that he understands the memorial schemes that Yates discovers as similar to the categories Kant describes as making knowledge and experience possible.

20. Hillman, *Myth of Analysis*, 178–79.

21. Ernst Cassirer, *The Phenomenology of Knowledge*, vol. 3 of *The Philosophy of Symbolic Forms*, trans. Ralph Manheim (New Haven: Yale University Press, 1957; rpt. 1973), 191.

22. Hillman, *Myth of Analysis*, 104–5.

23. Ibid., 97.

24. Ibid., 189–90.

25. Ibid., 217.

26. Ernst Cassirer, *Mythical Thought*, vol. 2 of *The Philosophy of Symbolic Forms*, trans. Ralph Manheim (New Haven: Yale University Press, 1955; rpt. 1971), 157.

27. Ernst Cassirer, *Language and Myth*, trans. Susanne Langer (New York: Harper and Brothers, 1946; rpt. New York: Dover, 1953), 33.

28. Cassirer, *Mythical Thought*, 206.

29. Hillman, *The Myth of Analysis*, 42–44.

30. Ibid., 8.

31. Ibid., 216–17.

32. Ibid., 288. Here Hillman is quoting W. F., Otto, *The Homeric Gods*, trans. M. Hadas (New York: Pantheon, 1964), 78.

33. Hillman, *Myth of Analysis*, 26.

34. Ibid., 296.

35. Cassirer, *The Phenomenology of Knowledge*, 92–103.

36. Hillman, *The Myth of Analysis*, 18.

37. Ibid., 28.

38. Ibid., 31–32.

39. Ibid., 34–36.

40. Ibid., 293.

6. THE MAGIC MIRROR OF MYTH . . .

1. Ernst Cassirer, *The Myth of the State* (New Haven: Yale University Press, 1946; rpt. 1970), 6.

2. Mircea Eliade, *The Sacred and the Profane: The Nature of Religion*, trans. Willard Trask (New York: Harper & Row, 1961), 12.

3. Roland Barthes, *Mythologies*, trans. Annette Lavers (New York: Hill and Wang, 1972; rpt. 1986), 124–25.

4. Hillman, *The Myth of Analysis*, 28–36.

5. Ibid., 288.

6. My remarks on ontological reduction are suggested by John Dewey in his discussion of the "precarious and stable" features of existence and how these are dealt with in traditional metaphysical speculation, and by Justus Buchler, in his discussion of "ontological parity." John Dewey, "Existence as Precarious and Stable," in *The Later Works of John Dewey, Vol. 1 (1925): Collected Articles and "Experience and Nature,"* ed. J. A. Boydston (Carbondale, Ill.: Southern Illinois University Press, 1981) and Justus Buchler, *Metaphysics of Natural Complexes*, 2nd edition, ed. K. Wallace, A. Marsoobian, and R. Corrington (Albany: SUNY Press, 1990).

7. Spirit may remain within the forms of religious consciousness, exhibiting itself as the supreme deity or perhaps as Brahma as described in the

Upanishads. Or, Spirit may break out of the bonds of the mythical by apprehending itself as consciousness-as-such in nonreligiously determined symbolic forms. See Cassirer, *Language and Myth*, 76–83; and *Mythical Thought*, 244–54.

8. Barthes, *Mythologies*, 146–57.

9. Ibid., 131.

10. Hillman, *The Myth of Analysis*, 82–88.

11. Cassirer, *Language and Myth*, 35–36, 71–73.

12. Cassirer, *The Myth of the State*, chapter 18.

13. Barthes, *Mythologies*, especially the conclusion.

14. Eliade, *The Myth of the Eternal Return*, chapter 4.

15. Ibid., chapter 3.

16. Hillman, *The Myth of Analysis*, 90–93.

CONCLUSION: THE NATURE OF CULTURE

1. Snohomish Tribal Story, "Pushing Up the Sky," in *Indian Legends of the Pacific Northwest*, ed. Ella E. Clark, as told by Chief William Shelton (Berkeley: University of California Press, 1953).

2. For an account of the Aristotle to whom naturalists owe a debt, see John Herman Randall, Jr., *Aristotle* (New York: Columbia University Press, 1960).

3. This locution comes from Justus Buchler's *Metaphysics of Natural Complexes*, 2nd edition, ed. K. Wallace, A. Marsoobian, and R. Corrington (Albany: SUNY Press, 1990), 1. Professor Buchler has had a great influence on my philosophic perspective, and his ideas are embedded in this work. Because of the pervasive influence, the reader will not find every allusion made explicit.

4. John Herman Randall, Jr., "The Nature of Naturalism," in *Naturalism and the Human Spirit*, ed. Krikorian (New York: Columbia University Press, 1944), 357.

5. See especially Justus Buchler, "Communication," in *Toward a General Theory of Human Judgment*, 2nd edition (New York: Dover, 1979); and George Herbert Mead, "Mind," in *The Social Psychology of George Herbert Mead* (Chicago: University of Chicago Press, 1956).

6. This is an extremely clumsy and not very helpful way of speaking about nature. If I speak about "what is," or "what exists," we are immedi-

ately drawn to a distinction between these and "what is not," or "what does not exist." And of course, then we are drawn into the metaphysical mistake of exclusion. Justus Buchler has, in fact, given us a useful language in which to speak of "whatever is, in whatever way." He uses the phrase, "natural complex." This phrase is certainly the key to Buchler's work. He writes,

> [W]hatever is discriminated in any respect or in any degree is a natural complex. . . . Precisely what kind of complex anything discriminated turns out to be; in what way its status, its location, its connections are to be interpreted; what traits it may or should be said to have after investigation or any other form of experience; is a distinct type of issue. Anything identified or discovered or imagined or discerned or inferred or sensed or posited or encountered or apprehended or made or acted upon—no matter whether deliberately or not—is here said to be "discriminated." Although whatever is in any way discriminated is a natural complex, it does not follow that all natural complexes are discriminated. (*Metaphysics of Natural Complexes*, 1–2.)

Though I think "natural complex" is a perfectly fine substitution for "what is," or "whatever exists," its introduction to the main discussion might prove distracting.

7. Please see Buchler's discussion of ontological priority and ontological parity in *Metaphysics of Natural Complexes*, 30–51.

8. To the naturalist, the question "Does God exist?" is not so much impossible to answer as it is perhaps foolish to ask. Of course God exists. The question is, "In what manner does God exist?" Certainly God exists as an object of faith, as a comfort to the believer in times of distress, as rationale for holy wars, and in many other ways. For a naturalist discussion of theological issues, see Robert S. Corrigton, "Ordinality and the Divine Natures," in *Nature's Perspectives: Prospects for Ordinal Metaphysics*, ed. Armen Marsoobian, Kathleen Wallace, and Robert S. Corrington (Albany: SUNY Press, 1991).

9. For an interesting discussion of the realism/antirealism debate in pragmatism, see J. David Lewis and Richard L. Smith, *American Sociology and Pragmatism: Mead, Chicago Sociology, and Symbolic Interaction* (Chicago: University of Chicago Press, 1980).

10. William Dennes, "The Categories of Naturalism," in *Naturalism and the Human Spirit*, 289.

11. Dewey, I believe, made a mistake in confounding the naturalist method with the method of *biological* science. His conception of human behavior was narrow, at least narrower than I'm proposing. His description of

the human process locates human being within the biological sphere, which of course is true, but he often limits human being to this sphere. This weakness appears, for example, in his contention that human experience is always one of problem solving. This may be the case in some respects, but certainly contemplation is a trait of human life, as is obeying the law of gravity when we jump from a building. See especially, "Existence as Precarious and Stable," in *The Later Works of John Dewey, Vol. 1*; and "The Live Creature," in *The Later Works of John Dewey, Vol. 10*.

12. Quoted by John Herman Randall, Jr., in "The Nature of Naturalism," 362.

13. John Herman Randall, Jr., *Nature and Historical Experience: Essays in Naturalism and in the Theory of History* (New York: Columbia University Press, 1958). See especially the essay "Substance as a Cooperation of Processes: A Metaphysical Analysis."

14. I do not wish to give the impression of "nature" as an all-encompassing, self-enclosed entity. Nor do I wish to discuss the many problems there are in thinking of the "ground" of whatever is, in whatever way that it is, as a "whole" with relations only to its "parts." For an excellent analysis of these and other problems, see Justus Buchler, "Probing the Idea of Nature," first published in *Process Studies* 8.3 (Fall 1978): 157–68; reprinted in 2nd edition of *Metaphysics of Natural Complexes*.

15. I would argue further, that we are born into *many* social groups, and that individual identity is "located" not only in the cumulative total of social memberships, but in the relations holding among and between the variety of groups.

16. Ernst Cassirer, *An Essay on Man: An Introduction to a Philosophy of Culture* (New Haven: Yale University Press, 1944; rpt. 1970), 23–24.

17. Mead's concept of sociality is very close to Whitehead's principle of concresence. However, Mead is not committed to the Whiteheadian notion that everything is related to everything else. For Mead, emergence or adjustment is always relative to a local context. See especially, George Herbert Mead, "Emergence and Identity," and "The Social Nature of the Present" in *The Philosophy of the Present*, ed. Arthur E. Murphy (Chicago: University of Chicago Press, 1932; rpt. 1980).

18. See especially George Herbert Mead, part 2 of *Mind, Self, and Society*, ed. Charles W. Morris (Chicago: University of Chicago Press, 1934; rpt. 1974).

19. The sense of nature as "providingness" comes from Justus Buchler. He writes, "Nature in the barest sense is the presence and availability of complexes. It is the provision and determination of traits—providing-

ness, if we must strengthen the emphasis, but not providence, not prov-
identness. It provides man, for instance, with the possibilities, the cir-
cumstances, and the substance of judgment." (*Metaphysics of Natural
Complexes*, 3.)

20. There is, of course, a problem in indicating the scope of any social organism. In some sense, the human race, from its moment of speciation, is an
integral organism, unbroken through millennia. On the other hand, we
can identify further specifications within this broad terrain. If culture is
the set of significant gestures of the social organism, constitutive of the
environment of human being, then we must distinguish somehow
between "sectors" of this organism. I would suggest that as "nature"
and "natures" both make sense within this perspective, so do "culture"
and "cultures."

21. John Dewey, *Experience and Nature.*

22. D. W. Winnicott, "The Location of Cultural Experience," in *Playing
and Reality* (New York: Penguin, 1971), 112–21.

23. Winnicott, "Creativity and its Origins," in *Playing and Reality.*

24. Lawrence E. Cahoone, *The Dilemma of Modernity: Philosophy, Culture and Anti-Culture* (Albany: SUNY Press, 1988). Cahoone's work is a
compelling account of the history of modern philosophy, in its subjec-
tivist traits, as it works itself through precisely this oscillation.

Bibliography

Atwood, Margaret. *You are Happy*. New York: Harper & Row, 1974.

Auerbach, Erich. *Mimesis: The Representation of Reality in Western Literature*. Trans. Willard Trask. Princeton: Princeton University Press, 1953.

Barthes, Roland. *Elements of Semiology*. Trans. Annette Lavers and Colin Smith. New York: Hill and Wang, 1968; rpt. 1978.

———. *Mythologies*. Trans. Annette Lavers. New York: Hill and Wang, 1972; rpt. 1986.

———. "Science versus Literature." In *Introduction to Structuralism*. Ed. Michael Lane. New York: Basic Books, 1970. Reprinted from *The Times Literary Supplement*, 28 September 1967.

———. "To Write: An Intransitive Verb?" In *The Structuralist Controversy: The Language of Criticism and the Science of Man*. Ed. Richard Macksey and Eugenio Donato. Baltimore: Johns Hopkins University Press, 1970; rpt. 1979.

Bascom, William. "The Forms of Folklore: Prose Narratives." *Journal of American Folklore* 78 (1965).

Blumenberg, Hans. *Work on Myth*. Trans. Robert M. Wallace. Cambridge, MA: MIT Press, 1985.

Buchler, Justus. *Metaphysics of Natural Complexes*. Ed. Kathleen Wallace and Armen Marsoobian. Albany: SUNY Press, 1990.

———. *Toward a General Theory of Human Judgment*. New York: Columbia University Press, 1951; rpt. New York: Dover, 1979.

Cahoone, Lawrence E. *The Dilemma of Modernity: Philosophy, Culture and Anti-Culture*. Albany: SUNY Press, 1988.

Campbell, Joseph. *The Hero with a Thousand Faces*. New York: Pantheon, 1949.

——— . *The Flight of the Wild Gander: Explorations in the Mythological Dimension*. New York: Viking, 1969.

——— . "Mythical Themes in Creative Literature and Art." In *Myths, Dreams, and Religion*. Ed. Joseph Campbell. New York: E. P. Dutton, 1970.

Cassirer, Ernst. *An Essay on Man: An Introduction to a Philosophy of Culture*. New Haven: Yale University Press, 1944; rpt. 1970.

——— . *Language*. Vol. 1 of *The Philosophy of Symbolic Forms*. Trans. Ralph Manheim. New Haven: Yale University Press, 1955; rpt. 1971.

——— . *Language and Myth*. Trans. Suzanne Langer. New York: Dover, 1953.

——— . *The Logic of the Humanities*. Trans. Clarence Smith Howe. New Haven: Yale University Press, 1960; rpt. 1974.

——— . *The Myth of the State*. New Haven: Yale University Press, 1946; rpt. 1970.

——— . *Mythical Thought*. Vol. 2 of *The Philosophy of Symbolic Forms*. Trans. Ralph Manheim. New Haven: Yale University Press, 1955; rpt. 1971.

——— . *The Phenomenology of Knowledge*. Vol. 3 of *The Philosophy of Symbolic Forms*. Trans. Ralph Manheim. New Haven: Yale University Press, 1957; rpt. 1973.

——— . "'Spirit' and 'Life' in Contemporary Philosophy." In *The Philosophy of Ernst Cassirer*. Ed. Paul Schillp. New York: Tudor, 1958.

——— . *Substance and Function and Einstein's Theory of Relativity* (published as one book). Trans. William Curtis Swabey and Marie Collins Swabey. New York: Dover, 1953.

——— . *Symbol, Myth, and Culture*. Ed. Donald Phillip Verene. New Haven: Yale University Press, 1979.

Clark, Ella E. *Indian Legends of the Pacific Northwest*. Berkeley: University of California Press, 1953.

Corrington, Robert S. "Ordinality and the Divine Natures." In *Nature's Perspectives: Prospects for Ordinal Metaphysics*. Ed. Armen Marsoobian, Kathleen Wallace, and Robert S. Corrington. Albany: SUNY Press, 1991.

Dennes, William. "The Categories of Naturalism." In *Naturalism and the Human Spirit*. Ed. Yervant H. Krikorian. New York: Columbia University Press, 1944.

De Saussure, Ferdinand. *Course in General Linguistics*. Trans. Wade Baskin. Ed. Charles Bally and Albert Sechehaye. New York: McGraw-Hill, 1966.

Dewey, John. *The Later Works, 1925–1953*. Ed. J. A. Boydston. Carbondale and Edwardsville: Southern Illinois University Press, 1981–90.

Eliade, Mircea. *Myth and Reality*. Trans. Willard Trask. Ed. Ruth Nanda Ashen. New York: Harper & Row, 1963.

——— . *The Myth of the Eternal Return, Or, Cosmos and History*. Trans. Willard Trask. Princeton: Princeton University Press, 1954; rpt. 1974.

——— . *The Sacred and the Profane: The Nature of Religion*. Trans. Willard Trask. New York: Harper & Row, 1961.

Frazer, Sir James. *The New Golden Bough* (abridged). Ed. Theodor Gaster. New York: Mentor, 1964.

Frye, Northrup. *Anatomy of Criticism: Four Essays*. Princeton: Princeton University Press, 1957.

Graves, Robert. *The Greek Myths: 1*. Baltimore: Penguin, 1955.

Gropius, Walter. *Bauhaus: 1919–1928*. Trans. P. Morton Shand. New York: The Museum of Modern Art, 1937.

Hamilton, Edith. *Mythology*. New York: Mentor, 1953.

Hillman, James. *The Myth of Analysis: Three Essays*. In *Archetypal Psychology*. Evanston, IL: Northwestern University Press, 1972; rpt. New York: Harper & Row, 1978.

——— . *Re-Visioning Psychology*. New York: Harper & Row, 1978.

Honko, Lauri. "The Problem of Defining Myth." In *The Myth of the State*. Ed. Haralds Biezais. Stockholm: Scripta Instituti Donneriani Aboensis, 1972.

Keller, Catherine. *From a Broken Web: Separation, Sexism, and Self*. Boston: Beacon Press, 1986.

Kirk, G. S. "On Defining Myths." *Phronesis: A Journal for Ancient Philosophy*, suppl. vol. 1 (1973).

Lacan, Jacques. *Écrits*. Trans. Alan Sheridan. New York: W. W. Norton, 1977.

———. *The Four Fundamental Concepts of Psycho-Analysis*. Ed. Jacques-Alain Miller. Trans. Alan Sheridan. New York: W. W. Norton, 1981.

Langer, Suzanne. *Problems of Art*. New York: Scribners, 1957.

Lauter, Estella. *Women as Mythmakers: Poetry and Visual Art by Twentieth-Century Women*. Bloomington: Indiana University Press, 1984.

Lévi-Strauss, Claude. *The Elementary Structures of Kinship*. Trans. James Harle Bell and Richard von Sturmer. Ed. Rodney Needham. Boston: Beacon Press, 1969.

———. *The Raw and the Cooked: Introduction to a Science of Mythology*. Trans. John and Doreen Weightman. New York: Harper, 1969.

———. "The Structural Study of Myth." In *Structural Anthropology*. Trans. Claire Jacobson and Brooke Grundfest Schoepf. New York: Basic Books, 1963.

———. *Tristes Tropiques*. Trans. John and Doreen Weightman. New York: Atheneum, 1975.

Lewis, J. David and Richard L. Smith. *American Sociology and Pragmatism: Mead, Chicago Sociology, and Symbolic Interaction*. Chicago: University of Chicago Press, 1980.

Malinowski, Bronislaw. *Magic, Science, and Religion and Other Essays*. Garden City, NY: Doubleday Anchor, 1954.

Mead, George Herbert. *Mind, Self, and Society*. Ed. Charles W. Morris. Chicago: University of Chicago Press, 1934; rpt. 1974.

———. *The Philosophy of the Present*. Ed. Arthur E. Murphy. Chicago: University of Chicago Press, 1932; rpt. 1980.

———. *The Social Psychology of George Herbert Mead*. Reprinted as *On Social Psychology*. Ed. Anselm Strauss. Chicago: University of Chicago Press, 1956.

Monod, Jacques. *Chance and Necessity: An Essay on the Natural Philosophy of Modern Biology*. Trans. Austryn Wainhouse. New York: Vintage, 1972.

Neville, Robert Cummings. *The Cosmology of Freedom*. New Haven: Yale University Press, 1974.

———. *Reconstruction of Thinking*. Albany: SUNY Press, 1981.

Nuyen, A. T. "The Fragility of the Self: From Bundle Theory to Deconstruction." *The Journal of Speculative Philosophy* 6.2 (1992).

Otto, Rudolph. *The Idea of the Holy.* Trans. John W. Harvey. New York: Oxford University Press, 1923; rpt. 1958.

Otto, W. F. *The Homeric Gods.* Trans. M. Hadas. New York: Pantheon, 1964.

Panofsky, Irwin. *Idea: A Concept in Art Theory.* Trans. Joseph J. S. Peake. New York: Harper & Row, 1968.

Plato. *The Republic.* Trans. B. Jowett. New York: Vintage.

Quine. W. V. O. "Ontological Relativity." In *Ontological Relativity and Other Essays.* New York: Columbia University Press, 1969.

Randall, J. H., Jr. *Aristotle.* New York: Columbia University Press, 1960.

————. *Nature and Historical Experience: Essays in Naturalism and in the Theory of History.* New York: Columbia University Press, 1958.

————. "The Nature of Naturalism." In *Naturalism and the Human Spirit.* Ed. Yervant H. Krikorian. New York: Columbia University Press, 1944.

Ricouer, Paul. *The Symbolism of Evil.* Trans. Emerson Buchanan. Boston: Beacon Press, 1969.

Winnicott, D. W. *Playing and Reality.* New York: Penguin, 1971.

Winch, Peter. "Understanding a Primitive Society." In *Understanding and Social Inquiry.* Ed. Fred R. Dallmayr and Thomas A. McCarthy. Notre Dame: University of Notre Dame Press, 1977.

Yates, Frances A. *The Art of Memory.* Chicago: University of Chicago Press, 1966.

Index

aphasia, 57
Apollo, 142, 145–47, 156–58, 162, 177, 186
archē, 89, 132, 137, 143–44, 187
archetypes, 7, 169–70, 172, 175–77, 181, 188
    See also Hillman, James
Aristotle, 193
astrology, 71, 76, 124
Atwood, Margaret, 8
Auerbach, Erich, 50n. 18 (219)

Baeten, Harold, 88n. 92 (222)
Barthes, Roland, 16, 18, 38, 95–117, 163–65, 167–69, 171–72, 174–75, 177, 180, 184–85, 200–02, 211
    and Cassirer, Ernst, 16–17, 95, 109–16, 141–43, 183
    and Eliade, Mircea, 141–43
    and Hillman, James, 141–43
    See also under specific subjects
Bascom, William, 27
biological existence, 49–51, 54, 92–93, 203–05
    and myth, 14, 28–29, 48, 58–59, 71–73, 76–78, 80–83, 123–25, 127–29, 131, 133–34, 139, 143, 145, 152–53, 155–62, 172, 174, 181, 188–89
bisexuality, 169–70
Blumenberg, Hans, 32–34

Buchler, Justus, 173n. 6 (229), 194n. 3 (230), 195n. 5 (230), 196n. 6 (230–31), 197n. 7 (231), 198, 202n. 14 (232), 206n. 19 (232–33)

Cahoone, Lawrence E., 208n. 24 (233)
Campbell, Joseph, 28–29
Cassirer, Ernst, 6, 10–17, 26–27, 41–93, 163–65, 171–74, 177–80, 183–84, 193, 200–02, 208, 211
    and Barthes, Roland, 16–17, 95, 109–16, 141–43, 183
    and Eliade, Mircea, 16–17, 119–21, 123–39, 141–43
    and Hillman, James, 17, 141–43, 149–52, 154–60
    See also under specific subjects
causality, mythical, 61–62
Circe, 8
coniunctio, 169–70, 172, 175–76
Corrington, Robert S., 197n. 8 (231)
creativity, 20–21, 91, 131–32, 146–47, 155, 158–62, 165, 169, 172, 175, 181, 183–89, 203, 211–13
    See also freedom, as unbounded creativity; human being, as self-creative

241